Nobel Writers on

For Joanna

Nobel Writers on Writing

Edited by

OTTAR G. DRAUGSVOLD

McFarland & Company, Inc., Publishers
Jefferson, North Carolina, and London

The present work is a reprint of the library bound edition of Nobel Writers on Writing, *first published in 2000 by McFarland.*

LIBRARY OF CONGRESS CATALOGUING-IN-PUBLICATION DATA

Nobel writers on writing / edited by Ottar G. Draugsvold.
          p.   cm.
     Includes bibliographical references and index.

     ISBN 978-0-7864-6609-2
     softcover binding : 50# alkaline paper ∞

     1. Literature, Modern — 20th century — History and
criticism.   2. Nobel Prizes.   I. Draugsvold, Ottar G., 1946–
PN771.N59   2011
809'.04 — dc21   00-35119

BRITISH LIBRARY CATALOGUING DATA ARE AVAILABLE

Front cover design by David K. Landis (Shake It Loose Graphics)

Manufactured in the United States of America

McFarland & Company, Inc., Publishers
  Box 611, Jefferson, North Carolina 28640
    www.mcfarlandpub.com

Contents

Acknowledgments

The speeches for 1968 through 1990 appeared in full in *Nobel Lectures: Literature 1968–1980* and *Nobel Lectures: Literature 1981–1990*, published by World Scientific Publishing Company, Ltd. The excerpts in this book are reprinted with permission of World Scientific Publishing Company and the Nobel Foundation. I wish to thank Ms. Kim Tan of World Scientific Publishing for providing copies of the speeches from 1968 through 1990.

Dr. Henry Singer of the American Nobel Committee was very helpful in the initial stages of research for this book. I greatly appreciate his giving spirit and good advice.

Ms. Kristina Fallenius of the Information Department of the Nobel Foundation has been a source of much needed information throughout the preparation of the manuscript for this book. It seemed no matter how obscure the question, she was able and willing to provide accurate information in a timely manner. I am grateful for her help.

My wife, Joanna, served as first reader and copy editor for the preparation of the materials in this anthology. The final form of this book is, in large part, a tribute to her persistence.

Preface

Fiction may be nothing more than an amusement, like television, movies, bowling, or bridge, something to fill the hours with passing interest. Reading can perform a cathartic function as an imaginative release from an odious reality. Sometimes the written word provides entry into worlds where profound meaning can be intuited. Great fiction and poetry fills all three roles for, "Fiction does not give us only what we want; more importantly, it may give us things we hadn't even known we wanted."[1]

The treasures uncovered in great reading often come piecemeal, as if the reader were digging deeper with each new experience of fiction. The process is cybernetic. A developing reader engaged with great writing changes with each exposure as he or she pursues the essential truths of fiction. Some insights arrive with a staggering suddenness. Others may percolate for years before rising to the surface. Defining the intrinsic rewards of great reading, however, becomes illusive. Walter Kerr describes:

> We must be prepared, after all of our preliminary sacrifice, to come away empty handed, with nothing left to us but a memory of delight, an increase in wellness so deep and so central and so invisibly distributed throughout the psyche that it cannot even be located, let alone measured and codified for a future use.[2]

The intention of this anthology is to make the works and insights of many of the great writers of the twentieth century more accessible to the next century's readers. As Mark Twain wrote, "The man who doesn't read good books has no advantage over the man who can't."[3] The writers profiled here are among those who woo us with their imagery, astonish us with their imaginations, and leave us, at times, breathless with wonder at their beauty of expression. Annie Dillard asks the right question about fiction: "Why are we reading, if not in hope of beauty laid bare, life heightened and its deepest mystery probed?"[4]

1

The list of Nobel Laureates in Literature is a good place to begin looking for such life changing passages. These men and women created new worlds with bare words so enticing that they lead us like native guides into unexplored territory. We become actors in their dramas, created from a literary tradition that stretches back to our pre-literate ancestors. The vibrancy of their voices ensures that their works will continue to be read as long as our language survives. The staying power of these writers also recommends their works to current writers who wrestle with voice, texture, dialogue, pace, characterization, plot, syntax and the myriad of other elements that constitute the writing of literature.

Academics have tended in recent years to rope off the works of great writers with "no trespassing" signs, treating vivid, living writing as a private wine cellar, reserved only for those who are initiated and installed as its stewards. Readers without special credentials are discouraged from gazing upon these sacred texts, much less venturing an opinion on such holy relics. It's as if the great poets and storytellers toiled exclusively for an audience of university professors. This miserly thinking renders great writing inaccessible to its intended audience. Joseph Campbell, the eminent twentieth century mythologist, described the impact of such reductive thinking: "We are looking for an experience of life but we're shoving ourselves off the experience by naming, translating, and classifying every experience that comes to us."[5] Professors of literature name, codify, and classify according to their own arcana. After such autopsies are complete, what had once been pulsing organic matter (wrenched from the creativity and soul of the writer) is transformed into a desiccated carcass.

With the exception of Henri Bergson, *none* of the Nobel writers included in this collection were academic intellectuals. They occupy a different, less contentious space, one that accepts intellectualism for what it is: a piece of the human experience that offers an incomplete view of the whole. Reading great fiction means to experience "poetry, words, images that jump at the right moment, that break open old worlds with surprise, abrasion and pace"[6]; this is the essence of writing "poetry in a prose flattened world."[7] The analysis of great works by academic intellectuals is no substitute for the fresh reading of the works themselves. The call of stories reaches deep into the heart and soul of each reader.

Writing is a solitary life. Seclusion allows eccentric realms of the personality to flourish, free from controls imposed by teamwork and cooperation, allowing writers to be "more themselves" than most of us. The compulsion and self-discipline of writing turn authors continually inward, making them less tractable than other people. Some use the occasion of the Nobel Prize to focus a spotlight on a worthy, but little known, area of fiction. Many answer the critics who previously condemned their work. The social role of the writer and its perils (from the threat of censorship to imprisonment) absorb others. Most allude to a personal impetus that inspired their work and ultimately placed them on the rostrum in Stockholm.

The approach of each laureate's address exposes a fragment of his or her artistic vision. There is no reason to expect that a solitary poet, playwright or novelist who has chosen to work in the mystical world of fiction would be a good speaker or be adept at constructing a cogent lecture. To many, receiving the Prize was both strange and painful ground on which to speak of their deepest concerns. "An artist blindly follows his nose with hands outstretched, and only after he has struck the rock and brought forth the form hidden within it does he theorize and explain what is forever inexplicable."[8] I have edited their presentations only to pare down length and discard dated material. (This collection is not intended to reprint the speeches *as speeches* or lectures *as lectures*.) The Nobel presentations give an unusual view of each writer's work and serve as an enticement for readers to explore the fiction of these illustrious prize winners.

Nobel Prize recipients are allowed forty-five minutes of presentation at the award ceremony. They can use the time as they see fit. The 1997 winner, Dario Fo, handed out cartoons to illustrate his topic. Most winners chose a speech or lecture format. The key contrast between the two forms is that the speech, like a play or poem, is meant to be immediately understood, each word and sentence striking home *as* it is spoken. The speech is, in this sense, time-bound in the particular, written and delivered to a particular audience at a particular time. The lecture is not so tightly constrained. The arguments in a lecture can be more complex, the references more obscure, and more than one reading may be necessary to gain a full understanding.

Given the basic difference between the two forms, one might expect that poets and playwrights who write words to be savored as they are spoken would be more likely to give speeches, while novelists who write words to be consumed as they are read, would choose the more formal lecture. However, the rampant individuality of the authors upsets such forecasts. Several winners could not attend the ceremony and sent an acceptance speech to be read by a stand-in. Neither Hemingway nor Solzhenitsyn made the trip to Stockholm. Pär Lagerkvist read a myth that he had written decades before. The only two authors to decline the Prize, Jean-Paul Sartre and Boris Pasternak, sent telegrams explaining their refusals. The reactions to the award over the past century have been as individual as the authors themselves.

Many notable writers have not won the Nobel Prize for Literature, including Joseph Conrad, Henrik Ibsen, Franz Kafka, Marcel Proust, James Joyce, Leo Tolstoy and Mark Twain. The Swedish Academy frequently passed over "lesser known" writers whose fame grew (over time) to bleach the repute of some who won. I do not criticize the Academy's efforts. The timing of the awards in relation to each writer's career and lifeline (the Prize has never been awarded posthumously) often eliminates worthy potential laureates. In spite of such prominent omissions, the Academy's selections consistently rank among the greatest writers of the twentieth century.

The Nobel award does suffer, however, from a Eurocentric bias. The choices are often skewed by barriers of language. It has been much easier for the Nobel Committee to assess writers of major European languages than to perform the same task for writers in other languages. Although the list of Nobel laureates clearly isn't an exhaustive record of great twentieth century writers, it is a starting point that delivers great riches for the contemporary reader and writer alike.

From the inception of the Prize, the Academy selected writers for the *body* of their work rather than for a "most outstanding work."[9] Only nine writers have specific titles mentioned in their citations from the Swedish Academy. The procedure for arriving at the podium in Stockholm is direct. The Academy solicits nominations from a variety of likely sources: national literary societies, academies, university professors and previous winners. Nominations must reach the Academy before February 1 of the year in question. The Academy then appoints a working committee, the Nobel Committee, to evaluate the nominations, using specialists as necessary (e.g. for works written in languages the Committee cannot read). The Committee recommends a winner to the Swedish Academy where a voice vote is taken in early October. The choice is announced immediately after the balloting, and the Prize is then officially awarded at the Concert Hall in Stockholm, Sweden, on December 10, the anniversary of Alfred Nobel's death.

A majority vote is required, although the Swedish Academy has a permanent membership of eighteen, resulting in occasional ties. The Academy may award the prize jointly, having done so four times: Mistral and Echegaray (1904), Gjellerup and Pontoppidan (1917), Agnon and Sachs (1966) and Johnson and Martinson (1974). However, the Academy is under no obligation to issue a prize each year. Seven times no prize has been awarded.

Imagine that you are one of the eighteen members of the Swedish Academy, appointed by the King of Sweden for life (receiving a small silver token with the image of Gustav III for attending weekly meetings, every Thursday at 5:00 P.M.). The date is February 2. The Academy has received dozens, perhaps hundreds, of nominations to be considered, some in languages that no one on the Committee can even read. The Committee has until the summer recess, May 31, to render the long list down to five finalists. When meetings resume the week of September 15, the Committee has less than one month to reach agreement on the award. It is a daunting task.

The Nobel Committee has often seemed to choose recipients for their novelty of vision, subject or technique. The charge in Alfred Nobel's will stipulates that only writers of an "idealistic tendency" be selected. Ironically, this clause barred Henrik Ibsen from the Prize, although Nobel himself admired the author's work. In the early years of the committee the social criticism of Ibsen's work, especially *An Enemy of the People*, *The Pillar of Society*, and *Ghosts* distanced the Norwegian writer from the "ideal, pure, and elevated" traits sought by the electors. The Committee has more broadly inferred the founder's intention since World War II, thus allowing for such writers as Samuel Beckett and Jean-Paul Sartre to enter into the realm of the anointed.

The Nobel Committee has occasionally chosen writers for charting new territory on the map of serious literature. Pearl Buck exposed the world to Chinese peasants, and Naguib Mahfouz brought the enigmatic land of Egypt into current literature. Others, like Mikhail Sholokhov, Miguel Asturias and Isaac Bashevis Singer, dragged their respective ethnic groups from the shadows into the light. Some writers introduced new concepts to literature: Bergson, for example, with his notion of time and space, became a new well of imaginative technique from which ensuing writers, such as Joyce and Faulkner, drank deeply.

Of the ninety-five recipients since 1901, I have selected thirty-one for inclusion in this book. The reasons for omission are several, but none have to do with my own judgment on the quality of their writing nor on the literary importance of each writer. I simply omitted writers who had little to say in their addresses at the Award ceremony. Many of the winners in the early part of the century presented a personal autobiography (my mother was born in... I attended Velmer Academy... I met my wife, etc.) at the Award ceremony. Others said essentially nothing beyond "thanks a lot." Most of the notable statements date from Faulkner's stirring speech in 1949. The majority of writers included in this collection received the

Nobel Award after that date. From among those noteworthy addresses, I
have selected only those laureates whose lectures and speeches would appeal
to a broad range of readers and writers. Such a choice is highly personal.
Another editor would have selected a different list.

Each chapter is divided into three parts: an introduction to the author
and the laureate's address (usually edited). A bibliography of the author's
work available in English is provided in the back matter of this book. Each
component is intended to aid the reader in pursuing further reading of the
author.

The introductions are based on the assumption that fiction, whether
it be poetry or prose, is written for an intelligent reader, not for an academic specialist. No attempt has been made to mold my remarks to fit the
current (or traditional) academic "take" on the writer in question. Instead,
I have attempted to portray the broad sweep of the author's themes and
works. Like a long-range snapshot, the picture is one of many possible
likenesses, not a definitive image. Writers leave a distinct and sometimes
vacillating literary trail of their development, as writers and as people,
dooming any attempt to bind them with a conceptual straightjacket. Flannery O'Connor clarified the value and function of commentary on fiction.
"The meaning of fiction is not abstract meaning but experienced meaning, and the purpose of making statements about the meaning of a story
is only to help you to experience that meaning more fully."[10]

My goal in compiling this anthology is to pique readers' interest in
previously unread authors. To that end I have applied a scalpel, and at
times a hatchet, to the Nobel acceptances of the writers profiled. I hope
that in the process I haven't violated the integrity of any speeches or lectures. References to then current literary frays have been cut, unless the
areas of contention have remained broad and continuing. Dated material,
unless well known, has also been deleted. It is a daunting task to edit the
published work of great writers. However, the presentations were intended
for the time and place in which they were given, generally not meant to
be enduring testaments in their totality. I have retained those elements of
the acceptance that continue to speak to readers and writers of today.

The bibliographies serve as a guide for future reading. These lists are
as inclusive as possible. However, even long dead writers like Camus and
Hemingway have had new titles published in recent years. There is no reason to expect that the bibliographies listed here will remain inclusive in
the future.

Writing, like other art forms, demands deft handling of technical
detail. Mastering the skill, hatching a unique style, even creating a new

paradigm may be a precondition of great art, but it is never its aim. One of the great visual artists, Auguste Rodin, clearly defined the meaning of art almost a century ago:

> Art is contemplative. It is the pleasure of the mind which searches into nature and which there divines the spirit by which nature herself is animated. It is the joy of the intellect which sees clearly into the universe and which re-creates it, with conscientious vision. Art is the most sublime mission of man, since it is the expression of thought seeking to understand the world and make it understood. It is alchemy.[11]

The world's great writers infuse their craft with imaginative wisdom beyond both reason and experience. Milan Kundera defined this process: "The writer inscribes himself on the spiritual map of his time, of his country, on the map of the history of ideas."[12] The Nobel Prize winners extend the established boundaries of their discipline, and, with their audacity and insight, breathe life into their characters. The writers included in this collection used the occasion of the awarding of the Nobel Prize to convey to the world some of the ecstasy, loss, anger, obsession and love that drove them to their accomplishments.

1. Bjørnstjerne Bjørnson

Nothing can grow to power in a people which does not have root in its history.

— Bjørnstjerne Bjørnson[1]

It would be easy to view the selection of Bjørnstjerne Bjørnson (1832–1910) by the Nobel Committee as the selection of a favorite son, a writer with only local influence and little repute outside of his native Norway. Despite his writing Norway's national anthem, such a view of decided nepotism would be wrong. Bjørnson was, in fact, a transitional figure in European literature, bridging the chasm between an old agricultural society and the emerging urban culture of early twentieth century Europe.

Bjørnson wrapped the new around the old in a vibrantly human bandage. Like a strong wind blowing over Scandinavia, he invigorated his readers for the struggle of accepting the modern. He spoke to the disturbed tranquillity in the Norwegian heart as its people faced dislocation and the pace of a modern era. His novels, plays and poetry seem larger than life, poised with an optimism like that of Walt Whitman in *Leaves of Grass.* An exultant personality, his statement, "I believe and live without moderation,"[2] created a national optimism for the future.

Social class and the group were his foci. As a novelist and playwright, Bjørnson portrayed the assimilation of peasants into a modern, confusing society. He challenged the creaky political, religious, social and literary structure of his day, pointing the way to a future with confidence. He introduced social realism, with all its directness and brutality, to the Scandinavian stage along with an acceptance of the changing roles within the family structure. As a poet he evoked the beauty and history of Norway with the love of a naturalist and the ardor of a patriot. When attacked he responded, "I will live in

9

Norway; I will thrash and be thrashed in Norway; I will sing and die in Norway — of that you may be certain."[3]

Mythology and national identity formed a framework for Bjørnson's imagination. As Louis L'Amour imbued the American cowboy with a simple but rigid morality, Bjørnson molded the Norse sagas of the mythic past into modern themes. The hero on his journey, traveling through extraordinary natural hazards and supernatural peril, succeeds through strength of will. But Bjørnson did more than replenish myths with modern language; he also complicated these fables by highlighting both the ennobling and the destructive power of great willfulness. For Bjørnson, prevailing over adversity was important but not paramount. "God help us if our sense of fair play is not the strongest of all our feelings."[4] Taming the will with morality to create a better community was Bjørnson's challenge of living.

Central to Bjørnson's concept of the fully realized life is the relationship he explored between humankind and the Infinite. Bjørnson challenged conventional religion. He was troubled by "the thought that much of the best human energy goes to waste because it is devoted to the pursuit of ideals that are indeed beyond the strength of man to realize."[5] This is both the bane of the hero and that of modern man if he accepts the precepts of Christianity. "What frightened Bjørnson in the great religious personalities was their lack of 'sound and straight humanity,' their morbid tendency toward the impossible, which unsettled the balance of life on earth."[6] Bjørnson, ever human, could not bring himself to condemn the "bigoted sincerity of the saints"[7]; instead, he shows us their narrowness, gloom and loneliness, instilling a respect and compassion for those spirited away on religious ecstasy. His exuberant, outgoing personality would not submit to "the tyranny of the supernatural, the infinite, the boundless" (*Beyond Human Might*). He abhorred the Christian idea that the purpose of life was to achieve a place in heaven.

Bjørnson's view of poetry was neither romantic nor individualistic. "The poet does the prophet's deeds"[8] is how he expressed his view of the art. His was an embracing sensibility. "Our instinct of preservation demands abundance. If life had no abundance it would stop. Every picture which does not possess it is a false picture."[9] Compassion is at the heart of his poetic insight, while Bjørnson called this warmth of feeling for his fellow creature a "clarity of the heart."[10]

Similar to Yeats' effect in Ireland, Bjørnson (along with Henrik Ibsen) largely created modern Scandinavian theater. When he began writing, most of the plays produced in Norway were translations of French and other European playwrights. The sagas of the North became the basis of Bjørnson's early assault on the prevailing theater.

Bjørnson's characters do not wallow in an individual and personal psychology, as do Ibsen's. Rather Bjørnson looked at the group, particularly the family and its pressures. In *Magnhild* and *Leonarda* he treats the issue of virtue as a law of the heart in conflict with socially proscribed morality. Are we not required, he asks, to dissolve immoral marriages? In *Love and Geography* he challenges the notion that the husband, Tygesen, has the right to behave in any manner he desires. By ignoring his wife and family in pursuit of business, Tygesen forfeits his proper role as the head of the clan. Unlike Ibsen, Bjørnson strives for a morality that works for the majority, the group unit, not for the exceptional individual. Does not a woman have the same right to demand virginity of her groom as he has to demand it of his bride? In Bjørnson's view a home which does not offer reasonable freedom to *all* its members is doomed to perish. This is, indeed, a very modern notion.

1903

"— as a tribute to his noble, magnificent, and versatile work as a poet, which has always been distinguished by both the freshness of its inspiration and the rare purity of its spirit—"

...Let me, in the interest of brevity, evoke a picture I have had in my mind since my early youth, whenever I think of human progress. I see it as an endless procession in which men and women move steadily along. The line they follow is not invariably straight but it does take them forward. They are urged on by an irresistible force, purely instinctive at first but eventually more and more conscious. Not that human progress is even entirely a matter of conscious effort, and no man has ever been able to make it so. It is in this no man's land between conscious progress and subconscious forging ahead that imagination is at work. In some of us, the gift of prescience is so great that it enables us to see far ahead to the new paths along which human progress will travel.

Nothing has ever molded our conscience so strongly as our knowledge of what is good and what is evil. Therefore, our sense of good and evil is so much a part of our conscience that, to this day, no one can disregard it and feel at ease with himself. That is why I have always been so puzzled by the idea that we writers should lay down our sense of good and evil before we take up our pens. The effect of this reasoning would be to turn our minds into cameras indifferent to good and evil, to beauty and ugliness alike!

I do not want to dwell here on the extent to which modern man — always assuming he is a sane individual — can shake off a conscience that is the heritage of millions of years, and by which all the generations of mankind have been guided to the present day. I shall merely ask why those who subscribe to this theory choose certain images instead of others? Is their choice a purely mechanical one? Why are the pictures that present themselves to their imagination almost invariably shocking? Are they sure that it is not they, in fact, who have chosen them?

I do not think we need to wait for the answer. They can no more shake off the ideas that have come down to them through centuries of inherited morality than we can. The only difference between them and ourselves is that, whereas we serve these ideas, they try to rebel against them. I should quickly add here that not all is immortal that appears to be so. Many of today's guiding ideas were revolutionary ones in the past. What I do say is that the writers who reject tendentiousness and purpose in their work are the very ones who display it in every word they write. I could draw countless examples from the history of literature to show that the more a writer clamors for spiritual freedom, the more tendentious his work is liable to be. The great poets of Greece were equally at home with mortals and immortals. Shakespeare's plays were a great Teutonic Valhalla with brilliant sunshine at times and violent tempests at others. The world to him was a battlefield, but his sense of poetic justice, his sublime faith in life and its infinite resources guided the battles.

We may invoke from their graves, as often as we wish, the characters of Molière and Holberg, to see nothing but a procession of figures in frilly costumes and wigs who, with affected and grotesque gestures, fulfill their mission. They are as tendentious as they are verbose.

I spoke just now of our Teutonic Valhalla. Did not Goethe and Schiller bring something of the Elysian fields into it? The sky was loftier and warmer with them, life and art happier and more beautiful. We may perhaps say that those who have basked in this warmth, in this sunshine — young Tegner, young Oehlenschlager, and young Wergeland, not forgetting Byron and Shelley — have all had something of the Greek gods in them.

This time and this trend are gone now but I should like to mention two great men who belong to it. First, I think of my old friend in Norway who is now ill [Ibsen]. He has lit many a beacon along our Norwegian coast to guide the mariner, to warn him of the danger that lies ahead. I think, too, of a grand old man in a neighboring country to the east [Tolstoy], whose light shines forth and gives happiness to many. Their spirit, their many years of work, were lit by a purpose that was even brighter, like a flame in the evening wind.

I have said nothing here of the effect of tendentiousness on art, which it can make or mar.... If tendentiousness and art appear in the same proportion, all is well. Of the two great writers I have mentioned, it may well be that the former's warnings are so severe as to be frightening. And the latter may lure us with the charms of an ideal that passes human understanding and therefore frightens, too. But what is necessary is that our courage to live is strengthened, not weakened. Fear should not turn us back from the paths which open before us. The procession must go on. We must be confident that life is fundamentally good, that even after frightening disasters and the most tragic events, the earth is bathed in a flood of strength whose sources are eternal. Our belief in it is its proof.

In more recent time, Victor Hugo has been my hero. At the bottom of his brilliant imagination lies the conviction that life is good and it is that which makes his work so colorful. There are those who talk of his shortcomings, of his theatrical mannerisms. Let them. For me, all his deficiencies are compensated by his joie de vivre. Our instinct of self-preservation insists on this, for if life did not have more good than evil to offer us, it would have come to an end long ago. Any picture of life that does not allow for this fact is a distorted picture. It is wrong to imagine, as some do, that it is the dark aspects of life which are bad for us. That is not true.

Weaklings and egotists cannot abide harsh facts but the rest of us can. If those who choose to make us tremble or blush were also able to hold out a promise that, for all that may befall us, life has happiness to offer us, we might say to ourselves: all right, we are faced in this plot and in these words with a mystery that is part of life, and we should be roused to fear or amusement according to the author's will. The trouble is that writers seldom achieve more than a sensation, and often not even that! We feel doubly dissatisfied, because the author's attitude to life is so negative and because he is not capable of leading us. Incompetence is always galling.

The greater the burden a man takes upon his shoulders, the stronger he must be to carry it. No words are unmentionable, no action or horror beyond powers of description, if one is equal to them.

A meaningful life — this is what we look for in art, in its smallest dewdrops as in its unleashing of the tempest. We are at peace when we have found it and uneasy when we have not.

The old ideas of right and wrong, so firmly established in our consciousness, have played their part in every field of our life; they are part of our search for knowledge and our thirst for life itself. It is the purpose of all art to disseminate these ideas and, for that, millions of copies would not be one too many.

This is the ideal I have tried to defend, as a respectful servant and enthusiast. I am not one of those who believe that an artist, a writer, is exempt from responsibility. On the contrary, his responsibility is greater than that of other men because he who is at the head of the procession must lead the way for those who follow.

2. *William Butler Yeats*

Hammer your thought into unity.... For years I tested all I did
by that sentence.
                                    — *Selected Poems and Three Plays*

Placing most writers within a category helps us to empathize
with their work more easily; however, labeling William Butler Yeats
(1865–1939) seems to weaken our grasp on the most influential Irish
poet of this century. The scope of Yeats' vision often eluded both
his friends and enemies, each group tending to embrace a fragment
of his work as if it were the nucleus. An attempt to reconcile tensions and incompatibilities among the diverse elements of consciousness was Yeats' true artistic ambition. "The end of art is the
ecstasy awakened by the presence before an ever-changing mind of
what is permanent in the world" (*Essays and Introductions*). To make
his sense of mission comprehensible, Yeats conceived a universal system of intermingling opposites, based on mystical experience, pic-
tured as rotating gyres forever whirling into one another's centers,
merging and then separating.

Yeats practiced occultism and was profoundly influenced by
theosophy, an intellectual movement of the early twentieth century
which offered a synthesis of science, religion and philosophy. Yeats
claimed, "The mystical life is the center of all that I do and all that
I think and all that I write."[1] Mystical experience defies adequate
description, and Yeats' epiphanies are no exception. Yet these mystical episodes furnished the inspiration and deep structure of his
works. Among his principles was the idea that the borders of our
minds are permeable, allowing (under proper conditions) many
minds to flow into one, creating a single energy (or synergy). Memory also is plastic and can become one with the one Great Memory,
the memory of Nature herself.

15

Yeats evoked the Great Mind and the Great Memory with symbols: "Whatever the passions of man have gathered about becomes a symbol in the Great memory, and in the hands of him who has the secret it is a worker of wonders, a caller-up of angels or of devils" (*Essays and Introductions*). The importance of ritual in his work flows from his profound appreciation of the function of symbols, a "system of evocation and mediation — to reunite the perception of the spirit, of the dream, with natural beauty."[2]

Although Yeats' poetry can be read at many levels, with varying meanings (some of which served temporary political or social functions), he was not a man of his times. *Mourn and Then Onward*,[3] his elegy for Parnell, caused many to see him as a political writer. He wasn't. Romantics, anti-modernists, republicans, and elitists: all at one time or another claimed Yeats as one of their own, only to feel rejected and betrayed when he ignored their agendas. "I hate and still hate with an ever growing hatred the literature of the point of view" ("A General Introduction to My Work" in *Essays and Introductions*). In fact, he was at odds with the enlightenment and the ascendancy of the scientific-technological imperative of his times.

Yeats was an ardent proponent for the primacy of literature as a cultural force. "I believe that literature is the principal voice of the conscience, and that it is its duty age after age to affirm its morality against the special moralities of clergymen and churches, and of kings and parliaments and peoples."[4] When he lacked a vocabulary to express his particular vision, he invented one by using conventional terms in unusual ways.

> When I spoke of emotions as the first thing and last in education, I did not mean excitement. In the completely emotional man the least awakening of feeling is a harmony, in which every chord of every feeling vibrates.... Excitement is the feature of an insufficiently emotional nature, the harsh discourse of the vibration of but one or two chords [*Autobiographies*].

The spoken word was for Yeats *the* vehicle with which to achieve his unity. "I have spent my life in clearing out of poetry every phrase written for the eye, and bringing all back to syntax that is for ear alone" ("Introduction for My Plays" in *Essays and Introductions*). One of the difficulties of discussing Yeats' works are his numerous revisions as he approached ever nearer to his goal. *Cuchulain's Fight with the Sea* reached its final form in 1933, yet it was first published in 1892. It had taken him a lifetime to acquire the final simplicity he sought.

Yeats' writing anticipated some of the major trends in both theater and linguistics. His concern for the impact of language on the imaginative, cognitive and spiritual life of people predates much of linguistic philosophy. He was a harbinger of the "theater of the absurd." His *Purgatory* is a precursor to Samuel Beckett's *Waiting for Godot*.[5] Experimenting with techniques of the Japanese Noe theater to depict poetically spiritual truths and psychological realities which could not be expressed using conventional means, Yeats moved the Irish-English theater out of its Victorian stupor.

Yeats struggled to fold many phenomena into one intense unifying experience in order to produce a systematic poetry so inclusive it would be possible "to hold reality and justice in a single thought." The singular idea he sought was god-like in its inclusiveness. He successfully fused an idyllic past, with all its symbolism, into modern form in order to "lessen the solitude without destroying its peace."[6]

1923

"— for his always inspired poetry, which in a highly artistic form gives expression to the spirit of a whole nation —"

The Irish Dramatic Movement

I have chosen as my theme the Irish Dramatic Movement because when I remember the great honor that you have conferred upon me, I cannot forget many known and unknown persons.... I wish to tell the Royal Academy of Sweden of the labors, triumphs, and troubles of my fellow workers.

The modern literature of Ireland, and indeed all the stir of thought which prepared to the Anglo-Irish War, began when Parnell fell from power in 1891. A disillusioned and embittered Ireland turned away from parliamentary politics; an event was conceived and the race began, as I think, to be troubled by the event's long gestation. Dr. Hyde founded the Gaelic League, which was for many years to substitute for political argument a Gaelic grammar, and for political meetings village gatherings, where songs were sung and stories told in the Gaelic language. Meanwhile I had begun a movement in English, in the language in which modern Ireland thinks and does its business; founded certain societies where clerks, working men, men of all classes, could study those Irish poets, novelists, and historians who had written in English, and as much of Gaelic literature as had been translated into English. But the great mass of our people, accustomed to interminable political speeches, read little, and so from the very start we felt that we must have a theater of our own. The theaters of Dublin had nothing about them that we could call our own. They were empty buildings hired by the English traveling companies and we wanted Irish plays and Irish players. When we thought of these plays we thought of everything that was romantic and poetical, for the nationalism we had called up — like that every generation had called up in moments of discouragement — was romantic and poetical. It was not, however, until I met in 1896 Lady Gregory, a member of an old Galway family, who had spent her life between two Galway houses, the house where she was born and the house into which she was married, that such a theater became possible. All about her lived a peasantry who told stories in a form of English which has much of its syntax from Gaelic, much of its vocabulary from Tudor English, but it was very slowly that we discovered in that speech of theirs our most powerful dramatic instrument, not indeed until she began to write. Though my plays were written without dialect and in English blank verse, I think she was attracted to our movement because their subject matter differed but little from the subject matter of the country stories.

I have in Galway a little old tower, and when I climb to the top of it I can see at no great distance a green field where stood once the thatched cottage of a famous country beauty, the mistress of a small local landed proprietor. I have spoken to old men and women who remember her, though all are dead now, and they spoke of her as the old men upon the wall of Troy spoke of Helen; nor did man and woman differ in their praise. One old woman, of whose youth the neighbors cherished a scandalous tale, said of her, "I tremble all over when I think of her"; and there was another old woman on the neighboring mountain who said, "The sun and the moon never shone on anybody so handsome, and her skin was so white that it looked blue, and she had two little blushes on her cheeks." And there were men that told of the crowds that gathered to look at her upon a fair day, and of a man "who got his death swimming a river," that he might look at her.

...It seemed as if the ancient world lay all about us with its freedom of imagination, its delight in good stories, in man's force and woman's beauty, and that all we had to do was to make the town think as the country felt; yet we soon discovered that the town could only think town thought.

In the country you are alone with your own violence, your own heaviness, and with the common tragedy of life, and if you have any artistic capacity you desire beautiful emotion; and, certain that the seasons will be the same always, care not how fantastic its expression. In the town, where everybody crowds upon you, it is your neighbor not yourself that you hate and, if you are not to embitter his life and your own life, perhaps even if you are not to murder him in some kind of revolutionary frenzy, somebody must teach reality and justice. You will hate that teacher for a while, calling his books and plays ugly, misdirected, morbid or something of that kind, but you must agree with him in the end. We were to find ourselves in a quarrel with public opinion that compelled us against our own will and the will of our players to become always more realistic, substituting dialect for verse, common speech for dialect.

...We could experiment and wait, with nothing to fear but political misunderstanding. We had little money and at first needed little, twenty-five pounds given by Lady Gregory and twenty pounds by myself and a few pounds picked up here and there. And our theatrical organization was preposterous, players and authors all sat together and settled by vote what play should be performed and who should play it. It took a series of disturbances, weeks of argument, during which no performance could be given, before Lady Gregory and John Synge and I were put in control. And our relations with the public were even more disturbed. One play was violently attacked by the patriotic press because it described a married peasant woman who had a lover, and when we published the old Aran folk tale upon which it was founded, the press said the story had been copied from some decadent author of Pagan Rome. Nobody reading today can understand why.... *The Rising of the Moon*, now an Irish classic, could not be performed for two years because of political hostility.... The players would not perform it because they said it was an unpatriotic act to admit that a policeman was capable of patriotism.

...Every political party had the same desire to substitute for life, which never does the same thing twice, a bundle of reliable principles and assertions. Nor did religious orthodoxy like us any better than political; my *Countess Cathleen* was denounced by Cardinal Logue as an heretical play, and when I wrote that we would like to perform "foreign masterpieces," a Nationalist newspaper declared that "a foreign masterpiece is a very dangerous thing." The little halls where we performed could hold a couple of hundred people at the utmost and our audience was often not more than twenty or thirty, and we performed but two or three times a month and during our periods of quarreling not even that. But there was no lack of leading articles, we were from the first a recognized public danger. Two events brought us victory, a friend gave us a theater, and we found a strange man of genius, John Synge.

...I had met John Synge in Paris in 1896. Somebody had said, "There is an Irishman living on the top floor of your hotel; I will introduce you." I was very poor, but he was much poorer.... He was the man that we needed because he was the only man I have ever known incapable of a political thought or of a humanitarian purpose. He could walk the roadside all day with some poor man without any desire to do him good, or for any reason except that he liked him. He was to do for Ireland, though more by his influence on other dramatists than by his direct influence, what Robert Burns did for Scotland.

I did not, however, see what was to come when I advised John Synge to go to a wild island off the Galway coast and study its life because that life "had never been expressed in literature." When he found the wild island he became happy for the first time, escaping as he said "from the nullity of the rich and the squalor of the poor."

When I had landed from a fishing yawl on the middle of the island of Aran, a few months before my first meeting with Synge, a little group of islanders, who had gathered to watch a stranger's arrival, brought me to "the oldest man upon the island." He spoke but two sentences, speaking them very slowly, "If any gentleman has done a crime we'll hide him. There was a gentleman that killed his father and I had him in my house three months till he got away to America." It was a play founded on that old man's story Synge brought back with him. A young man arrives at a little public house and tells the publican's daughter that he has murdered his father. He so tells it that he has all her sympathy, and every time he retells it, with new exaggeration and additions, he wins the sympathy of somebody or other, for it is the countryman's habit to be against the law. The countryman thinks the more terrible the crime the greater must the provocation have been. The young man himself under the excitement of his own story becomes gay, energetic and lucky. He prospers in love and comes in first at the local races and bankrupts the roulette table afterwards. Then the father arrives with his head bandaged but very lively, and the people turn upon the impostor. To win back their esteem he takes up a spade to kill his father in earnest, but horrified at the threat of what had sounded so well in the story, they bind him to hand over the police. The father releases him and father and son walk off together, the son, still buoyed up by his imagination, announcing that he will be master henceforth. Picturesque, poetical, fantastical, a masterpiece of style and of music, the supreme work of our dialect theater, it roused the populace to fury.

We played it under police protection, seventy police in the theater the last night, and five hundred, some newspaper said, keeping order in the streets outside. It is never played before any Irish audience for the first time without something or other being flung at the players.

We are burdened with debt, for we have come through war and civil war and audiences grow thin when there is firing in the streets. We have, however, survived so much that I believe in our luck, and think that I have a right to say I end my lecture in the middle or even perhaps at the beginning of the story. But certainly I have said enough to make you understand why, when I received from the hands of your King the great honor your Academy has conferred upon me, I felt that a young man's ghost should have stood upon one side of me and at the other a living woman in her vigorous old age.

3. Henri Bergson

[Man's] physical nature is inextricably intertwined with his bodily frame; he is not spirit plus soul, plus body; but spirit, soul and body interfused; a sensuous-rational being, continuous with the world in which he lives. All being is of one tissue.

— Henri Bergson[1]

Henri Bergson's (1859–1941) writing inspired wide ranging reconsideration of many of the fundamental concepts of human experience: time, matter, energy, intelligence and intuition. His provocative analyses lifted him among the most influential writers of the first half of the twentieth century. A fiction writer's philosopher, he introduced into literature the concept of Stream of Consciousness, which James Joyce, Virginia Woolf and William Faulkner were to develop as a new and illuminating fictional technique. Bergson raised up intuition as a separate form of intelligence: "The light that shines on life's pathway, that illumines personality, liberty and our kinship with the ideal, is intuition."[2] He challenged our commonly held ideas of time. "Extension is space without quality — but succession without distinction is the fundamental feature of consciousness, duration."[3] His was a new view of the material world, encompassing spontaneity, which he believed had been ignored by scientists. Throughout his career Bergson attempted to reveal the illusions of scientists that biased not only their results but also their methods of inquiry.

Bergson's "intuition" is far from an innate hormonal response. Rather, he claimed that intuition is a manner of perceiving the world directly, and therefore more accurately, than with the intellect. He believed the intellect to be a functional tool, most useful for getting along in the world by creating categories. However, intellect becomes an obstacle to understanding the inner life of man. "All the molds crack," he said. "They are too narrow, above all, too rigid, for what we try to put into them."[4] Using a metaphor from the new medium of moving pictures, he said that trying to understand innate human nature with intellect was attempting to comprehend a movie by looking at only a few frames of film. He attacked the then prevalent notion that science was capable, even theoretically, of a fundamental understanding of the human consciousness.

Henri Bergson was successful in coining epigrams that attracted wide attention: "creative evolution," "élan vital," along with "the Stream of Consciousness," became concepts infusing a non-mechanical world concept into legitimate intellectual discourse. He encouraged a retreat into the self. "We live for the external world rather than for ourselves; we speak rather than think; we are acted upon rather than act ourselves. To act freely is to recover possession of oneself, and to get back into pure duration."[5]

Bergson applied a similar analysis to time, distinguishing sharply between time as measured by instruments and time as experienced, which he called duration. "Duration is the continuous progress of the past which gnaws into the future and which swells as it advances," for "the past in its entirety is prolonged into the present and abides there actual and acting."[6] His "creative evolution" embraced the flux that is by its very nature constantly producing something new. "Matter is a flux and not a thing, a process derived from the spiritual process of life by inversion. It is, so to speak, life that has lost, or is losing, its vitality, it is existence almost devoid of duration and descending in the direction of space."[7] This is at once both a restatement of Heraclitus' dictum that one cannot step into the same river twice and an application of the new physics of atomic and sub-atomic matter.

Bergson understood the process of creative writing and commented on it as no philosopher had since Aristotle in the *Poetics*. "Pure art detaches us from the instrumental mechanisms that condition everyday life; it frees us from our social selves by awakening our deepest emotions or by refining our external perceptions beyond the requirements of practical existence."[8] He envisioned writing that expressed the unpredictable flow of inner experience which rivets us to that moment. He understood also the prerequisites of vibrant characterization. "Each of us has his own way of loving and hating; and this love or this hatred reflects his whole personality."[9] The writer's task is to make his inherently unique vision felt in its particularity, while employing a confining language that tends to force all variety into rigid molds. An advocate of the "special role" of the artist, he believed it necessary "to brush aside the utilitarian symbols, the conventional and socially accepted generalities, in short, everything that veils reality from us, in order to bring us face to face with reality itself."[10] Bergson also understood that words convey meaning not only by their denotative and connotative definitions but also through rhythm, cadence, sentence length, pace and juxtaposition. He had a poet's understanding of the function of language.

Henri Bergson's analysis of human psychology brought him to a full understanding of comedy as well. "It is really a kind of automatism that makes us laugh — an automatism, as we have already remarked, closely akin to mere absentmindedness. To realize this more fully, it need only be noted that a comic character is generally comic in proportion to his ignorance of himself. The comic person is unconscious" (*Laughter: An Essay on the Meaning of the Comic*).

Bergson brought to legitimate public discussion an exuberant human-centered philosophy, one that recognized the fecundity and unique nature of each individual. He denied the authority of sterile, mechanistic world views, substituting — in their stead — his vigorous organic notions of flux and vital impulse. "Many people are hard, narrow, and unhappy, and are living without the faith, hope, and peace which should be every man's possession, because their minds are imprisoned in a little rigid, mechanical philosophy into which they are vainly trying to compress life."[11]

Although he was strongly inclined to convert to Catholicism late in life, Bergson gave his reasons for remaining Jewish in his will, dated 1937. "I have preferred to remain with those who tomorrow will be persecuted."[12] He refused an exemption by Vichy officials from the requirement that all Jews must register as such. At eighty-one years of age he lined up outdoors to register himself as a Jew. A few weeks later he died of pneumonia, having caught a cold while waiting to register.

> Mankind lies groaning, half crushed beneath the weight of its own progress. Men do not sufficiently realize that their future is in their own hands.... Theirs the responsibility, then, for deciding if they want merely to live, or intend to make just the extra effort required for fulfilling ... the essential function of the universe, which is a machine for the making of gods [*An Introduction to Metaphysics*].

1927

"— in recognition of his rich and vitalizing ideas and the brilliant skill with which they have been presented—"

...I thank the Swedish Academy from the bottom of my heart. It has bestowed upon me an honor to which I should not have dared aspire. I recognize its value even more, and I am even more moved by it, when I consider that this distinction, given to a French writer, may be regarded as a sign of sympathy given to France.

The prestige of the Nobel Prize is due to many causes, but in particular to its twofold idealistic and international character: idealistic in that it has been designed for works of lofty inspiration; international in that it is awarded after the production of different countries has been minutely studied and the intellectual balance sheet of the whole world has been drawn up. Free from all other considerations and ignoring any but intellectual values, the judges have deliberately taken their place in what the philosophers have called a community of the mind. Thus they conform to the founder's explicit intention. Alfred Bernhard Nobel declared in his will that he wanted to serve the causes of idealism and the brotherhood of nations. By establishing a peace Prize alongside the high awards in the arts and sciences, he marked his goal with precision. It was a great idea. Its originator was an inventive genius and yet he apparently did not share an illusion widespread in his century. If the nineteenth century made tremendous progress in mechanical inventions, it too often assumed that these inventions, by the sheer accumulation of their material effects, would raise the moral level of mankind. Increasing experience has proved, on the contrary, that the technological development of a society does not automatically result in the moral perfection of the men living in it, and that an increase in the material means at the disposal of humanity may even present dangers unless it is accompanied by a corresponding spiritual effort. The machines we build, being artificial organs that are added to our natural organs, extend their scope, and thus enlarge the body of humanity. If that body is to be kept entire and its movements regulated, the soul must expand in turn; otherwise its equilibrium will be threatened and grave difficulties will arise, social as well as political, which will reflect on another level the disproportion between the soul of mankind, hardly changed from its original state, and its enormously enlarged body. To take only the most striking example: one might have expected that the use of steam and electricity, by diminishing distances, would by itself bring about a moral *rapprochement* between peoples. Today we know that this was not the case and that antagonisms, far from disappearing, will risk being aggravated if a spiritual progress, a greater effort toward brotherhood, is not accomplished. To move toward such a *rapprochement* of souls is the natural tendency of a foundation with an international character and an idealistic outlook which implies that the entire civilized world is envisaged from a purely intellectual point of view as constituting one single and identical republic of minds. Such is the Nobel Foundation.

It is not surprising that this idea was conceived and realized in a country as highly intellectual as Sweden, among a people who have given so much attention to moral questions and have recognized that all others follow from them, and who, to cite only one example, have been the first to grasp that the political problem par excellence is the problem of education.

Thus the scope of the Nobel Foundation seems to widen as its significance is more deeply realized, and to have benefited from it becomes an honor all the more deeply appreciated. No one is more fully aware of this than I am. I wished to say so before this illustrious audience, and I conclude, as I began, with the expression of my profound gratitude.

4. Sinclair Lewis

Ah, smugness! That's the enemy.

—*Arrowsmith*

The small-town America of Sinclair Lewis (1885–1951) bears little resemblance to the bucolic ideal popularized by Norman Rockwell. Smallville, U.S.A., "had cultivated caution until they had lost the power to be interested" (*Dodsworth*). Lewis parodied the cupidity of prestigious social groups like, "scientists, whom Great Britain so much valued that she gave them titles almost as high as those which she rewarded distillers, cigarette-manufacturers, and the owners of obscene newspapers" (*Arrowsmith*). Critics (missing his real target by a wide margin) have claimed that Lewis hated fundamentalists, based on his parody of evangelical fundamentalism in *Elmer Gantry*. However, he didn't limit his ridicule to either Protestants or the religious: "The Roman Catholic Church is superior to the militant Protestant Church. It does not compel you to give up your sense of humor, or your pleasant vices. It merely requires you to give up your honesty, your reason, your heart and soul" (*Elmer Gantry*).

Lewis knew that every society extorts conformity and compliance from its members. What irked him was the unreflective nature of the American version of such coercion. With an avuncular style he unwrapped the mythology shrouding our institutions:

> The University of Winnemac is a mill to turn out men and women who will lead moral lives, play bridge, drive good cars, be enterprising in business and occasionally mention books, though they are not expected to have time to read much [*Arrowsmith*].

While Lewis created character types, then made them itch, he did so with a grin. Even the Reverend Elmer Gantry — a hypocrite,

29

sneak, coward, philanderer and boob — is a "bad boy" who hasn't learned his lesson, but he is not an evil man. Gantry's flailing attempts to manipulate the world to do his bidding make him much like us. At one point Gantry hires fake converts to bolster the tent meeting of his new love, evangelist Sharon Falconer, only to end up having to bribe them to stay away when they threaten to expose the fraud. And Gantry suffers the real frustrations of his calling, "year after year again of standing in the pulpit and knowing your congregation won't remember what you've said seven minutes after you've said it."

Critics have treated Lewis harshly. Telling the truth is not the surest path to popularity, nor is calling business people "human cash registers" nor academic administrators "men of measured merriment." He exposed the dehumanizing forces of rampant American capitalism, much as Dickens had done for the English industrial revolution a century earlier: When Martin suggested that all milk should be pasteurized, Pickerbaugh worried, "No, no Martin, don't think we could do that. Get so much opposition for the dairymen and landlords. Can't accomplish anything in this work unless you keep from offending people" (*Arrowsmith*).

The medical and educational establishments, in Lewis' view, were willing vassals to a rampaging economic system. Typical of Lewis' downbeat style, Gottlieb, "a benefactor of mankind" (*Arrowsmith*), not only isn't viewed as such, he isn't even very interesting, while the vacuous "Almus Pickerbaugh [in the same novel] had published scientific papers — often. He had published them in the 'Midwest Medical Quarterly,' of which he was one of fourteen editors." Lewis relates how this enterprising, but not very bright, doctor also found a germ that caused epilepsy and two germs that caused cancer. "Usually it took him a fortnight to make the discovery, write the report, and have it accepted" (*Arrowsmith*). Lewis' deadpan reporting underscores the very foolishness he parodies.

No American writer prior to Lewis examined the social dynamics of urban America with such microscopic intensity. His barb pricked every special interest group it touched — religious, educational, medical, and economic — at a time when the president of the United States was quoted as saying, "the business of America is business." Lewis should be remembered for his audacity if for nothing else.

Sinclair Lewis was not a great novelist. His writing does not consist of beautiful phrases, of sweeping vistas of man's fate, nor of piercing insights into the psychology of the individual. Rather, he studied the social dynamics of the herd and the impact of that herd on the individual, exposing powerful undercurrents with such minute detail that "he could have manufactured wax flowers that would make a man with hay fever sneeze."[1] It is this dedication to the facts and their specificity that gives Lewis' novels their staying power. He broke a fresh trail in depicting group dynamics. "Without his writing one cannot imagine modern American literature," said Mark Schorer, his biographer in *Sinclair Lewis: An American Life*.[2] No American writer after reading Lewis' scathing probes has dared to romanticize small-town life. Sinclair Lewis' penetrating insight into our national hypocrisy reads as poignantly today as it did when he wrote, giving him a well earned place among the Nobel laureates in Literature.

1930

"—for a vigorous and graphic art of description and his ability to create, with humor, new types of characters—"

The American Fear of Literature

...I wish, in this address, to consider certain trends, certain dangers, and certain high and exciting promises in present-day American literature. To discuss this with complete and unguarded frankness — and I should not insult you by being otherwise than completely honest, however indiscreet — it will be necessary for me to be a little impolite regarding certain institutions and persons of my own greatly beloved land.

...I have for myself no conceivable complaint to make, and yet for American literature in general, and its standing in a country where industrialism and finance and science flourish and the only arts that are vital and respected are architecture and the film, I have a considerable complaint.

...There is in America a learned and most amiable old gentleman who has been a pastor, a university professor, and a diplomat. He is a member of the American Academy of Arts and Letters and no few universities have honored him with degrees.... This scholar stated, and publicly, that in awarding the Nobel Prize to a person who has scoffed at American institutions as much as I have, the Nobel Committee and the Swedish Academy had insulted America.... I should have supposed that to a man so learned as to have been made a Doctor of Divinity, a Doctor of Letters

… would have reasoned: "Although personally I dislike this man's books, nevertheless the Swedish Academy has in choosing him honored America by assuming that the Americans are no longer a puerile backwoods clan, so inferior that they are afraid of criticism, but instead a nation come of age and able to consider calmly and maturely any dissection of their land, however scoffing." I should even have supposed that so international a scholar would have believed that Scandinavia, accustomed to the works of Strindberg, Ibsen, and Pontoppidan, would not have been peculiarly shocked by a writer whose most anarchistic assertion has been that America, with all her wealth and power, has not yet produced a civilization good enough to satisfy the deepest want of human creatures.

…In America most of us — not readers alone but even writers — are still afraid of any literature which is not a glorification of everything American, a glorification of our faults as well as our virtues. To be not only a best-seller in America but to be really beloved, a novelist must assert that all American men are tall, handsome, rich, honest, and powerful at golf; that all country towns are filled with neighbors who do nothing from day to day save go about being kind to one another; that although American girls may be wild, they change always into perfect wives and mothers; and that, geographically, America is composed solely of New York, which is inhabited entirely by millionaires; of the West, which keeps unchanged all the boisterous heroism of 1870; and of the South, where everyone lives on a plantation perpetually glossy with moonlight and scented with magnolias.

It is not today vastly more true than it was twenty years ago that such novelists of ours as you have read in Sweden, novelists like Dreiser and Willa Cather, are authentically popular and influential in America…. We still most revere the writers for the popular magazines who in a hearty and edifying chorus chant that the America of a hundred and twenty million population is still as simple, as pastoral, as it was when it had but forty million; that in an industrial plant with ten thousand employees, the relationship between the worker and the manager is still as neighborly and uncomplex as in a factory of 1840, with five employees; that the relationships between father and son, between husband and wife, are precisely the same in an apartment in a thirty-story palace today, with three motor cars awaiting the family below and five books on the library shelves and a divorce imminent in the family next week, as were those relationships in a rose-veiled five-room cottage in 1880; that, in fine, America has gone through the revolutionary change from rustic colony to world empire without having in the least altered the bucolic and Puritanic simplicity of Uncle Sam.

I am, actually, extremely grateful to the ... academician for having somewhat condemned me. For since he is a leading member of the American Academy of Arts and Letters, he has released me, has given me the right to speak as frankly of that Academy as he has spoken of me. And in any honest study of American intellectualism today, that curious institution must be considered.

Before I consider the Academy, however, let me sketch a fantasy which has pleased me the last few days in the unavoidable idleness of a rough trip on the Atlantic. I am sure that you know, by now, that the award to me of the Nobel Prize has by no means been altogether popular in America. Doubtless the experience is not new to you. I fancy that when you gave the award even to Thomas Mann, whose *Zauberberg* seems to me to contain the whole of intellectual Europe, even when you gave it to Kipling, whose social significance is so profound that it has been rather authoritatively said that he created the British Empire, even when you gave it to Bernard Shaw, there were countrymen to those authors who complained because you did not choose another.

And I imagined what would have been said had you chosen some American other than myself. Suppose you had taken Theodore Dreiser.

Now to me, as to many other American writers, Dreiser more than any other man, marching alone, usually unappreciated, often hated, has cleared the trail from Victorian and Howellsian timidity and gentility in American fiction to honesty and boldness and passion for life. Without his pioneering, I doubt if any of us could, unless we liked to be sent to jail, seek to express life and beauty and terror.... If you had given the Prize to Mr. Dreiser ... you would have heard that his style is cumbersome, that his choice of words is insensitive, and that his books are interminable. And certainly respectable scholars would complain that in Mr. Drieser's world, men and women are often sinful and tragic and despairing, instead of being forever sunny and full of song and virtue, as befits authentic Americans.

And had you chosen Mr. Eugene O'Neill, who has done nothing much in American drama save to transform it utterly, in ten or twelve years, from a false world of neat and competent trickery to a world of splendor and fear and greatness, you would have been reminded that he has done something far worse than scoffing — he has seen life as not to be neatly arranged in the study of a scholar but as a terrifying, magnificent, and often quite horrible thing akin to the tornado, the earthquake, the devastating fire.

And had you given Mr. James Branch Cabell the Prize, you would have been told that he is too fantastically malicious. So would you have been told that Miss Willa Cather, for all the homely virtue of her novels concerning the peasants of Nebraska, has in her novel, *The Lost Lady*, been so untrue to America's patent and perpetual and possibly tedious virtuousness as to picture an abandoned woman who remains, nevertheless, uncannily charming even to the virtuous, in a story without any moral; that Mr. Henry Mencken is the worst of all scoffers; that Mr. Sherwood Anderson viciously errs in considering sex as important a force in life as fishing; that Mr. Upton Sinclair, being a Socialist, sins against the perfectness of American capitalistic mass production ... and that Mr. Ernest Hemingway is not only too young but, far worse, uses language which should be unknown to gentlemen; that he acknowledges drunkenness as one of man's eternal ways to happiness, and asserts that a soldier may find love more significant that the hearty slaughter of men in battle.

It is my fate in this paper to swing constantly from optimism to pessimism and back, but so is it the fate on anyone who writes or speaks of anything in America — the most contradictory, the most depressing, the most stirring, of any land in the world today.

Thus, having with no muted pride called the roll of what seem to me to be great men and women in American literary life today, and having indeed omitted a dozen other names of which I should like to boast were there time, I must turn again and assert that in our contemporary American literature, indeed in all American arts save architecture and the firm, we — yes, we who have such pregnant and vigorous standards in commerce and science — have no standards, no healing communication, no heroes to be followed nor villains to be condemned, no certain ways to be pursued, and no dangerous paths to be avoided.

The American novelist or poet or dramatist or sculptor or painter must work alone, in confusion, unassisted save by his own integrity.

That, of course, has always been the lot of the artist. The vagabond and criminal François Villon had certainly no smug and comfortable refuge in which elegant ladies would hold his hand and comfort his starveling soul and more starved body. He, veritably a great man, destined to outlive in history all the dukes and puissant cardinals whose robes he was esteemed unworthy to touch, had for his lot the gutter and the hardened crust.

Such poverty is not for the artist in America. They pay us, indeed, only too well; the writer is a failure who cannot have his butler and motor and his villa at Palm Beach, where he is permitted to mingle almost in equality with the barons of banking. But he is oppressed ever by something worse than poverty — by the feeling that what he creates does not matter, that he is expected by his readers to be only a decorator or a clown, or that he is good-naturedly accepted as a scoffer whose bark probably is worse than his bite and who probably is a good fellow at heart, who in any case certainly does not count in a land that produces eighty-story buildings, motors by the million, and wheat by the billions of bushels. And he has no institution, no group, to which he can turn for inspiration, whose criticism he can accept and whose praise will be precious to him.

The American Academy of Arts and Letters ... does not include Theodore Dreiser, Henry Mencken, our most vivid critic, George Jean Nathan, who though still young, is certainly the dean of our dramatic critics, Eugene O'Neill, incomparably our best dramatist, the really original and vital poets, Edna St. Vincent Millay and Carl Sandburg, Robinson Jeffers and Vachel Lindsay and Edgar Lee Masters. It does not include the novelists and short-story writers, Willa Cather, Joseph Hergesheimer, Sherwood Anmderson, Ring Lardner, Ernest Hemingway, Louis Bromfield, Wilbur Daniel Steele, Fannie Hurst, Mary Austin, James Branch Cabell, Edna Ferber, nor Upton Sinclair.... I should not expect any Academy to be so fortunate as to contain all these writers, but one which fails to contain any of them, which thus cuts itself off from so much of what is living and vigorous and original in American letters, can have no relationship whatever to our life and aspirations. It does not represent the literary America of today — it represents only Henry Wadsworth Longfellow.

...I am reluctantly considering the Academy because it is so perfect an example of the divorce in America of intellectual life from all authentic standards of importance and reality.... Our universities and colleges, or gymnasia, most of them, exhibit the same unfortunate divorce.... I can think of [only] four of them, Rollins College in Florida, Middlebury College in Vermont, the University of Michigan, and the University of Chicago ... which have shown an authentic interest in contemporary creative literature.

But the paradox is that in the arts our universities are as cloistered, as far from reality and living creation, as socially and athletically and scientifically as they are close to us. To a true-blue professor of literature in an American university, literature is not something that a plain human being, living today, painfully sits down to produce. No; it is something dead; it is something magically produced by superhuman beings who must, if they are to be regarded as artists at all, have died at least one hundred years before the diabolical invention of the typewriter. To any authentic don, there is something slightly repulsive in the thought that literature could be created by any ordinary human being, still to be seen walking the streets, wearing quite commonplace trousers and coat and looking not so unlike a chauffeur or a farmer. Our American professors like their literature clear and cold and pure and very dead.

...There has recently appeared in America, out of the universities, an astonishing circus called "the New Humanism." Now of course "humanism" means so many things that it means nothing. It may infer anything from a belief that Greek and Latin are more inspiring than the dialect of contemporary peasants to a belief that any living peasant is more interesting than a dead Greek. But it is a delicate bit of justice that this nebulous word should have been chosen to label this nebulous cult. Insofar as I have been able to comprehend them ... this newest of sects reasserts the dualism of man's nature. It would confine literature to the fight between man's soul and God, or man's soul and evil.... So the whole movement results in the not particularly novel doctrine that both art and life must be resigned and negative. It is a doctrine of the blackest reaction introduced into a stirringly revolutionary world.

Strangely enough, this doctrine of death, this escape from the complexities and danger of living into the secure blankness of the monastery, has become widely popular among professors in a land where once would have expected only boldness and intellectual adventure, and it has more than ever shut creative writers off from any benign influence which might conceivably have come from the universities.

...It was with the emergence of William Dean Howells that we first began to have something like a standard, and a very bad standard it was.

...Mr. Howells was one of the gentlest, sweetest, and most honest of men, but he had the code of a pious old maid whose greatest delight was to have tea at a vicarage. He abhorred not only profanity and obscenity but all of what H. G. Wells has called "the jolly coarseness of life." ... He was actually able to tame Mark Twain, perhaps the greatest of our writers, and to put that fiery old savage into an intellectual frock coat and top hat. But, all this time, while men like Howells were so effusively seeking to guide America into becoming a pale edition of an English cathedral town, there were surly and authentic fellows — Whitman and Melville, then Dreiser and James Huneker and Mencken — who insisted that our land had something more than tea-table gentility.

And so, without standards, we have survived. And for the strong young men, it has perhaps been well that we should have no standards. For, after seeming to be pessimistic about my own and much beloved land, I want to close this dirge with a very lively sound of optimism.

I have, for the future of American literature, every hope and every eager belief. We are coming out, I believe, of the stuffiness of safe, sane, and incredibly dull provincialism. There are young Americans today who are doing such passionate and authentic work that it makes me sick to see that I am a little too old to be one of them.

There is Ernest Hemingway, a bitter youth, educated by the most intense experience, disciplined by his own high standards, an authentic artist whose home is in the whole of life; there is Thomas Wolfe, a child of, I believe, thirty or younger, whose one and only novel, *Look Homeward, Angel*, is worthy to be compared with the best in our literary production, a Gargantuan creature with great gusto of life; there is Thornton Wilder, who in an age of realism dreams the old and lovely dreams of the eternal romantics; there is John Dos Passos, with his hatred of the safe and sane standards of Babbitt and his splendor of revolution; there is Stephen Benet, who to American drabness has restored the epic poem with his glorious memory of old John Brown; there are Michael Gold, who reveals the new frontier of the Jewish East Side, and William Faulkner, who has freed the South from hoopskirts; and there are a dozen other young poets and fictioneers, most of them living now in Paris, most of them a little insane in the tradition of James Joyce, who, however insane they may be, have refused to be genteel and traditional and dull.

I salute them, with a joy in being not yet too far removed from their determination to give to the America that has mountains and endless prairies, enormous cities and lost far cabins, billions of money and tons of faith, to an America that is as strange as Russia and as complex as China, a literature worthy of her vastness.

5. Pearl S. Buck

> The best government in the world, the best religion, the best tra-
> ditions of any people, depend upon the good or evil of the men
> and women who administer them.
>
> — *My Several Worlds*

A controversial choice for the Nobel Prize in Literature (considered by many to be too light a writer for such an accolade), Pearl
Buck's *The Good Earth* ranked second in popularity only to Mark
Twain's writings in worldwide readership. Pearl Buck (1892–1973)
may not be a deeply provocative writer, but she was an accomplished
storyteller. She tells tales, primarily set in China, brimming with
human vacillation between evil and good, bigotry and wisdom. And
her selection was consistent with the Nobel tradition. A survey of
her work reveals elements that must have been instrumental in the
1938 decision.

She introduced "the Chinese peasant" into world literature,
paving the way for others in later years (Mahfouz, Asturias,
Sholokhov, Singer and Morrison) to receive Nobel laurels for intro-
ducing other "new" populations to world literature. Buck, who was
raised in China by her missionary parents and spoke Chinese as her
first language, lived among the Chinese peasantry for over thirty
years, making her well placed to interpret China to the West. She
attempted to create a context for understanding behaviors and attitudes that to the Western sensibility seemed either incomprehensible or irretrievably backward, including infanticide of female babies
and child slavery.

A strong adherent of the "idealistic" in human relations, she
emphasized the similarities between Chinese and non–Chinese peoples in her writing. Few Westerners understood China in general,
or the Chinese peasantry in particular, well enough to accomplish

the task of humanizing China for the West. Wang Lung, the protagonist in *The Good Earth,* has a soul no different from that of an
Iowa farmer. Buck exposes his failings and his strengths to under-
score this point. In a wonderfully concise phrase, Buck tells us that
after years of struggling to gain prosperity, Wang Lung "took into
his head to eat dainty foods." A single phrase announces a major
transformation of Wang Lung's psyche from that of a hard-working
farmer to that of the founder and patriarch of a great house. In *Sons*
she exposes the fraud behind a fierce War Lord (Wang Lung's son):
"The truth was that Wang the Tiger could not be cruel unless he
was angry, and indeed this was a weakness in a lord of war that he
could only kill in anger." A moralist, Buck chose to remain unso-
phisticated in order to personally preserve a vibrant bond with the
basic truths of human existence. Still, she had a finely grained insight
of the subtleties of relationship: "The bond between them was only
of flesh, and it could be easily broken. David was not a man of lust.
Passion he had, but it was entangled with spirit and mind ... she
could hold him by the strands that touched his heart ... [but] she
did not possess him" (*Peony*).

One of the central themes in Pearl Buck's work is the wisdom
of tolerance: religious, cultural and individual. She believed that
Westerners had something to learn from China in applying subtlety
and patience as alternatives to power and aggression toward achieving a goal. In *Peony* she confronts anti–Semitism, both among Westerners living in China and between Chinese and Jews. In an
insightful description of Christian reaction to Jewish tradition, Kung
Chen explains why Jews have encouraged reactions against them in
diverse parts of the world: "None on earth can love those who declare
that they alone are the sons of God." In the same novel a Buddhist
priest, chanting on the edge of the funeral of an old Jewish merchant, explains to the merchant's son: "Your father, although a foreigner, had a large heart, and he never separated himself from any
man. We wish to honor him with what we have, and we have nothing except our religion" (*Peony*).

Buck opened her big heart to the world, and the world
responded. These words were shouted by a parishioner in her father's
church as people began leaving during one of his less interesting ser-
mons: "Do not offend this good foreigner! He is making a pilgrim-
age in our country so that he may acquire merit in heaven. Let us
help him to save his soul!" (*My Several Worlds*). It is difficult to imagine such religious understanding occuring in a church or temple in
the United States.

Pearl Buck also illustrated the wisdom of a time honored tactic employed by the Chinese in dealing with foreign invasions, i.e., that of assimilation. Rather than take a combative attitude toward others, invasions by foreigners (along with their beliefs) were met with welcome. The Chinese people embraced strangers, drew them close, formed partnerships and intermarried so that within a generation or two they were no longer foreign.

Buck learned from and shared with the China of her upbringing a gentleness and consideration for the feelings of others, a respect for the importance of ancestry, family and tradition, along with a wry sense of reality. "But somewhere I had learned from Thoreau, who doubtless learned it from Confucius, that if a man comes to do his own good for you, then must you flee that man and save yourself" (*My Several Worlds*). She was a writer whose peasant heart cut through the pretense of difference so successfully that her works resonated throughout the world.

Her stories emphasize the idealistic tendency specified in Alfred Nobel's will: strong attachment to the earth, family, ancestry and tolerance among peoples of diverse backgrounds, making her a most deserving recipient of the Prize.

> There should be a deep attachment, heart should be tied to heart between parent and child, for unless the child learns how to love a parent profoundly, I believe that he will never learn how to love anyone else profoundly, and not knowing how to love means the loss of the meaning of life and its fulfillment [*My Several Worlds*].

1938

"—for her rich and truly epic descriptions of peasant life in China and for her biographical masterpieces—"

© The Nobel Foundation, 1938

The Chinese Novel

When I came to consider what I should say today it seemed that it would be wrong not to speak of China. And this is none the less true because I am an American by birth and by ancestry and though I live now in my own country and shall live there, since there I belong. But it is the Chinese and not the American novel which has shaped my own efforts in writing. My earliest knowledge of story, of how to tell and write stories, came to me in China. It would be ingratitude on my part not to recognize this today. And yet it would be presumptuous to speak before you on the subject of the Chinese novel for a reason wholly personal. There is another reason why I feel that I may properly do so. It is that I believe the Chinese novel has an illumination for the Western novel and for the Western novelist.

When I say Chinese novel, I mean the indigenous Chinese novel, and not that hybrid product, the novels of modern Chinese writers who have been too strongly under foreign influence while they were yet ignorant of the riches of their own country.

The novel in China was never an art and was never so considered, nor did any Chinese novelist think of himself as an artist. The Chinese novel, its history, its scope, its place in the life of the people, so vital a place, must be viewed in the strong light of this one fact. It is a fact no doubt strange to you, a company of modern Western scholars who today so generously recognize the novel.

...If the Chinese scholars ever knew of the growth of the novel, it was only to ignore it the more ostentatiously. Sometimes, unfortunately, they found themselves driven to take notice, because youthful emperors found novels pleasant to read. Then these poor scholars were hard put to it. But they discovered the phrase "social significance," and they wrote long literary treatises to prove that a novel was not a novel but a document of social significance. Social significance is a term recently discovered by the most modern of literary young men and women in the United States, but the old scholars of China knew it a thousand years ago, when they, too, demanded that the novel should have social significance, if it were to be recognized as an art.

...The art of literature, so I was taught, is something devised by men of learning. Out of the brains of scholars came rules to control the rush of genius, that wild fountain which has its source in deepest life. Genius, great or less, is the spring, and art is the sculptured shape, classical or modern, into which the waters must be forced, if scholars and critics were to be served. But the people of China did not so serve. The waters of the genius of story gushed out as they would, however the natural rocks allowed and the trees persuaded, and only common people came and drank and found rest and pleasure.

The preface of *Fah Shu Ching*, one of the most famous of Buddhist books, says, "When giving the words of gods, these words should be given forth simply." This might be taken as the sole literary creed of the Chinese novelist, to whom, indeed, gods were men and men were gods.

For the Chinese novel was written primarily to amuse the common people. And when I say amuse I do not mean only to make them laugh, though laughter is also one of the aims of the Chinese novel. I mean amusement in the sense of absorbing and occupying the whole attention of the mind. I mean enlightening that mind by pictures of life and what that life means. I mean encouraging the spirit not by rule-of-thumb talk about art, but by stories about the people in every age, and thus presenting to people simply themselves. Even the Buddhists who came to tell about gods found that people understood gods better if they saw them working through ordinary folk like themselves.

...Story was what they wanted. And when I say story, I do not mean mere pointless activity, not crude action alone. The Chinese are too mature for that. They have always demanded of their novel character above all else. *Shui Hu Chuan* they have considered one of their three greatest novels, not primarily because it is full of the flash and fire of action, but because it portrays so distinctly one hundred and eight characters that each is to be seen separate from the others. Often I have heard it said of that novel in tones of delight, "When anyone of the hundred and eight begins to speak, we do not need to be told his name. By the way the words come from his mouth we know who he is." Vividness of character portrayal, then, is the first quality which the Chinese people have demanded of their novels, and after it, such portrayal shall be by the character's own action and words rather than by the author's explanation.

...Nor was the novel in China shaped, as it was in the West, by a few great persons. In China the novel has always been more important than the novelist. There has been no Chinese Defoe, no Chinese Fielding or Smollett, no Austen or Brontë or Dickens or Thackeray, or Meredith or Hardy, any more than Balzac or Flaubert. But there were and are novels as great as the novels in any other country in the world, as great as any could have written, had he been born in China. Who then wrote these novels of China?

...A good novelist, or so I have been taught in China, should be above all else *tse ran*, that is, natural, unaffected, and so flexible and variable as to be wholly at the command of the material that flows through him. His whole duty is only to sort life as it flows through him and in the vast fragmentariness of time and space and even to discover essential and inherent order and rhythm and shape. We should never be able, merely by reading pages, to know who wrote them, for when the style of a novelist becomes fixed, that style becomes his prison. The Chinese novelists varied their writing to accompany like music their chosen themes.

These Chinese novels are not perfect according to Western standards.

They are not always planned from beginning to end, nor are they compact, any more than life is planned or compact. They are often too long, too full of incident, too crowded with character, a medley of fact and fiction as to material, and a medley of romance and realism as to method, so that an impossible event of magic or dream may be described with such exact semblance of detail that one is compelled to belief against all reason. The earliest novels are full of folklore, for the people of those times thought and dreamed in the ways of folklore. But no one can understand the mind of China today who has not read these novels, for the novels have shaped the present mind, too, and the folklore persists in spite of all the Chinese diplomats and Western-trained scholars would have us believe to the contrary. The essential mind of China is still that mind of which George Russell wrote when he said of the Irish mind, so strangely akin to the Chinese, "that mind which in its full imagination believes anything. It creates ships of gold with masts of silver and white cities by the sea and rewards and fairies, and when that vast folk mind turn to politics it is ready to believe anything."

...It is as though for centuries the novel had been developing unnoticed and from deep roots among the people, spreading into the trunk and branch and twig and leaf to burst into this flowering in the Yuan dynasty, when the young Mongols brought into the old country they had conquered their vigorous, hungry, untutored minds and demanded to be fed. Such minds could not be fed with the husks of the old classical literature, and they turned therefore the more eagerly to the drama and the novel, and in this new life, in the sunshine of imperial favor, though still not with literary favor, there came two of China's three great novels, *Shui Hu Chuan* and *San Kuo*—*Hung Lou Meng* being the third.

I wish I could convey to you what these three novels mean and have meant to the Chinese people. But I can think of nothing comparable to them in Western literature. We have not in the history of our novel so clean a moment to which we can point and say, "There the novel is at its height." These three are the vindication of that literature of the common people, the Chinese novel. They stand as completed monuments of that popular literature, if not of letters. They, too, were ignored by men of letters and banned by censors and damned in succeeding dynasties as dangerous, revolutionary, decadent. But they lived on, because people read them and told them as stories and sang them as songs and ballads and acted them as dramas, until at last grudgingly even the scholars were compelled to notice them and to begin to say they were not novels at all but allegories, and if they were allegories perhaps then they could be looked upon as literature after all, though the people paid no heed to such theories and never read the long treatises which scholars wrote to prove them. They rejoiced in the novel they had made as novels and for no purpose except for joy in story and in story through which they could express themselves.

...*Hung Lou Meng*—The Dream of the Red Chamber—seized hold of the people primarily because it portrayed the problems of their own family system, the absolute power of women in the home, the too great power of the matriarchy, the grandmother, the mother, and even the bond-maids, so often young and beautiful and fatally dependent, who became too frequently the playthings of the sons of the house and ruined them and were ruined by them. Women reigned supreme in the Chinese house, and because they were wholly confined in its walls and often illiterate, they ruled to the hurt of all. They kept men children, and protected them from hardship and effort when they should not have been so protected. Such a one was Chia Pao Yu, and we follow him to his tragic end in *Hung Lou Meng*.

But I can mention only a small fraction of the hundreds of novels which delight the common people of China. And if those people knew of what I was speaking to you today, they would after all say, "Tell of the great three, and let us stand or fall by *Shui Hu Chuan* and *San Kuo* and *Hung Lou Meng*." In these three novels are the lives which the Chinese people lead and have long led, here are the songs they sing and the things at which they laugh and the things which they love to do. Into these novels they have put the generations of their being and to refresh that being they return to these novels again and again, and out of them they have made new songs and plays and other novels. Some of them have come to be almost as famous as the great originals, as for example *Ching P'ing Mei*, that classic of romantic physical love, taken from a single incident in *Shui Hu Chuan*.

The instinct which creates *the arts* is not the same as that which produces art. The creative instinct is, in its final analysis and in its simplest terms, an enormous extra vitality, a super-energy, born inexplicably in an individual, a vitality great beyond all the needs of his own living—an energy which no single life can consume. This energy consumes itself then in creating more life, in the form of music, painting, writing, or whatever is its most natural medium of expression. Nor can the individual keep himself from this process, because only by its full function is he relieved of the burden of this extra and peculiar energy—an energy at once physical and mental, so that all his senses are more alert and more profound than another man's, and all his brain more sensitive and quickened to that which his senses reveal to him in such abundance that actuality overflows into imagination. It is a process proceeding from within. It is the heightened activity of every cell of his being, which sweeps not only himself, but all human life about him, or in him, in his dreams, into the circle of his activity.

From the product of this activity, art is deducted — but not by him. The process which creates is not the process which deduces the shapes of art. The defining of art, therefore, is a secondary and not a primary process. And when one born for the primary process of creation, as the novelist is, concerns himself with the secondary process, his activity becomes meaningless. When he begins to make shapes and styles and techniques and new schools, then he is like a ship stranded upon a reef whose propeller, whirl wildly as it will, cannot drive the ship onward. Not until the ship is in its element again can it regain its course.

And for the novelist the only element is human life as he finds it in himself or outside himself. The sole test of his work is whether or not his energy is producing more of that life. Are his creatures alive? That is the only question. And who can tell him? Who but those living human beings, the people? Those people are not absorbed in what art is or how it is made — are not, indeed, absorbed in anything very lofty, however good it is. No, they are absorbed only in themselves, in their own hungers and despairs and joys and above all, perhaps, in their own dreams. These are the ones who can really judge the work of the novelist, for they judge by the single test of reality. And the standard of the test is not to be made by the device or art, but by the simple comparison of the reality of what they read, to their own reality.

6. T.S. Eliot

The end of all our exploring
Will be to arrive where we started
And know the place for the first time

—*Little Gidding*

The supernatural seeps into and out of T.S. Eliot's (1888–1965) work: "Man is man because he can recognize supernatural realities, not because he can invent them" (*Selected Essays*). Prufrock, the vacillating coward in Eliot's most famous verse, is too distracted to ever be made whole:

> Do I dare
> Disturb the universe,
> Shall I part my hair behind?
> Do I dare to eat a peach?
> I shall wear white flannel trousers,
> and walk upon the beach.
> [*The Love Song of J. Alfred Prufrock*]

Eliot and Yeats discovered a new species of poetry, one that either repelled or attracted subsequent twentieth century poets. None could ignore their work. Eliot brought the sensibility of a fragmented soul, "a bundle of broken mirrors,"[1] to poetry as Shostakovich brought discordance to music. Gone the lyric phrasing, romantic ideals, and transcendent emotion — in their place a collage of stark images and discontinuity that became modernism. No topic, no perspective was beyond modernist expression:

> Feet rising and falling,
> Eating and drinking, Death and dung.
>
> [*East Coker*]

47

The goal was "to strip poems to their bare bones to use poetry to go beyond poetry, like music heard so deeply that it is not heard at all" (*The Dry Salvages*). Fragmented souls may vibrate to discordant images, but estrangement wasn't Eliot's message; we must, he said, go through alienation to arrive at eternal wholeness. "A wrong attitude towards nature implies, somewhere, a wrong attitude towards God, and that the consequence is an inevitable doom" (*The Idea of a Christian Society*). There is no mistaking Eliot's bleak warning. "And the wind shall say: 'Ere were a decent godless people/Their only monument the asphalt road/And a thousand lost golf balls" (*The Rock*).

Eliot wrote of and for an audience suffering "tumid apathy with no concentration" (*Burnt Norton*), decrying "a sense of unreality that pervades a world that has lost the rhythm of the seasons ... such a world is unreal"[2] He skated on the black ice separating knowledge of things from the experience of truth: "As for us, we know too much, and are convinced of too little" (*Selected Essays*). Everything he wrote was grounded in this thirst for a deep meaningful relationship with God.

> You are not here to verify,
> Instruct yourself, or inform curiosity
> Or carry a report. You are here to kneel.
>
> [*Little Gidding*]

Eliot's interior monologues explore a Buddhist vision fused to Henri Bergson's notions of time and space.

> At the still point of the turning world. Neither flesh nor fleshless;
> Neither from nor towards: at the still point, there the dance is.
> ...Where past and future are gathered.
> Except for the point, the still point,
> There would be no dance,
> and there is only the dance.
>
> [*Burnt Norton*]

He believed that "man can embody truth but he cannot know it"[3]:

> There is a meaning not given by but given to experience.
> We had the experience but missed the meaning,
> And approach to the meaning restores the experience
> In a different form, beyond any meaning
> We can assign to happiness.
>
> [*The Dry Salvages*]

Eliot the critic introduced the notions of "objective correlative" and "dissociation of sensibility" into the vocabulary of dramatic criticism. "The only way of expressing emotion in the form of art is by finding an 'objective correlative,' in other words, a set of objects, a situation, a chain of events which shall be the formula of that *particular* emotion; such that when the external facts, which must terminate in sensory experience, are given, the emotion is immediately evoked"("Hamlet," *Selected Prose of T.S. Eliot*). Dissociation of sensibility flows the other way — inept language forces the audience further from the dramatic essence. Eliot's Zen-like description of the act of criticism satisfies his criterion of objective correlation:

> You don't really criticize any author to whom you have never surrendered yourself... you have to give yourself up, and then recover yourself, and the third moment is having something to say, before you have wholly forgotten both surrender and recovery. Of course the self recovered is never the same as the self before it was given [*T.S. Eliot: The Man and His Work*].

He warns starkly against reversing the process; reading to prove one's point he labeled conquest the opposite of surrender.

Eliot undertook the daunting task of resurrecting the verse drama in modern times, inviting a comparison with Shakespeare. He explained, "The human soul, in intense emotion, strives to express itself in verse. It is not for me, but for the neurologists, to discover why this is so, and why and how feeling and rhythm are related" (*Selected Essays*).

Eliot shook the world for its failure to live, to comprehend, to understand, and to accept. "The worst that can be said about most of our malefactors, from statesmen to thieves, is that they are not men enough to be damned."[4] Here is Thomas Sterns Eliot, haunted by the failure of metaphysical nerve, enticing us to take the bold step into uncertainty:

> The awful daring of a moment's surrender
> Which an age of prudence can never retract
> By this, and this only, we have existed.
>
> [*The Wasteland*]

1948

"—for his outstanding, pioneer contribution to present-day poetry—"

...I must try ... to express myself in an indirect way, by putting before you my own interpretation of the significance of the Nobel Prize in Literature. If this were simply the recognition of merit, or of the fact that an author's reputation has passed the boundaries of his own country and his own language, we could say that hardly any one of us at any time is, more than others, worthy of being so distinguished. But I find in the Nobel Award something more and something different from such recognition. It seems to me more the election of an individual, chosen from time to time from one nation or another, and selected by something like an act of grace, to fill a peculiar role and to become a peculiar symbol. A ceremony takes place, by which a man is suddenly endowed with some function which he did not fill before. So the question is not whether he was worthy to be so singled out, but whether he can perform the function which you have assigned to him: the function of serving as a representative, so far as any man can be, of something of far greater importance than the value of what he himself has written.

Poetry is usually considered the most local of all the arts. Painting, sculpture, architecture, music, can be enjoyed by all to see or hear. But language, especially the language of poetry, is a different matter. Poetry, it might seem, separates people instead of uniting them.

But on the other hand we must remember, that while language constitutes a barrier, poetry itself gives us a reason for trying to overcome the barrier. To enjoy poetry belonging to another language, is to enjoy an understanding of the people to whom that language belongs, an understanding we can get in no other way. We may think also of the history of poetry in Europe, and of the great influence that the poetry of one language can exert on another; we must remember the immense debt of every considerable poet to poets of other languages than his own; we may reflect that the poetry of every country and every language would decline and perish, were it not nourished by poetry in foreign tongues. When a poet speaks to his own people, the voices of all the poets of other languages who have influenced him are speaking also. And at the same time he himself is speaking to younger poets of other languages, and these poets will convey something of *his* vision of life and something of the spirit of *his* people, to their own. Partly through his influence on other poets, partly through translation, which must be also a kind of recreation of his poems by other poets, partly through readers of his language who are not themselves poets, the poet can contribute toward understanding between peoples.

In the work of every poet there will certainly be much that can only appeal to those who inhabit the same region, or speak the same language, as the poet. But nevertheless there is a meaning to the phrase "the poetry of Europe" and even to the word "poetry" the world over. I think that in poetry people of different countries and different languages — though it be apparently only through a small minority in any one country — acquire an understanding of each other which, however partial, is still essential. And I take the award of the Nobel Prize in Literature, when it is given to a poet, to be primarily an assertion of the supra-national value of poetry. To make that affirmation, it is necessary from time to time to designate a poet: and I stand before you, not on my own merits, but as a symbol, for a time, of the significance of poetry.

7. William Faulkner

> Memory believes before knowing remembers. Believes longer than
> recollects, longer than knowing even wonders.
>
> —*Light in August*

Only a few writers in the twentieth century acted as channel markers designating new waters for others to follow. William Faulkner (1897–1962) is one of these few. His rise to pre-eminence was slow and uncertain; by 1945 all seventeen of his novels were out of print. His works are dense, with remote locales evoked in verbose language and characters wrapped in moral dilemmas impregnated with history. He writes like an American Dostoyevsky, slogging thigh deep through innocence, incest, corruption, guilt, slavery and decadence among the bogs of memory and fable, chimera and fact. His fictional county, Yoknapatawpha, means "water flowing slow through the flatland" in native Chickasaw Indian dialect. His characters live downstream, coping with a river that falls and rises independent of human volition. We surrender to such a river because we must, even when it deposits the flotsam of the past over our plans for the present.

A vivid sense of the inevitability of personal history permeates Faulkner's reality. None of his characters is free in the sense of a "new man." All are encumbered: "A man will talk about how he'd like to escape from living folks. But it's the dead folks that do him the damage. It's the dead ones that lay quiet in one place and don't try to hold him, that he can't escape from" (*Light in August*). With perfect pitch for the arrhythmic beating of the human heart, Faulkner pities his characters as they grope for happiness. "Don't make me have to pray yet. Dear God, let me be damned a little longer," prays Miss Burden in *Light in August*, offering hope of extending a forbidden sexual affair with Joe Christmas.

With compassion Faulkner champions social sins. "You forget that lying is a struggle for survival ... little puny man's way of draggin' circumstance about to fit his preconception of himself as a figure in the world"(*Sartoris*). On the propensity of people to mind their neighbors' business, he writes, "A man ... will pass up a hundred chances to do good for one chance to meddle where meddling is not wanted" (*Light in August*). His ironic voice was applied particularly to women: "And the ladies called upon her ... even in her own house, while they told her how to run it and what to wear and what to make her husband eat" (*Light in August*). But the whole species is, in his view, fractious. "The last sound on the worthless earth will be two human beings trying to launch a homemade space ship and already quarreling about where they are going next" ("UNESCO Address" in Meriwether).[1]

Faulkner gloried in the subtlety of the natural world and wrote of it with a poet's ear. Every outdoorsman can identify with atmosphere that strikes the senses before thought occurs. "I could smell the cold" (*The Sound and the Fury*). He knew the elusiveness of deer as only a hunter knows deer:

> Then the buck was there. He did not come into sight; he was just there, looking not like a ghost but as if all of light were condensed in him and he were the source of it, not only moving in it but disseminating it, already running, seen first as you always see the deer, in that split second after he has already seen you [*Go Down, Moses*].

He applied a keen sensitivity to small, often unnoticed details that give his interior monologues the power to evoke more than they describe. "It was only as he put his hand on the door that he became aware of complete silence beyond it, a silence which he at eighteen knew that it would take more than one person to make" (*Light in August*).

Faulkner read the debris of the human predicament — the agony, endurance and hope of humanity playing itself out in his fictional "postage stamp" of the world: "That's what they mean by the womb of time: the agony and the despair of spreading bones, the hard girdle in which lie the outraged entrails of events" (*As I Lay Dying*). His values were conservative, old fashioned and antagonistic to the emergence of American commercialism:

> Reality cannot be bought. It can only be had by love. The right attitude toward nature and man is love. And love is the opposite of the lust for power over nature or over other men, for God gave the earth to man not to hold for himself and his descendants' inviolable title

forever ... and all the fee He asked was pity and humility and
sufferance and endurance and the sweat of his face for bread [*The
Bear*].

William Faulkner tends to surround an event with significance
while the act itself is scarcely reported. He tested the tensile strength
of Henri Bergson's notion of duration, using stream-of-conscious-
ness monologues as a major narrative line. No other American had
applied the technique with such dedication, skill and complexity as
did Faulkner. None spoke a dialect so particular and peculiar that it
became universal. Faulkner answered the call issued by Walt Whitman to an earlier generation of American writers in "Passage to
India":

> Who shall soothe these feverish children?
> Who justify these restless explorations?
> Who speak the secret of impassive earth?
> Who bind it to us?

1949

*"—for his powerful and artistically unique contribution to the modern
American novel—"*

I feel that this award was not made to me as a man, but to my work —
a life's work in the agony and sweat of the human spirit, not for glory and
least of all for profit, but to create out of the materials of the human spirit
something which did not exist before. So this award is only mine in trust.
It will not be difficult to find a dedication for the money part of it com-
mensurate with the purpose and significance of its origin. But I would like
to do the same with the acclaim too, by using this moment as a pinnacle
from which I might be listened to by the young men and women already
dedicated to the same anguish and travail, among whom is already that
one who will some day stand here where I am standing.

Our tragedy today is a general and universal physical fear so long sustained by now that we can even bear it. There are no longer problems of
the spirit. There is only the question: When will I be blown up? Because
of this, the young man or woman writing today has forgotten the problems of the human heart in conflict with itself which alone can make good

writing because only that is worth writing about, worth the agony and the sweat.

He must learn them again. He must teach himself that the basest of all things is to be afraid: and, teaching himself that, forget it forever, leaving no room in his workshop for anything but the old verities and truths of the heart, the old universal truths lacking which any story is ephemeral and doomed — love and honor and pity and pride and compassion and sacrifice. Until he does so, he labors under a curse. He writes not of love but of lust, of defeats in which nobody loses anything of value, of victories without hope, and, worst of all, without pity or compassion. His griefs grieve on no universal bones, leaving no scars. He writes not of the heart but of the glands.

Until he relearns these things, he will write as though he stood among and watched the end of man. I decline to accept the end of man. It is easy enough to say that man is immortal simply because he will endure: that when the last dingdong of doom has clanged and faded from the last worthless rock hanging tideless in the last red and dying evening, that even then there will still be one more sound: that of his puny inexhaustible voice, still talking. I refuse to accept this. I believe that man will not merely endure: he will prevail. He is immortal, not because he alone among creatures has an inexhaustible voice, but because he has a soul, a spirit capable of compassion and sacrifice and endurance. The poet's, the writer's, duty is to write about these things. It is his privilege to help man endure by lifting his heart, by reminding him of the courage and honor and hope and pride and compassion and pity and sacrifice which have been the glory of his past. The poet's voice need not merely be the record of man, it can be one of the props, the pillars to help him endure and prevail.

8. Bertrand Russell

I want to stand at the rim of the world and peer into the darkness beyond, and see a little more than others have seen, of the
strange shapes of mystery that inhabit that unknown night.

— Bertrand Russell[1]

If one trait characterized Bertrand Russell's (1872–1970) active
life, it was his iconoclastic attitude towards the snug (and smug)
English upper class institutions of which he was a product (Russell
Viscount Amberley, 3rd Earl Russell of Kingston Russell). Russell
never fit into that milieu. He adamantly opposed all forms of received
dogma that had passed unquestioned from generation to generation.
A prolific writer, he cast skeptical and often sardonic eyes on the foolishness of our species, earning him three separate and quite distinct
reputations: logician, social philosopher, and anti-war activist.

As a major philosophical writer of this century, Russell wrote
for common readers, crediting them with the capacity to grasp and
appreciate his arguments. He established a vaunted reputation as a
logician prior to the First World War with the publication of *Principia Mathematica* (in collaboration with Alfred North Whitehead).
Sometimes described as the greatest logician since Aristotle, Russell's fundamental contribution to the field was demonstrating the
limitations of logic. He insisted that knowledge derived from logic
is provisional: "Logic is the art of *not* drawing conclusions."[2] Just as
Aristotle had tutored Plato, Russell tutored Ludwig Wittgenstein
(who used Russell's theory of Logical Atomism as a springboard for
what became modern linguistic philosophy).

Bertrand Russell also gained a broad following for his discus-
sions of social philosophy. Political theory, war, physics, education,
sexual ethics, religion, psychology and prison reform fell under his

57

analytic gaze and graceful pen. His analysis of social psychology and those who manipulated it for their own ends informed his many opinions: "Obloquy is, to most men, more painful than death; that is one reason why, in times of collective excitement, so few men venture to dissent from the prevailing opinion" (*An Outline of Intellectual Rubbish*). He brazenly chided the Christian Church for its suppression of free thought and free expression.

> The church no longer contends that knowledge is in itself sinful, though it did so in its palmy days; but the acquisition of knowledge, even though not sinful, is dangerous, since it may lead to pride of intellect, and hence to a questioning of the Christian dogma [*Why I Am Not a Christian*].

His boldness drew quick attention to his arguments. In one sentence he undercuts the concept of the proper raising of children, while in the next he exposes the hypocrisy rife in relationships between men and women. Sweeping away the traditional family structure (sanctioned by church and society) as both unfair and illogical, Russell attacked the precepts of parental and male dominance:

> There is no greater reason for children to honor parents than for parents to honor children, except that while the children are young, the parents are stronger than the children. The same thing, of course, happened in the relations of men and women…. I defy anyone to find a basis for this view, except that men have stronger muscles than women [*New Hopes for a Changing World*].

Most widely known for his unorthodox views on sexual morality, Russell advocated both free love and open marriage. His appointment as a professor at City College of New York was annulled by an American court on the grounds that he advocated sexual immorality. Russell also championed the notion that common crime was a disease, not a moral lapse. He was jailed for his pacifism during World War I, and again briefly during the Vietnam War, for leading an illegal sit-in. He convened, along with Jean-Paul Sartre, an International War Crimes Tribunal charging the U.S. government with war crimes.

Russell used his experience and skills of analysis to confer his advice on readers. "The most savage controversies are those about matters as to which there is no good evidence either way" (*An Outline of Intellectual Rubbish*). On the subject of human vanity he advocates, "Do not attempt to live without vanity, since this is impossible, but choose the right audience from which to seek admiration." [3]

Russell reserved his most vehement censure for the church. He believed that "Man is a credulous animal, and must believe some-thing; in the absence of good grounds for belief, he will be satisfied with bad ones" (*An Outline of Intellectual Rubbish*). He considered religion a negative influence in human development:

> The three human impulses embodied in religion are fear, conceit, and hatred. The purpose of religion, one may say, is to give an air of respectability to these passions, provided they run in certain chan-nels [*Has Religion Made Useful Contributions to Civilization?*].

In the same book he defined religiosity as "a disease born of fear and a source of untold misery to the human race." But even in dealing with such a serious subject, Russell displays his self-deprecating wit:

> The whole conception of Sin is one which I find very puzzling, doubtless owing to my sinful nature. If "Sin" consisted in causing needless suffering, I could understand: but on the contrary, sin often consists in avoiding needless suffering [*An Outline of Intellectual Rubbish*].

Russell's opposition to the church wasn't based in opposition to spirituality but rather to unexamined doctrine. "The greatest men who have been philosophers have felt the need both of science and of mysticism."[4] Like Leo Tolstoy, Russell felt abject disappointment in the disparity between Christ's words and accepted church prac-tices.

> Churches may owe their origin to teachers with strong individual convictions, but these teachers have seldom had much influence upon the churches that they founded, whereas churches have had an enormous influence upon the communities in which they flourished. To take the case that is of most interest to members of Western civi-lization: the teaching of Christ, as it appears in the Gospels, has had extraordinarily little to do with the ethics of Christians [*Has Religion Made Useful Contributions to Civilization?*].

Russell realized that in the absence of a deity the ethical basis of human behavior had to be reconnoitered. He followed his atheism to its unhappy if logical conclusion — ethical relativism. He was disap-pointed by that position. "I find it quite intolerable to suppose when I say 'Cruelty is bad' I am merely saying that 'I dislike cruelty'" (*Prin-ciples of Social Reconstruction*). He attempted to find a way out of this dilemma with his notion of "compossible" desires, compossible mean-ing desires which are consistent with as many other desires as possi-ble. Russell used creativity as an example; the pleasures it gives us do not come at others' expense. Conversely, possessive impulses can only be satisfied by depriving others of the same achievement, what we now call a zero sum game.

Russell's eloquent yet homey style of expression, an absolute dedication to Truth, along with his enormous capacity for self-deprecating humor may explain an absence of vehement antipathy from his adversaries. He wrote with the flair of a humorist even when addressing the question of epistemology:

> The newspapers, at one time, said that I was dead, but after carefully examining the evidence I came to the conclusion that the statement was false. When the statement comes first and the evidence afterwards, there is a process called "verification" which involves confrontation of the statement with the evidence [*An Inquiry Into Meaning and Truth*].

Russell displayed his wit against prigs of all descriptions. When a violent feminist told him that "half of every man is a lunatic," he replied, "the better half." The humorless atheism of others became a pointed jibe in Russell's hands: "Saying prayers is the equivalent to believing that the Universe is governed by a being who changes his mind if you ask him to."[5]

On his twelfth birthday Russell's grandmother wrote in the Bible she gave to him: "Thou shalt not follow a multitude to do evil." If nothing else laudable could be said of Bertrand Russell, he at least adhered to that advice. He resolutely held his own counsel. In 1962 he wrote his own humorous epitaph. "On the occasion of my lamented but belated death... His life, for all its waywardness, had a certain anachronistic consistency, reminiscent of the aristocratic rebels of the early nineteenth century. His principles were curious, but, such as they were, they governed his actions."[6]

1950

"— in recognition of his varied and significant writings, in which he champions humanitarian ideals and freedom of thought—"

What Desires Are Politically Important?

I have chosen this subject for my lecture tonight because I think that most current discussion of politics and political theory take insufficient account of psychology.... It is neglect of such questions by the eminent men who sit in remote capitals, that so frequently causes disappointment. If politics is to become scientific, and if the event is not to be constantly surprising, it is imperative that our political thinking should penetrate more deeply into the springs of human action. What is the influence of hunger upon slogans? How does their effectiveness fluctuate with the number of calories in your diet? If one man offers you democracy and another offers you a bag of grain, at what stage of starvation will you prefer the grain to the vote? Such questions are far too little considered.

All human activity is prompted by desire. There is a wholly fallacious theory advanced by some earnest moralists to the effect that it is possible to resist desire in the interests of duty and moral principle. I say this is fallacious, both because no man ever acts from a sense of duty, but because duty has no hold on him unless he desires to be dutiful. If you wish to know what men will do, you must know not only, or principally, their material circumstances, but rather the whole system of their desires with their relative strengths.

There are some desires which, though very powerful, have not, as a rule, any great political importance. Most men at some period of their lives desire to marry, but as a rule they can satisfy this desire without having to take any political action.

...The desires that are politically important may be divided into a primary and a secondary group. In the primary group come the necessities of life: food, shelter and clothing. When these things become very scarce, there is no limit to the efforts that men will make, or to the violence they will display, in the hope of securing them.

...But man differs from other animals in one very important respect, and that is that he has some desires which are, so to speak, infinite, which can never be fully gratified, and which would keep him restless even in Paradise. The boa constrictor, when he has had an adequate meal, goes to sleep, and does not wake until he needs another meal. Human beings, for the most part, are not like this.

...Acquisitiveness — the wish to possess as much as possible of goods, or the title to goods — is a motive which, I suppose, has its origin in a combination of fear with the desire for necessaries.... But whatever may be the psychoanalysis of acquisitiveness, no one can deny that it is one of the great motives — especially among the more powerful, for, as I said before, it is one of the infinite motives. However much you may acquire, you will always wish to acquire more; satiety is a dream which will always elude you.

...Rivalry is a much stronger motive.... When the British Government very unwisely allowed the Kaiser to be present at a naval review at Spithead, the thought which arose in his mind was not the one which we had intended. What he thought was, "I must have a Navy as good as Grandmama's." And from this thought have sprung all our subsequent troubles. The world would be a happier place than it is if acquisitiveness were always stronger than rivalry. But in fact, a great many men will cheerfully face impoverishment if they can thereby secure complete ruin for their rivals. Hence the present level of taxation.

Vanity is a motive of immense potency. Anyone who has much to do with children knows how they are constantly performing some antic, and saying "Look at me." "Look at me" is one of the most fundamental desires of the human heart. It can take innumerable forms, from buffoonery to the pursuit of posthumous fame. There was a Renaissance Italian princeling who was asked by the priest on his deathbed if he had anything to repent of. "Yes," he said, "there is one thing. On one occasion I had a visit from the Emperor and the Pope simultaneously. I took them to the top of my tower to see the view, and I neglected the opportunity to throw them both down, which would have given me immortal fame." History does not relate whether the priest gave him absolution. One of the troubles about vanity is that it grows with what it feeds on.... It is scarcely possible to exaggerate the influence of vanity throughout the range of human life, from the child of three to the potentate at whose frown the world trembles. Mankind have even committed the impiety of attributing similar desires to the Deity, whom they imagine avid for continual praise.

But great as is the influence of the motives we have been considering, there is one which outweighs them all. I mean the love of power. Love of power is closely akin to vanity, but it is not by any means the same thing. What vanity needs for its satisfaction is glory, and it is easy to have glory without power.... Power, like vanity, is insatiable. Nothing short of omnipotence could satisfy it completely. And as it is especially the vice of energetic men, the causal efficacy of love of power is out of all proportion to its frequency. It is, indeed, by far the strongest motive in the lives of important men.

Love of power is greatly increased by the experience of power, and this applies to petty power as well as to that of potentates. In the happy days before 1914, when well-to-do ladies could acquire a host of servants, their pleasure in exercising power over the domestics steadily increased with age. Similarly, in any autocratic regime, the holders of power become increasingly tyrannical with experience of the delights that power can afford. Since power over human beings is shown in making them do what they would rather not do, the man who is actuated by love of power is more apt to inflict pain than to permit pleasure.... But it has other sides which are more desirable. The pursuit of knowledge is, I think, mainly actuated by love of power. And so are all advances in scientific technique.

...I come now to other motives which, though in a sense less fundamental than those we have been considering, are still of considerable importance. The first of these is love of excitement. Human beings show their superiority to the brutes by their capacity for boredom, though I have sometimes thought, in examining the apes at the zoo, that they, perhaps, have the rudiments of this tiresome emotion. However that may be, experience shows that escape from boredom is one of the really powerful desires of almost all human beings. When white men first effect contact with some unspoilt race of savages, they offer them all kinds of benefits, from the light of the gospel to pumpkin pie. These, however much as we may regret it, most savages receive with indifference. What they really value among the gifts that we bring to them is intoxicating liquor which enables them, for the first time in their lives, to have the illusion for a few brief moments that it is better to be alive than dead.... With civilized men ... it is, I think, chiefly love of excitement which make the populace applaud when war breaks out; the emotion is exactly the same as at a football match, although the results are sometimes somewhat more serious.

...Our mental make-up is suited to a life of very severe physical labor. I used, when I was younger, to take my holidays walking. I would cover twenty-five miles a day, and when the evening came I had no need of anything to keep me from boredom, since the delight of sitting amply sufficed. But modern life cannot be conducted on these physically strenuous principles. A great deal of work is sedentary, and most manual work exercises only a few specialized muscles.

...What is serious about excitement is that so many of its forms are destructive. It is destructive in those who cannot resist excess in alcohol or gambling. It is destructive when it takes the form of mob violence. And above all it is destructive when it leads to war. It is so deep a need that it will find harmful outlets of this kind unless innocent outlets are at hand. There are such innocent outlets at present in sport, and in politics so long as it is kept within constitutional bounds. But these are not sufficient, especially as the kind of politics that is most exciting is also the kind that does most harm. Civilized life has grown altogether too tame, and, if it is to be stable, it must provide harmless outlets for the impulses which our remote ancestors satisfied in hunting.... More seriously, pains should be taken to provide constructive outlets for the love of excitement. Nothing in the world is more exciting than a moment of sudden discovery or invention, and many more people are capable of experiencing such moments than is sometimes thought.

Interwoven with many other political motives are two closely related passions to which human beings are regrettably prone: I mean fear and hate. It is normal to hate what we fear, and it happens frequently, though not always, that we fear what we hate. I think it may be taken as the rule among primitive men, that they both fear and hate whatever is unfamiliar. They have their own herd, originally a very small one. And within one herd, all are friends, unless there is some special ground of enmity.... We love those who hate our enemies, and if we had no enemies there would be very few people whom we should love.

...There are two ways of coping with fear: one is to diminish the external danger, and the other is to cultivate Stoic endurance. The latter can be reinforced, except where immediate action is necessary, by turning our thoughts away from the cause of fear. The conquest of fear is of very great importance. Fear is in itself degrading; it easily becomes an obsession; it produces hate of that which is feared, and it leads headlong to excesses of cruelty. Nothing has so beneficent an effect on human beings as security.... There is, of course, the *odium theologicum*, and it can be a cause of enmity. But I think that this is an offshoot of herd feeling: the man who has a different theology feels strange, and whatever is strange must be dangerous. Ideologies, in fact, are one of the methods by which herds are created, and the psychology is much the same however the herd may have been generated.

...I do not think it can be questioned that sympathy is a genuine motive, and that some people at some times are made somewhat uncomfortable by the sufferings of some other people. It is sympathy that has produced the many humanitarian advances of the last hundred years.... Perhaps the best hope for the future of mankind is that ways will be found of increasing the scope and intensity of sympathy.

...Politics is concerned with herds rather than with individuals, and the passions which are important in politics are, therefore, those in which the various members of a given herd can feel alike. The broad instinctive mechanism upon which political edifices have to be built is one of co-operation within the herd and hostility towards other herds. The co-operation within the herd is never perfect. There are members who do not conform, who are, in the etymological sense, "egregious," that is to say, outside the flock. These members are those who have fallen below, or risen above, the ordinary level. They are: idiots, criminals, prophets, and discoverers. A wise herd will learn to tolerate the eccentricity of those who rise above the average, and to treat with a minimum of ferocity those who fall below it.

...I do not wish to seem to end upon a note of cynicism. I do not deny that there are better things than selfishness, and that some people achieve these things. I maintain, however, on the one hand, that there are few occasions upon which large bodies of men, such as politics is concerned with, can rise above selfishness, which, on the other hand, there are a very great many circumstances in which populations will fall below selfishness, if selfishness is interpreted as enlightened self-interest.

And among those occasions on which people fall below self-interest are most of the occasions on which they are convinced that they are acting from idealistic motives. Much that passes as idealism is disguised hatred or disguised love of power. When you see large masses of men swayed by what appear to be noble motives, it is as well to look below the surface and ask yourself what it is that makes these motives effective. It is partly because it is so easy to be taken in by a facade of nobility that a psychological inquiry, such as I have been attempting, is worth making. I would say, in conclusion, that if what I have said is right, the main thing needed to make the world happy is intelligence. And this, after all, is an optimistic conclusion, because intelligence is a thing that can be fostered by known methods of education.

9. Pär Lagerkvist

Religion in the true sense cannot be dispensed with. If the religious need is not satisfied in a natural way, it will seek satisfaction in an unnatural way as demonstrated by our time's worship of the state and of man.[1]

— Pär Lagerkvist[1]

Pär Fabian Lagerkvist's (1891–1974) simple narrative style masks a teeming background of spiritual tensions. A skillful storyteller, he frames myths, short stories and novellas that read as easily as any popular novel but reflect back to biblical and pre-biblical events with an eye to the present moment. Early in his career he chose Cubism as the paradigm he would follow in fiction, "dividing and relocating aspects of reality in order to arrive at a deeper and less obvious reality."[2]

Ambiguity reveals his many-faceted reality. In *The Holy Land* he stresses that the three crosses of Golgotha represent the Christian trinity, knowing full well that the lone cross dominates. Is he implying that the single cross denies our full humanity? He seems to be questioning Christ as a role model for humankind. In *The Sibyl* he takes the questioning further, asking of the Christ of the New Testament: "Is he himself really so loving? To those who love him he gives peace, they say, and he takes them up with him into his heaven; but they say, too, that he hurls those who don't believe in him into hell."

Prismatic, often inverted images are among his favorite and most powerful techniques. *The Dwarf* represents the complete inversion of normal human values and outlook. Understanding the Dwarf, an evil character who parallels the advisor of Machiavelli's Prince, forces the reader to reconsider normality. Yet Lagerkvist relieves the harrowing misery of his tales with passages of lyrical beauty:

67

How can one grasp anything of life — understand and penetrate men
and their lives — until one has learned from the sea? How can one
see through their empty strivings and odd ambitions until one has
looked out over the sea, which is boundless and sufficient in itself?
Until one has learned to think like the sea and not like these restless
creatures who fancy that they're going somewhere, and that this
going is the most important thing of all — that the goal is the meaning and purpose of their life. Until one has learned to be carried
along by the sea, to surrender to it utterly, and cease fretting about
right and wrong, sin and guilt, truth and falsehood, good and evil —
about salvation and grace and eternal damnation — about devil and
god and their stupid disputes. Until one has become as indifferent
and free as the sea and will let oneself be carried, aimless, out into
the unknown — surrender utterly to the unknown — to uncertainty
as the only certainty, the only really dependable thing when all's said
and done. Until one has learned all that [*Pilgrim at Sea*].

At the core of Pär Lagerkvist's writing are a bundle of intertwined beliefs making up, in composite, an understanding of the
relationship of God to humankind, humans to one another, and
humankind to God. What does it mean, he asks brutally, to be chosen by God, or possessed by the Holy Spirit? Is God just? Does God
understand his creatures? Lagerkvist brought to these questions a
religious atheism and an unswerving faith in humankind's ability to
both perceive the Truth and to endure it. "One must follow a private road, an uncharted way. The mystery of the divine cannot be
structured and mapped out for us. God, Christ, and the Church —
in their conventional forms — play no significant or meaningful part
in our spiritual quests."[3] Humans must, he believed, explore the
meaning of every facet of reality to gain spiritual transcendence:

> But the tree [of knowledge] cannot be otherwise, [the Lord said].
> Admittedly, it's rather complicated learning how to eat of it, but it
> must be complicated; it can't be helped. Some things you must find
> out for yourselves, or what's the point of your existence? You can't be
> spoon-fed the whole time. Personally, I think the tree is the finest
> thing I've created, and if you don't show yourselves worthy of it,
> human life won't be much to speak of. Tell them that ["Paradise" in
> *The Marriage Feast*].

This seems Lagerkvist's justification for asking the blunt questions of faith and its consequences. He understood the strain such
an interrogation placed on those who followed his lead, but he
believed the only alternative to such a quest was despair. Lagerkvist
knew that many of his fellow creatures were not vexed by the thirst
for spiritual enlightenment; they were not even aware that they were

in need of it. In a wonderfully concise and humorous piece of dialogue, he summarizes the mendacity of organized religion and the
hypocrisy of its tepid followers with a wry dialogue between a Bible
salesman and his customer:

> "No, we don't want any."
> "The lady next door bought it." (he lied)
> "Oh? Who?"
> "I don't know. She was elderly. Rather thin."
> "Oh?"
> "Yes, a very refined lady."
> "Oh, I know! Mrs. Berglov! Oh, did she buy it?..."
> "Yes, she had heard so much about it, but it is so hard to come by."
> "Oh — Oh, I'd better take that one then" ["God's Little Traveling
> Salesman" in *The Marriage Feast*].

In "The Executioner" (in *The Eternal Smile*) he again displays
a dark sense of humor concerning banality in the affairs of men.
"'Well, just fancy that — the executioner's here! Just wait till I tell
Herbert!' She went up to him and put her hand affably on his arm.
'My son's just dying to meet you: he's so fond of bloodshed, dear
boy.'" Even, it seems, the scourge of death can become a celebrity.

Lagerkvist's tales are replete with human sympathy, usually in
opposition to inherited and unquestioned morality. In *Barabbas*, the
character of Peter says of Barabbas, "We have no right to condemn
him. We ourselves are full of faults and shortcomings, and it is no
credit to us that the Lord has taken pity on us notwithstanding."
Lazarus also becomes a pivotal, an equivocal figure, a symbolic bridge
between humans and God. Resurrected for what? Resurrected to
what? Men and women must find their own answers.

Barabbas had seen Christ "surrounded by a dazzling light" and
is greatly relieved when the vision dimmed. "It showed that his eyes
were all right now, like everybody else's eyes" (*Barabbas*). This biblical metaphor of scales falling from the eyes recurs throughout
Lagerkvist's works, echoing Blake's dictum that a man is the measure of what he can see. "It is strange that I who can see the fires
which are so far away, cannot perceive the stars. I have never been
able to" (*The Dwarf*). Lagerkvist's main characters all suffer, many
from physical afflictions, yet it's the willful crippling of their souls
that interests him most. Physical deformities reflect diseases of the
spirit. "In appearance he was well-bred amiability personified, but
one cannot judge by people's faces. It is their bodies which show
them as the kind of animals they are" (*The Dwarf*).

Humans' innate capacity to wreak violence upon each other in the name of some higher calling is a theme throughout much of Lagerkvist's writing. In "Fragments,"[4] Arnold pulls shrapnel fragments from the wounds of the dead and dying to take back to his children. (He hopes to use them again as weapons.) The flat reporting style of "The Children's Campaign" (in *The Marriage Feast*) resounds a hollow echo of falsehood. The great battle of "The Children's Campaign" is reported to have killed 12,924 soldiers on each side. This purports to be the truth but the implausibility of the identical numbers makes it another war lie. When a small child, guilty of feeling homesick at Christmas, is shot as a deserter (for wandering off his post), this too is justified. There are few writers who bear such stark testimony to the cruelty of nationalistic policies and the easy and broad acceptance those policies gain among the populace. "In reality all of them want a war. It implies a simplification which comes as a relief. Everybody thinks that life is too complicated, and so it is as they live it" (*The Dwarf*).

Amidst these harrowing questions, Lagerkvist offers us redemption through love. Even the dreaded executioner has someone who loves him:

> "I shall be waiting for you. You know that when you come home, weary, with blood on your hands, I shall be waiting there among the birches. You will rest your head in my lap, and I shall kiss your burning forehead and wash the blood from you. I shall be waiting, and I shall love you" ["The Executioner" in *The Eternal Smile*].

Herod the Great, a murderous tyrant, finds love with Mariamne. So unsettling is the experience, he has her killed. Such is the power of evil — but the power of love is even greater as Herod dies with Mariamne's name on his lips (*Herod and Mariamne*). Fully developed human love abounds in "The Marriage Feast," a tender and powerful story of passion and misunderstanding.

Lagerkvist offers solace for those who find the courage to pursue the arduous path to spiritual fulfillment. In "The Masquerade of Souls" (in *The Marriage Feast*) he proclaims his conviction that the soul has its own land "and in that land there is always a festival." Using the imagery of the Bible he evokes fulfillment: "He knelt down to drink. ...The water was very chilly and had no taste at all ... and he who drank of it knew that he would never thirst again" (*The Holy Land*). This is the language of the Bible, Lagerkvist's instrument, which he uses to challenge its own message of received Truth in the twentieth century.

1951

"—for the artistic vigor and true independence of mind with which he endeavors in his poetry to find answers to the eternal questions confronting mankind—"

The Myth of Mankind

Once upon a time there was a world, and a man and a woman came to it on a fine morning, not to dwell there for any length of time, but just for a brief visit. They knew many other worlds, and this one seemed to them shabbier and poorer than those others. True, it was beautiful enough with its trees and mountains, its forests and copses, and skies above with ever-changing clouds and the wind which came softly at dusk and stirred everything so mysteriously. But, for all that, it was still a poor world compared to those they possessed far, far away. Thus they decided to remain here for only a short while, for they loved each other and it seemed as though nowhere else was their love so wonderful as in just this world. Here, love was not something one took for granted and that permeated everyone and everything, but was like a visitor from whom wondrous things were expected. Everything that had been clear and natural in their life became mysterious, sinister, and veiled. They were strangers abandoned to unknown powers. The love that united them was a marvel — it was perishable; it could fade away and die. So for a while they wished to remain in this new world they had found for themselves.

It was not always daylight here. After the light of day, dusk would fall upon all things, wiping out, obliterating them. The man and woman lay together in the darkness listening to the wind as it whispered in the trees. They drew closer to each other, asking: why are we here at all?

Then the man built a house for himself and the woman, a house of stones and moss, for were they not to move on shortly? The woman spread sweet-scented grass on the earthen floor and awaited him home at dusk. They loved each other more than ever and went about their daily chores.

One day, when the man was out in the fields, he felt a great longing come upon him for her whom he loved above all things. He bent down and kissed the earth she had lain upon. The woman began to love the trees and the clouds because her man walked under them when he came home to her, and she loved twilight too, for it was then that he returned to her.

It was a strange new world, quite unlike those other worlds they owned far, far away.

And so the woman gave birth to a son. The oak trees outside the house sang to him, he looked about him with startled eyes and fell asleep lulled by the sound of the wind in the trees. But the man came home at night carrying gory carcasses of slain animals; he was weary and in need of rest. Lying in the darkness, the man and woman talked blissfully of how they would soon be moving on.

What a strange world this was; summer followed by autumn and frosty winter, winter followed by lovely spring. One could see time pass as one season released another; nothing ever stayed for long. The woman bore another son and, after a few years, yet another. The children grew up and went about their business; they ran and played and discovered new things every day. They had the whole of this wonderful world to play with and all that was in it. Nothing was too serious to be turned into a toy. The hands of the man became calloused with hard work in the fields and in the forest. The woman's features became drawn and her steps less sprightly than before, but her voice was as soft and melodious as ever. One evening, as she sat down tired after a busy day, with the children gathered round her, she said to them, "Now we shall soon be moving from here. We will be going to the other worlds where our home is." The children looked amazed. "What are you saying, Mother? Are there any other worlds than this?" The mother's eyes met the husband's and pain pierced their hearts. Softly, she replied, "Of course there are other worlds," and she began to tell them of the worlds so unlike the one in which they were living, where everything was so much more spacious and wonderful, where there was no darkness, no singing trees, no struggle of any sort. The children sat huddled around her, listening to her story. Now and then, they would look up at their father as if asking, "Is this true, what Mother is telling us?" He only nodded and sat there deep in his own thoughts. The youngest son sat very close to his mother's feet; his face was pale, his eyes shone with a strange light. The eldest boy, who was twelve, sat further away and stared out. Finally, he rose and went out into the darkness.

The mother went on with her story and the children listen avidly. She seemed to behold some far-off country with eyes that stared unseeing; from time to time she paused as though she could see no more, remember no more. After a while, though, she would resume her story in a voice that grew fainter and fainter. The fire was flickering in the sooty fireplace; it shone upon their faces and cast a glow over the warm room. The father held his hand over his eyes. And so they sat without stirring until midnight. Then the door opened; a gust of cold air invaded the room and the eldest son appeared. He was holding in his hand a large black bird with blood gushing from its breast. This was the first bird he had killed on his own. He threw it down by the fire where it reeked of warm blood. Then, still without uttering a word, he went into a dark corner of the room at the back and lay down to sleep.

All was quiet now; the mother had finished her story. They gazed bewildered at each other, as if waking from a dream, and stared at the bird as it lay there dead, the red blood seeping from its breast, staining the floor about it. All arose silently and went to bed.

After that night, little was said for a time; each one went his own way. It was summer, bumblebees were buzzing in the lush meadows, the copses had been washed a bright green color by the soft rains of spring, and the air was crystal clear. One day, at noon, the smallest child came up to his mother as she was sitting outside the house. He was very pale and quiet and asked her to tell him about the other world. The mother looked at him in amazement. "Darling," she said, "I cannot speak of it now. Look, the sun is shining! Why aren't you out playing with your brothers?" He went quietly away and cried, but no one knew.

He never asked her again but only grew paler and paler, his eyes burning with a strange light. One morning, he could not get up at all, but just lay there. Day after day, he lay still, hardly saying a word, gazing into space with his strange eyes. They asked him where the pain was and promised that he would soon be out again in the sun and see all the fine new flowers that had come up. He did not reply, but only lay there not even seeming to see them. His mother watched over him and cried and asked him if she should tell him of all the wonderful things she knew, but he only smiled at her.

One night, he closed his eyes and died. They all gathered round him, his mother folded his small hands over his breast and, when the dusk fell, they sat huddled together in the darkening room and talked about him in whispers. He had left this world, they said, and gone to another world, a better and happier one, but they said it with heavy hearts and sighed. Finally, they all walked away frightened and confused, leaving him lying there, cold and forsaken.

In the morning, they buried him in the earth. The meadows were scented, the sun was shining softly, and there was gentle warmth everywhere. The mother said, "He is no longer here." A rose tree near his grave burst into blossom.

And so the years came and went. The mother often sat by the grave in the afternoons, staring over the mountains that shut everything out. The father paused by the grave whenever he passed it on his way, but the children would not go near it, for it was like no other place on earth.

The two boys grew up into tall strapping lads, but the man and the woman began to shrink and fade away. Their hair turned gray, their shoulders stooped, and yet a kind of peace and dignity came upon them. The father still tried to go out hunting with his sons, but it was they who coped with the animals when they were wild and dangerous. The mother, aging, sat outside the house and groped about with her hands when she heard them returning home. Her eyes were so tired now that they could only see at noon when the sun was at its highest in the sky. At other times, all was darkness about her and she used to ask why that was so. One autumn day, she went inside and lay down, listening to the wind as to a memory of long long ago. The man sat by her side and, together, they talked about things as if they were alone in the world once more. She had grown very frail but an inner light illuminated her features. One night, she said to them in her failing voice, "Now I want to leave this world where I have spent my life and go to my home." And so she went away. They buried her in the earth and there she lay.

Then it was winter once more and very cold. The old man no longer went out, but sat by the fire. The sons came home with carcasses and cut them up. The old man turned the meat on the spit and watched the fire turn a brighter red where the meat was roasting on it. When the spring came, he went out and looked at the trees and fields in all their greenery. He paused by each one and give it a nod of recognition. Everything here was familiar to him. He stopped by the flowers he had picked for her he loved the first morning they had come here. He stopped by his hunting weapons, now covered with blood, for one of his sons had taken them. Then he walked back into the house and lay down and said to his sons as they stood by his deathbed, "Now I must depart from this world where I have lived all my life and leave it. Our home is not here." He held their hands in his until he died. They buried him in the earth as he had bid them do, for it was there he wished to lie.

Now both the old people were gone and the sons felt a wonderful relief. There was a sense of liberation as though a cord tying them to something which was no part of them had been severed. Early next morning, they arose and went out into the open, savoring the smell of young trees and of the rain which had fallen that night. Side by side they walked together, the two tall youngsters, and the earth was proud to bear them. Life was beginning for them and they were ready to take possession of this world.

10. François Mauriac

I am a metaphysician who works in the concrete. I exploit a certain gift for creating atmosphere to make the Catholic universe of evil palpable, tangible, pungent. The theologians offer us an abstract idea of the sinner; I present him in flesh and blood.

—*Second Thoughts*

An estate in the Gironde region of Bordeaux, France, embroiled in bitter family strife, is Mauriac's (1885–1970) slate, with adults humiliating one another, using children like pieces in a chess match to be sacrificed to the higher goal of crippling one's opponent. Limiting his stage allows Mauriac to scrape the unsavory dregs of bourgeois family life, unearthing a vast Christian hypocrisy behind those respectable doors. He is the master of the prosperous middle class family scene.

Although his plots often slide from melancholy into despair, he draws his characters so acutely that we are continually pulled toward the hearths of Gironde. In *The Knot of Vipers*, Mauriac exhausts our energy in ironic sympathy for an embittered old man who complains in a letter to his wife, "My hatred grew, by slow degrees, as I came to realize how completely indifferent you were to me, how nothing really existed for you outside the circle of your pulling, screaming, greedy little scraps of humanity." Those "little scraps of humanity" are a reference to his children. The old man later moans, "If you had had any real love for me you could have saved me from my ingrained habit of never setting anything above immediate gain." The moral blindness the old man exhibits, of which he is unaware, rings as a major theme in Mauriac's works.

Children are treated cruelly by respectable members of their middle class families. "He knew in advance that his mother would wipe away the hasty salutation, and say, with disgust sounding in

75

her voice, 'You always make me so wet....'" The little boy, Guillaume, is speaking of his mother's automatic response to his good-night kiss in *The Weakling*. Children become pawns in these adult wars. Paula, Guillaume's mother, says, "We speak of 'making love': we should be able, too, to speak of 'making hate.' To make hate is comforting. It rests the mind and relaxes the nerves." The intensity, selfishness and lack of charity which Mauriac often depicts in his novels he terms pharisaism: "It is the turn of mind and that form of human experience where religion and lying meet" (*Second Thoughts*). Mauriac relentlessly attacks the pretense of respectable society. "Show men only in the official or public acts of their existence? One might as well spend one's time costuming puppets" (*Second Thoughts*).

The broad appeal of his stories attests to the universal nature of human self-righteousness. "Human love became self-aware only through pain, so that if we did not cause pain to another, we did not know that we were loved. Lovers know each other only through the suffering they inflict, the wounds they exchange" (*Second Thoughts*). Pain abounds in Mauriac's adult characters who meet the world with avarice, manipulation, revenge, resentment and jealousy. These grown-ups spare no effort to mask their baseness in acceptable garb. Mothers hate and abuse their young children, tyrannize them and transform their hatred of other adults into the punishment of a guiltless child. "What I detest about him is his youth.... I loathe and detest all young men, and Phili more than most," says a respectable father in *The Knot of Vipers*. Wives scorn their mothers-in-law, and mothers-in-law respond in kind. "To get the better of her mother-in-law, that was the only thing that mattered! It would be mere child's play to bring Fernand [her husband] to heel" (*Genetrix*). Not even death brings relief in these bitter alliances. Madam Cezanave relates her self-satisfied relief at denying her husband the smallest corner of human compassion on his death bed. "She would not let herself remember the secret sense of satisfaction that the end had come without her having to witness it" (*Genetrix*).

For all the misery in Mauriac's world, it is not one without joy and exultation. The ecstatic bliss of redemption — through Grace — always hovers in the background, a redemption of tainted humanity. "They must be ransomed as they are, with all their load of propensities and vices: they must be taken, ravished, saved, with all their sins still on them" (*Second Thoughts*). To be a child in Bordeaux means to live in innocence, a Grace before the Fall:

> His nature was purely instinctive, and what struck me more and more, as he grew older, was his purity, his unawareness of evil, his

utter disregard of it.... I never got the impression that, with him,
purity was something he had been taught, something of which he
was conscious. It had the limpid quality of water running over a
stony bed. It glittered on him like the dew of grass.... He had come
from the hand of the potter uncracked and lovely. I felt myself, in
comparison with him, deformed [*The Knot of Vipers*].

It may seem strange that this devoutly Catholic writer should
expend so much of his life's energy drawing portraits of evil and
repugnance. Mauriac found no contradiction in such a task. He
believed it to be inevitable. "It is the mark of our slavery and of our
wretchedness that we can, without lying, paint a faithful portrait only
of the passions" (*The Weakling and the Enemy*). Mauriac loathed any
attempt to pretend that we are better than we are, but he also knew
that we could be better. His exploration of the impact of this awareness gives his work its wide audience. Wistfulness, along with a firm
belief in redemption through Christ, are more than themes in Mauriac's work; they comprise the air and water of the world he chronicles. Mauriac masters light and shadow in portraying his characters.
He adds tone and texture, subtly evoking melancholy as sensually as
an Impressionist painter. His power to confess the human plight,
with compassion, makes him a writer of the universal, ever and
always grounded in the particular:

The man who has arrived, no matter what heights he may have
reached, discovers that what he finally comes to is the waiting room
where we all end up — and he watches the door that opens on the
void of eternity swing back and forth in the wind [*Second Thoughts*].

1952

*"—for the deep spiritual insight and the artistic intensity with which he
has in his novels penetrated the drama of human life—"*

...I never imagined that this little world of the past which survives
in my books, this corner of provincial France hardly known by the French
themselves where I spent my school holidays, could capture the interest
of foreign readers. We always believe in our uniqueness; we forget that the
books which enchanted us, the novels of George Eliot or Dickens, of Tolstoy or Dostoevsky, or of Selma Lagerlöf, described countries very different

from ours, human beings of another race and another religion. But nonetheless we loved them only because we recognized ourselves in them. The whole of mankind is revealed in the peasant of our birthplace, every countryside of the world in the horizon seen through the eyes of our childhood. The novelist's gift consists precisely in his ability to reveal the universality of this narrow world into which we are born, where we have learned to love and to suffer. To many of my readers in France and abroad my world has appeared somber. Shall I say that this has always surprised me? Mortals, because they are mortal, fear the very name of death; and those who have never loved or been loved, or have been abandoned and betrayed or have vainly pursued a being inaccessible to them without as much as a look for the creature that pursued them and which they did not love — all these are astonished and scandalized when a work of fiction describes the loneliness in the very heart of love. "Tell us pleasant things, said the Jews to the prophet Isaiah. Deceive us by agreeable falsehoods."

Yes, the reader demands that we deceive him by agreeable falsehoods. Nonetheless, those works that have survived in the memory of mankind are those that have embraced the human drama in its entirety and have not shied away from the evidence of the incurable solitude in which each of us must face his destiny until death, that final solitude, because finally we must die alone.

This is the world of a novelist without hope. This is the world into which we are led by your great Strindberg. This would have been my world were it not for the immense hope by which I have been possessed practically since I awoke to conscious life. It pierces with a ray of light the darkness that I have described. My color is black and I am judged by the black rather than by the light that penetrates it and secretly burns there. Whenever a woman in France tries to poison her husband or to strangle her lover, people tell me: "Here is a subject for you." They think that I keep some sort of museum of horrors, that I specialize in monsters. And yet, my characters differ in an essential point from almost any others that live in the novels of our time: they feel that they have a soul. In this post–Nietzschean Europe where the echo of Zarathustra's cry "God is dead" is still heard and has not yet exhausted its terrifying consequences, my characters do not perhaps all believe that God is alive, but all of them have a conscience which knows that part of their being recognizes evil and could not commit it. They know evil. They all feel dimly that they are the creatures of their deeds and have echoes in other destinies.

For my heroes, wretched as they may be, life is the experience of infinite motion, of an indefinite transcendence of themselves. A humanity which does not doubt that life has a direction and a goal cannot be a humanity in despair. The despair of modern man is born out of the absurdity of the world; his despair as well as his submission to surrogate myths: the absurd delivers man to the inhuman. When Nietzsche announced the death of God, he also announced the times we have lived through and those we shall still have to live through, in which man, emptied of his soul and hence deprived of a personal destiny, becomes a beast of burden more maltreated than a mere animal by the Nazis and by all those who today use Nazi methods. A horse, a mule, a cow has a market value, but from the human animal, procured without cost thanks to a well-organized and systematic purge, one gains nothing but profit until it perishes. No writer who keeps in the center of his work the human creature made in the image of the Father, redeemed by the Son, and illuminated by the Spirit, can in my opinion be considered a master of despair, be his picture ever so somber.

For his picture does remain somber, since for him the nature of man is wounded, if not corrupted. It goes without saying that human history as told by a Christian novelist cannot be based on the idyll because he must not shy away from the mystery of evil.

But to be obsessed by evil is also to be obsessed by purity and childhood. It makes me sad that the too hasty critics and readers have not realized the place which the child occupies in my stories. A child dreams at the heart of all my books; they contain the loves of children, first kisses and first solitude, all the things that I have cherished in the music of Mozart. The serpents in my books have been noticed, but not the doves that have made their nests in more than once chapter; for in my books childhood is the lost paradise, and it introduces the mystery of evil.

The mystery of evil — there are not two ways of approaching it. We must either deny evil or we must accept it as it appears both within ourselves and without — in our individual lives, that of our passions, as well as in the history written with the blood of men by power-hungry empires. I have always believed that there is a close correspondence between individual and collective crimes, and, journalist that I am, I do nothing but decipher from the day to day in the horror of political history the visible consequences of that indivisible history which takes place in the obscurity of the heart. We pay dearly for the evidence that evil is evil, we who live under a sky where the smoke of crematories is still drifting. We have seen them devour under our own eyes millions of innocents, even children. And history continues in the same manner. The system of concentration camps has struck deep roots in old countries where Christ has been loved, adored, and served for centuries. We are watching with horror how that part of the world in which man is still enjoying his human rights, where the human mind remains free, is shrinking under our eyes like the "peau de chagrin" of Balzac's novel.

Do not for a moment imagine that as a believer I pretend not to see the objections raised to belief by the presence of evil on earth. For a Christian, evil remains the most anguishing of mysteries. The man who amidst the crimes of history perseveres in his faith will stumble over the permanent scandal: the apparent uselessness of the Redemption. The well-reasoned explanations of the theologians regarding the presence of evil have never convinced me, reasonable as they may be, and precisely because they are reasonable. The answer that eludes us presupposes an order not of reason but of charity. It is an answer that is fully found in the affirmation of St. John: God is Love. Nothing is impossible to the living love, not even drawing everything to itself; and that, too, is written.

Forgive me for raising a problem that for generations has caused many commentaries, disputes, heresies, persecutions, and martyrdoms. But it is after all a novelist who is talking to you, and one whom you have preferred to all others; thus you must attach some value to what has been his inspiration. He bears witness that what he has written about in the light of his faith and hope has not contradicted the experience of those of his readers who share neither his hope nor his faith. To take another example, we see that the agnostic admirers of Graham Greene are not put off by his Christian vision. Chesterton has said that whenever something extraordinary happens in Christianity ultimately something extraordinary corresponds to it in reality. If we ponder this thought, we shall perhaps discover the reason for the mysterious accord between works of Catholic inspiration, like those of my friend Graham Greene, and the vast dechristianized public that devours his books and loves his films.

Yes, a vast dechristianized public! According to André Malraux, "the revolution today plays the role that belonged formerly to the eternal life." But what if the myth were, precisely, the revolution? And if the eternal life were the only reality?

Whatever the answer, we shall agree on one point: the dechristianized humanity remains a crucified humanity. What worldly power will ever destroy the correlation of the cross with human suffering? Even your Strindberg, who descended in the extreme depths of the abyss from which the psalmist uttered his cry, even Strindberg himself wished that a single word be engraved upon his tomb, the word that by itself would suffice to shake and force the gates of eternity: "o crux ave spes unica." After so much suffering even he is resting in the protection of that hope, in the shadow of that love. And it is in his name that your laureate asks you to forgive these all too personal words which perhaps have struck too grave a note. But could he do better, in exchange for the honors with which you have overwhelmed him, than to open to you not only his heart, but his soul? And because he has told you through his characters the secret of his torment, he should also introduce you tonight to the secret of his peace.

11. Ernest Hemingway

A writer's problem does not change.... It is always how to write
truly and, having found what is true, to project it in such a way
that it becomes a part of the experience of the person who reads
it. There is nothing more difficult to do.

— Ernest Hemingway[1]

No American writer of the twentieth century burned a deeper
brand on the writing community than did Ernest Hemingway
(1899–1961). Although his work appears to be clear, simple and
blunt, his style masks writing that is technical, complex and lyrical.
Other writers appreciated his virtuosity. In describing his approach
to fiction he said, "You know you're in if you hit a ratio of ten to
one — that is, if you get your writing to have a truth and a reality
ten times stronger than the original reality you are drawing on."[2]
When he hit his goal, the result was magnificent, as in his masterpiece novella, *The Old Man and the Sea*.

Hemingway's terse style became the standard by which many
American writers judged themselves in his wake. He achieved a reputation for writing in short sentences. The following passage from
"The Short Happy Life of Francis Macomber" demonstrates how
effectively he could use the short declarative structure:

The great American boy-men. Damned strange people. But he liked
this Macomber now. Damned strange fellow. Probably meant the
end of cuckoldry too. Well, that would be a damned good thing.
Damned good thing. Beggar had probably been afraid all his life.
Don't know what started it. But over now. Hadn't had time to be
afraid with the buff. That and being angry too. Motor car too.
Motor cars made it familiar. Be a damn fire eater now. He'd seen it
in the war work the same way. More of a change than any loss of
virginity. Fear gone like an operation. Something else grew in its

83

place. Main thing a man had. Made him into a man. Women knew it too. No bloody fear.

Hemingway writes with poetic intention, i.e., to make the reader feel the emotions he would have felt had he been the character himself. He set a new standard of immediacy in the portrayal of physical action, a highly technical feat. His depiction of the last seconds of the life of Francis Macomber illustrates this facility and belies the notion that Hemingway did not use long sentences.

> Wilson, who was ahead, was kneeling shooting, and Macomber, as he fired, unhearing his shot in the roaring of Wilson's gun, saw fragments like slate burst from the huge boss of the horns, and the head jerked, he shot again at the wide nostrils and saw the horns jolt again and fragments fly, and he did not see Wilson now and, aiming carefully, shot again with the buffalo's huge bulk almost on him and his rifle almost level with the on-coming head, nose out, and he could see the little wicked eyes and the head started to lower and he felt a sudden white-hot, blinding flash explode inside his head and that was all he ever felt.

Hemingway believed that the omission of major events strengthened the impact of a story by communicating an effect below the surface of the writing. "If a writer of prose knows enough about what he is writing about he may omit something that he knows and the reader, if the writer is writing truly enough, will have a feeling of those things as strongly as if the writer had stated them."[3] In "Out of Season" Hemingway implies the suicide of an old man, by hanging, without reporting it. In what many believe to he his finest short story, "The Big Two-Hearted River," a reprieve from war casts a dominant shadow without ever being mentioned. He often portrays the provisionary nature of courage without naming it, as in the following passage from "The Capital of the World":

> Too many times he had seen the horns, seen the bull's wet muzzle, the ear twitching, then the head go down and the charge, the hoofs thudding and the hot bull pass him as he swung the cape, to recharge as he swung the cape again, then again, and again, and again, to end winding the bull around him in his great media-veronica, and walk swingingly away, with bull hairs caught in the gold ornaments of his jacket from the close passes: the bull standing hypnotized and the crowd applauding.

Hemingway spared no effort in finding the precise word. He said of *A Farewell to Arms*, "I had rewritten the ending thirty-nine times in manuscript and now I worked it over thirty times in proof, trying to get it right. I finally got it right."[4] Ford Maddox Ford said of Hemingway's word choice: "[They] strike you, each one, as if they were pebbles fetched fresh from a brook. They live and shine, each in its place. So one of the pages has the effect of a brook-bottom into which you look down through the flowing water. The words from a tessellation, each in order beside the other."[5]

Hemingway aggravated many of his critics by refusing to take a "high-brow" view of literature. He championed Joseph Conrad when reading Conrad became unfashionable. Hemingway dexterously placed his critical appraisal of American literature in his novel, *Green Hills of Africa*: "All modern American literature comes from one book by Mark Twain called *Huckleberry Finn*. All American writing comes from that.... There was nothing before. There has been nothing as good since."

Critics have often charged Hemingway with a lack of empathy and understanding of women, a valid criticism. However, Hemingway understood men and the relationships between them with a fine-grained sensibility, penetrating the unspoken depths of their souls. Solzhenitsyn put his appraisal of Hemingway's writing in *The First Circle*: "An intelligent, morally good, boundlessly honest writer, a soldier, hunter, fisherman, drunkard and lover of women, quietly and frankly despising all falsehood, simple, very human, with the innocence of a genius."

The idea that Hemingway glorified war and violence is a misconception that tarnishes his reputation. He glorified courage, not violence. His dedication to the facts of warfare led him to assume a naturalist's pose and describe without pity or remorse (or any other abstraction) the residue of a battlefield after the firing has ceased.

> Until the dead are buried they change somewhat in appearance each day. The color change in Caucasian races is from white to yellow, to yellow-green, to black. If left long enough in the heat the flesh comes to resemble coal-tar, especially where it has been broken or torn, and it has quite a visible tarlike iridescence. The dead grow larger each day until sometimes they become quite too big for their uniforms, filling these until they seem blown tight enough to burst ["A Natural History of the Dead"].

As a writer Hemingway understood that only under extreme stress does the social mask that hides a man's true character dissolve to reveal the man. Hemingway constructed his stories like Sousa composed his marches, building to a crescendo, at which point the character of a man becomes naked. That apex is often, by its nature, fraught with the peril of defeat or death.

Hemingway writes stories of a male protagonist squarely facing a world of overwhelming forces where the only victory lies in the character of his response. The valiant answer courageously, which is, according to a definition Hemingway made famous, "grace under pressure." A bullfighter facing horned death with courage, skill, and grace is for Hemingway a man worthy of emulation. In Hemingway's world, no matter how many times a man has failed when tested, redemption is always possible through renewed courage. Once a man is redeemed, by his own effort of will, he is redeemed forever.

1954

"—for his powerful mastery of the art of storytelling, most recently displayed in The Old Man and the Sea, *and for his influence on contemporary style—"*

© The Nobel Foundation, 1954

Having no facility for speech-making and no command of oratory nor any domination of rhetoric, I wish to thank the administrators of the generosity of Alfred Nobel for this Prize.

No writer who knows the great writers who did not receive the Prize can accept it other than with humility. There is no need to list these writers. Everyone here may make his own list according to his knowledge and his conscience.

It would be impossible for me to ask the Ambassador of my country to read a speech in which a writer said all of the things which are in his heart. Things may not be immediately discernible in what a man writes, and in this sometimes he is fortunate; but eventually they are quite clear and by these and the degree of alchemy that he possesses he will endure or be forgotten.

Writing, at its best, is a lonely life. Organizations for writers palliate the writer's loneliness but I doubt if they improve his writing. He grows in public stature as he sheds his loneliness and often his work deteriorates. For he does his work alone, and if he is a good enough writer he must face eternity, or the lack of it, each day.

For a true writer each book should be a new beginning where he tries again for something that is beyond attainment. He should always try for something that has never been done or that others have tried and failed. Then sometimes, with great luck, he will succeed.

How simple the writing of literature would be if it were only necessary to write in another way what has been well written. It is because we have had such great writers in the past that a writer is driven far out past where he can go, out to where no one can help him.

I have spoken too long for a writer. A writer should write what he has to say and not speak it. Again I thank you.

12. Albert Camus

If the world were clear, art would not exist.

—"Absurd Creation" in
The Myth of Sisyphus and Other Essays

Often read as an existentialist writer, Albert Camus (1913–1960) denounced the philosophy of existentialism which he believed had succumbed to the outrage of absurdity. His well-publicized break with Sartre occurred over aesthetic and philosophical issues. "I do not have much liking for the too famous existential philosophy, and, to tell the truth, I think its conclusions false" ("Pessimism and Tyranny" in *Resistance, Rebellion and Death*). Surrendering to absurdity, Camus writes, is a failure of the "virile reticence" of revolt (*The Rebel*). We must recognize the absurd but not be cowed by it. "Accepting the absurdity of everything around us is one step, a necessary experience: it should not become a dead end. It arouses a revolt that can become fruitful" ("Three Interviews" in *Lyrical and Critical Essays*).

Camus erects a monument to the spiritual discomfort of twentieth century man, comparing his plight to that of a prisoner in a medieval torture chamber, called the little-ease, with dimensions so cramped the prisoner could neither stand nor lie down. In our modern era we can be paroled from discomfort if we adopt a humane stance. For Camus, only vibrant human connections defy absurdity, overwhelm injustice, ameliorate suffering, nurture sanity and prevail over death itself. "In a world whose absurdity appears to be so impenetrable, we simply must reach a greater degree of understanding among men, a greater sincerity. We must achieve this or perish" ("Three Interviews" in *Lyrical and Critical Essays*).

Meursault (*The Stranger*) never ventures beyond the dead end of absurdity, suffering an inability to empathize that reduces him to little more than a talking beast. Guilty and sentenced to the guillotine for murdering a man whom he did not know, Meursault can only admit to being annoyed at having committed the crime. An unreflective man, abstractions such as justice, love and remorse lie beyond Meursault; he views life merely as concrete and momentary. "My mind was always on what was coming next, today or tomorrow." Jean-Baptiste Clamence, the judge-penitent in *The Fall,* admits to the same now-and-next outlook, and we recognize in him a similar same failure of compassion. "No excuses ever, for anyone; that's my principle at the outset." Look what happens to us, Camus implies, when we lose our capacity to love one another.

In his novels, plays and essays, Camus displays a melancholy appreciation of our shared fate in a time of apocalyptic wars and ethnocentrism as ideology, resulting in government sponsored death camps. The events of his life in Europe and North Africa convinced him that "the real passion of the twentieth century is servitude" (*The Rebel*). Lamenting the strain on friendship and affection caused by service to inhuman abstractions, he writes, "They hurt each other without wanting to, just because each represented to the others the cruel and demanding necessity of their lives" (*The First Man*).

Camus grew up as a poor fatherless child in Algiers, and from that experience developed a piercing sympathy for the constricted world of the common man.

> On some evenings it would sadden Jacques to look at them. Until then he had only known the riches and joys of poverty. But now heat and boredom and fatigue were showing him their curse, the curse of work so stupid you could weep and so interminably monotonous that it made the days too long and, at the same time, life too short [*The First Man*].

His terse prose and sparse landscapes provide undistracted views of discouraged souls seeking meaning with no beacons to guide them. For Camus, the path leading from despair to significance forks: aesthetics form one trail, while rebellion (upholding the sanctity of the individual) forms the other. "And for us who have been thrown into hell, mysterious melodies and the torturing images of a vanished beauty will always bring us, in the midst of crime and folly, the echo of that harmonious insurrection which bears witness, throughout the centuries, to the greatness of humanity" (*The Rebel*). Camus found great solace in the cycles of nature, "Knowing that certain nights whose sweetness lingers will keep returning to the earth and sea after we are gone, yes, this helps us die" ("The Sea Close By" in *Lyrical and Critical Essays*).

Camus rejected Christianity, yet a visible Judeo-Christian backbone supports much of his work. The titles of his major novels read like a reverse chronology of the Bible: *The Rebel, The Stranger, The Plague, The Just, Exile and the Kingdom* and *The Fall.* "So many men are deprived of grace. How can one live without grace? One has to try it and do what Christianity never did: be concerned with the damned"(*Notebooks 1942–1951*). Camus believes that we need, in our time, to transform the Ark of the Covenant, to create a new covenant between the Individual and the Infinite because, "nothing can discourage the appetite for divinity in the heart of man" (*The Rebel*). Restoring the possibility of grace can occur only after we recognize the mutual bond fusing humanity together in a shared fate. We are all members of the herd, consciously or unconsciously.

As a writer Camus maintained his independence from both friends and enemies in the political and philosophical movements that attempted to subvert his writing to their own ends. While becoming a significant intellectual force in French and European culture, he never lost his affection for the joy and beauty of the working class. His position as a prestigious writer and, simultaneously, a common Frenchman, opened the door of life more widely for Camus than for others, permitting him a broad perspective. Camus combines a taut writing style, as well as profound insights on society, with the courage to report back from the abyss of despair, unblinking. "There is no love of life without despair about life" ("Preface," *Lyrical and Critical Essays*).

1957

"—for his important literary production, which with clearsighted earnestness illuminates the problems of the human conscience in our times—"

...I felt that shock and inner turmoil [at receiving the Nobel award]. In order to regain peace I have had, in short, to come to terms with a too generous fortune. And since I cannot live up to it by merely resting on my achievement, I have found nothing to support me but what has supported me through all my life, even in the most contrary circumstances: the idea that I have of my art and of the role of the writer.

...For myself, I cannot live without my art. But I have never placed it above everything. If, on the other hand, I need it, it is because it cannot be separated from my fellow men, and it allows me to live, such as I am, on one level with them. It is a means of stirring the greatest number of people by offering them a privileged picture of common joys and sufferings. It obliges the artist not to keep himself apart; it subjects him to the most humble and the most universal truth. And often he who has chosen the fate of the artist because he felt himself to be different soon realizes that he can maintain neither his art nor his difference unless he admits that he is like the others. The artist forges himself to the others, midway between the beauty he cannot do without and the community he cannot tear himself away from. That is why true artists scorn nothing: they are obliged to understand rather than to judge. And if they have to take sides in this world, they can perhaps side only with the society in which, according to Nietzsche's great words, not the judge but the creator will rule, whether he be a worker or an intellectual.

By the same token, the writer's role is not free from difficult duties. By definition he cannot put himself today in the service of those who make history; he is at the service of those who suffer it. Otherwise, he will be alone and deprived of his art.

...In all circumstances of life, in obscurity or temporary fame, cast in the irons of tyranny or for a time free to express himself, the writer can win the heart of a living community that will justify him, on the one condition that he will accept to the limit of his abilities the two tasks that constitute the greatness of his craft: the service of truth and the service of liberty. Because his task is to unite the greatest possible number of people, his art must not compromise with lies and servitude which, whenever they rule, breed solitude. Whatever our personal weaknesses may be, the nobility of our craft will always be rooted in two commitments, difficult to maintain: the refusal to lie about what one knows and the resistance to oppression.

For more than twenty years of an insane history, hopelessly lost like all the men of my generation in the convulsions of time, I have been supported by one thing: by the hidden feeling that to write today was an honor because this activity was a commitment — and a commitment not only to write. Specifically, in view of my powers and my state of being, it was a commitment to bear, together with all those who were living through the same history, the misery and the hope we shared.... And I even think that we should understand — without ceasing to fight it — the error of those who in an excess of despair have asserted their right to dishonor and have rushed into the nihilism of the era. But the fact remains that most of us, in my country and in Europe, have refused this nihilism and have engaged upon a quest for legitimacy. They have had to forge for themselves an art of living in times of catastrophe in order to be born a second time and to fight openly against the instinct of death at work in our history.

Every generation doubtless feels called upon to reform the world. Mine knows that it will not reform it, but its task is perhaps even greater. It consists in preventing the world from destroying itself. Heir to a corrupt history, in which are mingled fallen revolutions, technology gone mad, dead gods, and worn-out ideologies, where mediocre powers can destroy all yet no longer know how to convince, where intelligence has debased itself to become the servant of hatred and oppression, this generation starting from its own negations had to re-establish, both within and without, a little of that which constitutes the dignity of life and death. In a world threatened by disintegration, in which our grand inquisitors run the risk of establishing forever the kingdom of death, it knows that it should, in an insane race against the clock, restore among the nations a peace that is not servitude, reconcile anew labor and culture, and remake with all men the Ark of the Covenant. It is not certain that this generation will ever be able to accomplish this immense task, but already it is rising everywhere in the world to the double challenge of truth and liberty and, if necessary, know how to die for it without hate. Whenever it is found, it deserves to be saluted and encouraged, particularly where it is sacrificing itself. In any event, certain of your complete approval, it is to this generation that I should like to pass on the honor that you have just given me.

At the same time, after having outlined the nobility of the writer's craft, I should have put him in his proper place. He has no other claims but those which he shares with his comrades in arms: vulnerable but obstinate, unjust but impassioned for justice, doing his work without shame or pride in view of everybody, not ceasing to be divided between sorrow and beauty, and devoted finally to drawing from his double existence the creations that he obstinately tries to erect in the destructive movement of history. Who after all this can expect from him complete solutions and high morals? Truth is mysterious, elusive, always to be conquered. Liberty is dangerous, as hard to live with as it is elating. We must march toward these two goals, painfully but resolutely, certain in advance of our failing on so long a road. What writer would from now on in good conscience dare set himself up as a preacher of virtue? For myself, I must state once more that I am not of this kind. I have never been able to renounce the light, the pleasure of being, and the freedom in which I grew up. But although this nostalgia explains many of my errors and my faults, it has doubtless helped me toward a better understanding of my craft. It is helping me still to support unquestioningly all those silent men who sustain the life made for them in the world only through memory of the return of brief and free happiness.

13. John Steinbeck

What some people find in religion a writer may find in his craft
... a kind of breaking through to glory.

— Conversations with John Steinbeck

An outraged social conscience welded to an agonizing search for Good propelled John Steinbeck (1902–1968) toward Oslo and the Nobel Prize. An idealist, he condemned the numb respectability of his day for willfully ignoring the plight of the commoner. His life-long fascination with the King Arthur legend and a forty year friend-ship with the mythologist Joseph Campbell informed the mythical structure of many of Steinbeck's novels: *East of Eden, The Wayward Bus, The Grapes of Wrath, The Pearl, Tortilla Flat,* and *Of Mice and Men.*

The one unforgivable sin of Steinbeck's world is valuing any-thing higher than the suffering of common people. He writes with bitterness:

> Dump potatoes in the rivers and place guards along the banks to keep the hungry people from fishing them out. Slaughter the pigs and bury them.... There is a crime here that goes beyond denuncia-tion [*The Grapes of Wrath*].

To the issue of inhumanity Steinbeck brought an ear with per-fect pitch and an almost photographic eye for detail that could make a scene throb with life. His sorrow becomes pity, a pity that washes over all, bathed in remorse:

> Some of the owner men were kind because they hated what they had to do, and some of them were angry because they hated to be cruel ... and all of them were caught in something larger than themselves [*The Grapes of Wrath*].

In *The Moon Is Down*, Steinbeck reveals an ironic twist in warfare with his sympathy for the common people expressed by empathy for both sides in the conflict:

> The people of the conquered country settled in a slow silent, waiting, revenge.... Now it was the conqueror who was surrounded ... no man might relax his guard. If he did, he disappeared, and some snowdrift received his body.

Lanser, a Nazi colonel in charge of the region, knows his fate. He has known it all along and feels powerless, thinking to himself, "If home crumbled, they would not tell us, and then it would be too late. These people will not spare us. They will kill us all." According to Steinbeck, oppressors — as individuals — deserve our pity, if of a somewhat different sort than their victims. Toward the end of the novel, Mayor Orden and Doctor Winter — while awaiting their own executions — revive an ongoing disagreement between them concerning the exact phrasing of Socrates' death speech. They turn quite naturally to Colonel Lanser, as if he were an old school chum, to settle the dispute. He supplies the philosophic wisdom without hesitation, one gentleman to another. In that brief moment we know that the colonel isn't very different from the mayor and doctor; the colonel is ensnared in a different web. It is the vulnerability of each man to be a pawn in the mighty cause of war which must evoke our sorrow. *The Moon Is Down* was published in 1942, shortly after the United States entered the world conflict; Steinbeck didn't shrink from controversy.

The dust bowl farmers of the 1930s, trapped in years of drought and depression, were also tangled in a phenomenon too great to comprehend or combat. Their misery simply had to be endured. Steinbeck transforms their tenacity into a vibrant Christian allegory suffused with gritty details, endowing *The Grapes of Wrath* with a realistic feel. The title comes from the "Battle Hymn of the Republic," and in this, his best known work, Steinbeck melds social outrage with lyricism and sociological detail unmatched in his other novels. His allegorical style is nowhere more naked than in his love of the earth — the organic — and in his revulsion of abstractions from life. Chiding those whose success let them forget their first love, he berated corporate farming. "They farmed on paper; and they forgot the land, the smell, the feel of it, and remembered only that they owned it, remembered only what they gained and lost by it" (*The Grapes of Wrath*). His poetic narration of the inter-chapters of *The Grapes of Wrath* is reminiscent of Walt Whitman's *Leaves of Grass*:

In the last part of May the sky grew pale and the clouds that had
hung in high puffs for so long in the spring were dissipated. The sun
flared down on the growing corn day after day until a line of brown
spread along the edge of each green bayonet. The clouds appeared,
and went away, and in a while they did not try any more [*The
Grapes of Wrath*].

John Steinbeck frequently employed humor in his writing,
insuring a suspension of judgment of sufficient duration to allow the
reader to enter the unfamiliar domains of his characters. In *Tortilla
Flat* he elicits empathy not merely with the characters and their problems but also with their solutions:

One night he [Pilon] had a dollar. A man in front of the San Carlos
hotel had put the dollar in his hand, saying, "Run down and get
four bottles of ginger ale. The hotel is out." Such things were almost
miracles, Pilon thought. One should take them on faith, not worry
and question them. He took the dollar up the road to give to Danny,
but on the way he bought a gallon of wine, and with the wine he
lured two plump girls into his house [*Tortilla Flat*].

In the same novel we are treated to the riotous incident of Big
Joe and Pilon on the beach. Pilon steals Big Joe's pants (as Big Joe
sleeps), selling them for a quart of wine to Mrs. Torrelli. He then
steals them back from the good lady. When Pilon tells Big Joe how
he rescued the pants from the rapacious Mrs. Torrelli, Joe becomes
indignant at the woman's behavior and thankful to have such a good
friend watching over his interests. *Tortilla Flat* is a tale of feckless
friendship in a world of constructed illusions at odds with the constructed illusions of conventional society.

Steinbeck also experimented with new forms of fiction. His
novella, *Of Mice and Men*, was an experiment, a "copy book exercise." The novel, he thought, "might benefit by the discipline, the
terseness of a play" (*Conversations with John Steinbeck*). He invented
a new genre, the play-novelette, using fable to translate philosophical insight into fictional realism. The focal character of the story,
Lennie, isn't a real character at all; he's a force of nature, the repos-
itory of dreams, dreams that cannot come true. Steinbeck transforms
that dream from an amorphous "wouldn't it be nice to have..." and
nails it down to a plot with an owner and a price tag. He called *Of
Mice and Men* "a study of the dreams and pleasures of everyone in
the world."[1]

In Steinbeck's works the tough guys have warm hearts, and the
soft guys who sometimes act like fussy old ladies come equipped
with backbones of steel. Among major twentieth century writers, the

quality of Steinbeck's work varies more than most. At times he was guilty of excessive sentimentality, along with flat characterization, overworked foreshadowing and allowing unrealistic and overblown description to remain in his writing. But at his best his work compares favorably with that of the best international writers.

Philosophically, John Steinbeck was convinced of the existence of a group instinct in humans similar to, but different in character from, that found in schools of fish. He called it the "over-soul." Steinbeck searched for alternatives for individual consciousness uprooted by the pace of change and impersonal mass movements. He believed that neither escape into individualism nor immersion into the collective fully satisfied the moral needs of the individual. He sought creative alternatives beyond those readily apparent for the resilient human spirit, creating a fictional world in which human moral endurance survives all travails. We are indebted to Steinbeck for reminding us that the hunger of the human soul for meaning and the desperate need we each share for human companionship knows no class boundaries.

1962

"—for his realistic as well as imaginative writings, distinguished by a sympathetic humor and a keen social perception—"

...Such is the prestige of the Nobel award and of this place where I stand that I am impelled, not to squeak like a grateful and apologetic mouse, but to roar like a lion out of pride in my profession and in the great and good men who have practiced it through the ages.

Literature was not promulgated by a pale and emasculated critical priesthood singing their litanies in empty churches — nor is it a game for the cloistered elect, the tinhorn mendicants of low calorie despair.

Literature is as old as speech. It grew out of human need for it, and it has not changed except to become more needed.

The skalds, the bards, the writers are not separate and exclusive. From the beginning, their functions, their duties, their responsibilities have been decreed by our species.

Humanity has been passing through a gray and desolate time of confusion. My great predecessor, William Faulkner, speaking here, referred to it as a tragedy of universal fear so long sustained that there were no longer problems of the spirit, so that only the human heart in conflict with itself seemed worth writing about.

Faulkner, more than most men, was aware of human strength as well as of human weakness. He knew that the understanding and the resolution of fear are a large part of the writer's reason for being.

This is not new. The ancient commission of the writer has not changed. He is charged with exposing our many grievous faults and failures, with dredging up to the light our dark and dangerous dreams for the purpose of improvement.

Furthermore, the writer is delegated to declare and to celebrate man's proven capacity for greatness of heart and spirit — for gallantry in defeat — for courage, compassion and love. In the endless war against weakness and despair, these are the bright rally-flags of hope and of emulation.

I hold that a writer who does not passionately believe in the perfectibility of man has no dedication nor any membership in literature.

The present universal fear has been the result of a forward surge in our knowledge and manipulation of certain dangerous factors in the physical world.

It is true that other phases of understanding have not yet caught up with this great step, but there is no reason to presume that they cannot or will not draw abreast. Indeed it is a part of the writer's responsibility to make sure that they do.

With humanity's long proud history of standing firm against natural enemies, sometimes in the face of almost certain defeat and extinction, we would be cowardly and stupid to leave the field on the eve of our greatest potential victory.

Understandably, I have been reading the life of Alfred Nobel — a solitary man, the books say, a thoughtful man. He perfected the release of explosive forces, capable of creative good or of destructive evil, but lacking choice, ungoverned by conscience or judgment.

Nobel saw some of the cruel and bloody misuses of his inventions. He may even have foreseen the end result of his probing — access to ultimate violence — to final destruction. Some say that he became cynical, but I do not believe this. I think he strove to invent a control, a safety valve. I think he found it finally only in the human mind and the human spirit. To me, his thinking is clearly indicated in the categories of these awards.

They are offered for increased and continuing knowledge of man and of his world — for understanding and communication, which are the functions of literature. And they are offered for demonstrations of the capacity for peace — the culmination of all the others.

Less than fifty years after his death, the door of nature was unlocked and we were offered the dreadful burden of choice.

We have usurped many of the powers we once ascribed to God.

Fearful and unprepared, we have assumed lordship over the life or death of the whole world — of all living things.

The danger and the glory and the choice rest finally in man. The test of his perfectibility is at hand.

Having taken Godlike power, we must seek in ourselves for the responsibility and the wisdom we once prayed some deity might have.

Man himself has become our greatest hazard and our only hope.

So that today, St. John the Apostle may well be paraphrased: In the end is the Word, and the Word is Man — and the Word is with Men.

14. Mikhail Sholokhov

> You can never get away from it — sorrow, I mean. You can't run
> away from it and you can't bury yourself from it. That's how it
> is.
>
> — *The Don Flows Home to the Sea*

Mikhail Sholokhov (1905–1984) must surely be among the least
popular winners of the Nobel Prize in Literature. Much of the controversy enveloping Sholokhov comes not from his novels but from
his pronouncements; he attacked other Soviet Nobel laureates, calling Pasternak "a poet for old maids," and Solzhenitsyn a "Colorado
beetle who should have been exterminated."[1] Such is not the behavior of a writer currying favor among the international community.
But Sholokhov was not interested in Western opinion. He was, as
he declared, "first and foremost a Communist" and only secondly a
writer. He eventually became a member of the Communist Polit-
buro — the ruling cadre of the Soviet Union.

It would seem that he was little more than a clever ideologue
who wrote books. Yet Sholokhov was not a simple man. In the 1930s
he wrote Joseph Stalin a letter of protest against the abuses in the
collectivization of Kulaks, an act of conscience and courage.
Sholokhov suffered many a sparing bout with censors regarding his
own work. If, in the end, he succumbed by revising his own work,
he did at least fight for his creative authority.

Sholokhov's attacks on Pasternak and Solzhenitsyn spawned
hatred in the West. That animosity translated to claims that he did
not even write his masterpiece *The Quiet Don* (published in the West
in two volumes: *And Quiet Flows the Don* and *The Don Flows Home
to the Sea).* Stylistically he's been accused of lack of originality. Such
indictments seem justified. Although the same "literary crime" has
been committed by most great writers, including Shakespeare, the

charge is not often leveled against others. Sholokhov was castigated for being too simple and primitive in his lack of profound psychological complexity. This, of course, is to forget the wide-angle lens that defined his interest. He writes of a people, the Don Cossacks, in the middle of an endlessly confusing civil war where not only local autonomy and military advantage is in doubt but primary allegiances to church and ancestral heritage are threatened.

Criticism aside, *The Quiet Don* invites obvious comparison with *War and Peace*. If it fails to equal the majesty of Tolstoy's epic, it does stand comparison on its own merits. Few works by other authors do. Sholokhov practiced "truth-in-art" (in the sense that Tolstoy used the term to mean psychological realism). Sholokhov's Cossack villages, characters and landscapes are graphically portrayed with exquisite detail. The Cossacks' pride of independence, their prejudices, lust and reverence are vividly drawn as they struggle to retain their traditions through the wars and cultural revolution that shook Russia in the early twentieth century. Dynamically alive, Sholokhov's characters respond with resolution or despair and integrity or mendacity to the challenges of their time with all of the stupidity and nobility of which human beings are capable. His characters are vibrantly alive in an age of chaos. The nearest Western analog to the Cossacks and their plight are the Native Americans, trapped between a vibrant tribalism that they cannot return to and modern European notions of individualism and private property that obliterate their core beliefs about themselves and their universe.

Caught in the vortex of great global events, Gregor Melekhov, the courageous narrator, vacillates between fighting against the Bolsheviks, then with them, and finally in the end opposing them again. His lustful and tender affair with Aksinia weaves throughout the heroic epic with a sense of melancholy and longing. Not the slightest hint of Sholokhov's politics taints his characterizations. Gregor Melekhov, a natural leader of men and rooted in the love of his "mother country," demands our empathy. His turmoil stems from chaos, not from simplicity. Confusion is a technical device Sholokhov uses to create immediacy with a character's situation and to evoke those times of war, revolution and counter-revolution in readers who have not lived through such turmoil.

It is difficult to imagine a more lifelike record of the Don Cossacks than Sholokhov provides. While the separate scenes in his novels are easily accessible, the broad picture remains incomplete, his form reinforcing the message of confusion which drowns his characters. Imagine a group of agricultural people, with a horse-based warrior tradition stretching back to Ghengis Khan, confronted with the automobile, the airplane, urbanization, the Tsars, Germans, Mensheviks, White Russians, Bolsheviks and Stalin. Sholokhov's novels painted in the bright colors of lust and longing convey a time and place of pandemonium to readers living in a more predictable world.

1965

"—for the artistic power and integrity with which, in his epic of the Don, he has given expression to a historic phase in the life of the Russian people—"

...As I have already had occasion to testify in public, the feeling of satisfaction which this award arouses in me is not solely due to the international recognition of my professional merit and my individual characteristics as a writer. I am proud that this Prize has been awarded to a Russian, a Soviet writer. Here I represent a multitude of writers from my native land.

I have also previously expressed my satisfaction that, indirectly, this Prize is yet another recognition of the novel as a genre. I have not infrequently read and heard recent statements which have quite frankly astonished me, in which the novel has been declared an outdated form that does not correspond to present-day demands. Yet it is just the novel that makes possible the most complete comprehension of the world of reality, that permits the projection of one's attitude to this world, to its burning problems. One might say that the novel is the genre that most predisposes one to a profound insight into the tremendous life around us, instead of putting forward one's own tiny ego as the center of the universe. This genre, by its very nature, affords the very widest scope for a realistic artist.

Many fashionable currents in art reject realism, which they assume has served its time. Without fear of being accused of conservatism, I wish to proclaim that I hold a contrary opinion and am a convinced supporter of realistic art. There is a lot of talk nowadays about literary avantgardism with reference to the most modern experiments, particularly in the field of form. In my opinion the true pioneers are those artists who make manifest in their works the new content, the determining characteristics of life in our time.

Both realism as a whole and the realistic novel are based upon artistic experiences presented by great masters in the past. During their development, however, they have acquired important new features that are fundamentally modern.

I am speaking of a realism that carries within itself the concept of life's regeneration, its reformation for the benefit of mankind. I refer, of course, to the realism we describe as socialist. Its peculiar quality is that it expresses a philosophy of life that accepts neither a turning away from the world nor a flight from reality, a philosophy that enables one to comprehend goals that are dear to the hearts of millions of people and that lights up their path in the struggle.

Mankind is not divided into a flock of individuals, people floating about in a vacuum, like cosmonauts who have penetrated beyond the pull of Earth's gravity. We live on Earth, we are subject to its laws and, as the Gospel puts it, sufficient unto the day is the evil thereof, its troubles and trials, its hopes for a better future. Vast sections of the world's population are inspired by the same desires, and live for common interests that bind them together far more than they separate them. These are the working people, who create everything with their hands and their brains. I am one of those authors who consider it their highest honor and their liberty to have a completely untrammeled chance of using their pens to serve the working people.

This is the ultimate foundation. From it are derived the conclusion as to how I, a Soviet writer, view the place of the artist in the world of today.

The era we live in is full of uncertainty. Yet there is not one nation of Earth that desires a war. There are, however, forces that hurl whole nations into the furnaces of war. Is it not inevitable that the ashes from the indescribable conflagration of the Second World War should move the writer's heart? Is not an honest writer bound to stand up against those who wish to condemn mankind to self-destruction?

What, then, is the vocation and what are the tasks of an artist who sees himself, not as an image of a god who is indifferent to the sufferings of mankind, enthroned far above the heat of battle, but as a son of his people, a tiny particle of humanity?

To be honest with the reader, to tell people the truth — which may sometimes be unpleasant but is always fearless. To strengthen men's hearts in their belief in the future, in the belief in their own ability to build this future. To be a champion of peace throughout the world and with his words breed such champions whenever those words penetrate. To unite people in their natural, noble striving toward progress.

Art possesses a great ability to influence people's intellects and brains. I believe that anyone has the right to call himself an artist, if he channels this ability into creating something beautiful in the minds of men, if he benefits humanity.

My own people have not followed beaten tracks in their historical journey. Their journey has been that of the explorers, the pioneers for a new life. I have regarded and still regard it as my task as an author in all that I have written and in whatever I may come to write, to show my great respect for this nation of workers, this nation of builders, this nation of heroes, which have never attacked anyone but which knows how to put up an honorable defense of what it has created, of its freedom and dignity, of its right to build the future as it chooses.

I should like my books to assist people in becoming better, in becoming purer in their minds; I should like them to arouse love of one's fellow men, a desire to fight actively for the ideal of humanity and the progress of mankind. If I have managed to do this in some measure, then I am happy.

15. Miguel Ángel Asturias

Sweet is the land where one is born. It has no price. All other land is bitter.

— *The Green Pope*

"We can contribute an earthiness, a natural, animal force, a violence of new blood," writes Asturias (1899–1974), "that will enrich Western culture and broaden man's understanding of himself."[1] Thus the Guatemalan writer claims his turf as a Latin American writer at odds with his European cohorts. Land festers as an active agent in Asturias' fiction, infecting all. "The earth is the fundamental element, the earth is the mother, the earth is what conceives us, supports us, and afterwards protects us in her bosom."[2] With organic fluidity he embraces not only the present but also the mythic past. "Say the words of the psalm: "By the earth of which thou art made, by the fire which has burned thee, by the water which has filled thee, by the air of my voice which fills thee now with the name of the man I want to return, give him not peace until he returneth, let him not resist the call of earth" (*El Señor Presidente*).

Asturias does not describe but rather participates in "the magic of our climate and light [which] gives our stories a double aspect — from one side they seem dreams, from the other they are realities."[3] Asturias' novels emerge through the undergrowth of Guatemala as a natural element:

> Here my education began, and here too something began which
> must have had paramount influence on my artistic development. In
> this place there is a river.... In the waters of that river, at dusk ... I
> undoubtedly found a source of legend, enchantment, and purity. I
> went to school to learn the alphabet, but it was in the river, in those
> evenings, in those lights and leaves that I learned to know the magic
> of my country, the voice of my country.[4]

107

The aliases GMT, or GEO maker, for George Maker Thompson (protagonist of the Banana Trilogy, a fictionalized account of the history of the United Fruit Company) suggest an eerie spiritual force of global dimensions. He is, "a navigator in human sweat, a divinity who has anvils in the place of hands, great searchlights instead of eyes, chimney smoke instead of hair" (*The Green Pope*). The Company, an alien life force with no blood but numbers, draws lines and squares on the earth, putting a price tag on every living thing. Time, a province of the gods — measured in seasons and days and celebrated by festivals — is mechanized by The Company, cut into bits and pieces, counted and sold. And GMT becomes The Company, and The Company blossoms into a myth incorporated into Guatemalan reality.

Asturias saw firsthand the process of myth creation during the trial of Guatemala's former dictator, Manuel Estrada Cabrera. "When he was behind bars people said, no, that couldn't be Estrada Cabrera. The real Estrada Cabrera got away. This is some poor old man they've dumped in there."[5] *El Señor Presidente*, inspired by Cabrera, reads like a history of a wrathful Old Testament God angered by jealousy: "THOU SHALT HAVE NO OTHER GODS BEFORE ME."

Asturias' novels plunge through the "green hell" of Guatemala without losing their artistic bearings. The verdant texture of Asturias' fiction grows unconsciously in the reader through the writer's deft handling of figure and ground. Among the other strengths of his works are his lyrical description:

> Adelaido Lucero's lungs came up to his cheeks to draw in all the coastal air. He was stripped to the waist and was wearing a pair of pants more like a loincloth.... His callused, sweaty hands, hardened by work, kept on moving with the grace of a man afire. Squat, rise, squat, rise ... all the vertebrae of his spine were jutting out and his backbone was a copper-colored snake ... squat, rise, the hinge of his waist opening and closing, as they filled a platform car with rocks and stones [*Strong Wind*].

Asturias' early dedication to poetry, combined with his Mayan heritage, culminate in a veneration of the word. "The word has sacred significance, in the word everything, outside the word nothing.... The word must be as precise as possible, because the more precise it is the more completely does one take possession of the object or person."[6] Grounded in the history of Guatemala, Asturias wraps realism around deep mythic structure. While some have criticized his frequent use of myth integrated with realism, Asturias is comfortable with both the process and the outcome.

My novels are realistic precisely because they do include these aspects; because the witch doctor of the God Huracan assumes an overwhelming reality for the people of our country, because the storm which destroys the banana plantation may be very real, but for our Indians it also assumes magical proportions. This mentality molds the people's spirit and thinking in a very profound way.[7]

When his play *Audiencia* was staged in 1961, it caused a local scandal. "The public, the press, said it was against the Church, against the rich, that it was frankly leftist."[8] In fact, the play included a speech delivered before the high court several centuries ago by Fray Bartolome, attempting in 1700 to stanch the worst abuses of the Indian slavers by refusing absolution to settlers who bought slaves. Two hundred sixty-one years later, those words were still too radical for Guatemala to hear.

Asturias believed that achieving wholeness in a modern context requires reintegrating spirit into matter and embracing the reflections and ripples of matter within the realm of the spirit. His Mayan perspective captures the surrealistic stance of such an integration. The *Men of Maize* whose bodies are made of corn, blend perceptions that the Western mind can only desiccate and analyze as static concepts. It was Asturias' personal favorite among his works. His depiction of the web of life which connects Mayan myths to matter and memory gives his voice its haunting quality:

For the Indian, man is a transient being, a bird of passage, momentarily embodied in his individual self, from which he aspires to be released in order to join the whole again. His separateness and isolation are an anguish to him.[9]

1967

"—for the vividness of his literary work, rooted in national traits and Indian traditions—"

...The use of destructive forces, the secret which Alfred Nobel extracted from nature, made possible in our America the most colossal enterprises. Among them, the Panama Canal. A magic of catastrophe which could be compared to the thrust of our novels, called upon to destroy unjust structures in order to make way for a new life. The secret mines of the people, buried under tons of misunderstanding, prejudices, and taboos, bring to light in our narrative — between fables and myths — with blows of protest, testimony, and denouncement, dikes of letters which, like sands, contain reality to let the dream flow free or, on the contrary, contain the dream to let reality escape.

Cataclysms which engendered a geography of madness, terrifying traumas, such as the Conquest: these cannot be the antecedents of a literature of cheap compromise; and, thus, our novels appear to Europeans as illogical or aberrant. They are not shocking for the sake of shock effects. It is just that what happened to us was shocking. Continents submerged in the sea, races castrated as they surged to independence, and the fragmentation of the New World. As the antecedents of a literature these are already tragic. And from there we have had to extract not the man of defeat, but the man of hope, the blind creature who wanders through our songs. We are peoples from worlds which have nothing like the orderly unfolding of European conflicts, always human in their dimensions. The dimensions of our conflicts in the past centuries have been catastrophic.

Scaffoldings. Ladders. New vocabularies. The primitive recitation of the texts. The rhapsodists. And later, once again, the broken trajectory. The new tongue. Long chains of words. Thought unchained. Until arriving, once again, after the bloodiest lexical battles, at one's own expressions. There are no rules. They are invented. And after much invention, the grammarians come with their language-trimming shears. American Spanish is fine with me, but without the roughness. Grammar becomes an obsession. The risk of anti-grammar. And that is where we are now. The search for dynamic words. Another magic. The poet and the writer of the active word. Life. Its variations. Nothing prefabricated. Everything in ebullition. Not to write literature. Not to substitute words for things. To look for word-things, word-beings. And the problems of man, in addition. Evasion is impossible. Man. His problems. A continent that speaks. And which was heard in this Academy. Do not ask us for genealogies, schools, treatises. We bring to you the probabilities of a world. Verify them. They are singular. Singular is the movement, the dialogue, the novelistic intrigue. And most singular of all, throughout the ages there has been no interruption in the constant creation.

16. Aleksandr Solzhenitsyn

> None of us who lived close to her perceived that she was that one righteous person without whom, as the saying goes, no city can stand. Neither can the whole world.
>
> —*Matryona's House*

For Aleksandr Solzhenitsyn (1918–) conscience and justice comprise the soul, conscience functioning on a private level and justice acting in the social sphere. It is not possible, he contends, to be personally saved and unjust, nor is it likely that one can be just without being redeemed. A tautology, Solzhenitsyn's precept admits no division between justice and conscience. Many American readers view Solzhenitsyn as a caustic sociopolitical critic of Soviet society, while Solzhenitsyn actually writes of the soul. He engages both spiritual and political tasks in his writing without becoming didactic, a testimony to both his technical skill as a writer and to the source of his moral outrage. In the tradition of Dostoyevsky, Solzhenitsyn excoriates Soviet society for its moral corruption and the resultant crimes committed against its people, both as individuals and in groups. While Leo Tolstoy asks the one central question of humanity: "What must I do?" Solzhenitsyn answers, "What is the most precious thing in the world? Not to participate in injustices.... They have existed in the past and they will exist in the future. But let them not come about through *you*" (*The First Circle*).

As a religious writer Solzhenitsyn is not necessarily concerned with the form of government that rules. "It is not authoritarianism itself that is intolerable, but the ideological lies that are daily foisted upon us [the Soviets]" (*Letter to the Soviet Leaders*). Nonetheless, he is vitally interested in the practices and policies of *every* form of government. "We have to condemn publicly the very *idea* that some people have a right to repress others" (*The Gulag Archipelago*).

111

He addresses the Soviet Union with controlled rage leavened with black humor. Throughout *The First Circle* the stupidity and clumsiness of the Soviet system rings like a gong in a slapstick vaudeville routine. With deadpan delivery Solzhenitsyn discusses the working hours of Soviet prisoners. "The zeks [prisoners], to compensate for being deprived of all other rights, enjoyed a broader right to work [broader than the average citizen] — for twelve hours a day." This is slave labor redefined as privilege. Whether it be accidental damage to an old lathe and the resulting investigation which appears on the page like a comedy script for "The Three Stooges," or explaining how magazines purchased over-the-counter in the West become classified as secret and locked in fireproof safes (with a Marx Brothers ignorance of reality), the banality of the Soviet Communist system stretches our credulity. What would be ludicrous elsewhere becomes deadly in the Soviet Union. A prisoner is charged with "corrupting the morals of the enemies of the people"(*The First Circle*). In another instance, a service man with no battlefield experience is promoted to a front line general in World War I. The final scene of *The First Circle* echoes of the Western world's incomprehension of this Soviet reality. A French journalist observes vans transporting prisoners between islands of the Gulag, believing the signs which advertise food products painted on their sides; he concludes that "the provisioning of the capital is excellent," understanding nothing that he sees.

Solzhenitsyn unleashes his righteous anger, without restraint, on Stalin. The Soviet leader projected all blame for his own failures onto others; then he punished them for *his* sins. In a repressed and controlled state, this ploy succeeds. But there was one sin he could not lay at another's door: his own cowardly flight from Moscow when under threat of Nazi occupation. Stalin covered his shame with a new ploy. "He thereupon sent to prison every single person who remembered that panic on October 16"(*The First Circle*). Solzhenitsyn does not exaggerate; Stalin sent an estimated thirty million people to the Gulag during his reign. Most died. The rapid modernization of the Soviet Union was built on this foundation of slavery.

With biting satire Solzhenitsyn lacerates the corruption that feeds the status quo of the Soviet state, a state where the only free souls are prisoners who have already lost everything except their lives. In a parody of references to God from other works of literature, Solzhenitsyn uses twenty-six terms of supposed veneration to refer to Stalin, juxtaposing the accolades with text that exposes Stalin's baseness, dubbing him: Greatest Genius of Geniuses, Wise Teacher, Coryphaes of Sciences and Leader of All Progressive Humanity (*The*

First Circle). Stalin exposes himself as a psychopath in ensuing paragraphs. Solzhenitsyn portrays the Great Generalissimo as paranoid:

> He had not trusted his mother. And he had not trusted that God before whom he had bowed his head.... He did not trust his own fellow Party members.... He did not trust his fellow exiles. He did not trust the peasants.... He did not trust workers.... He did not trust members of the intelligentsia.... He did not trust soldiers and generals.... He did not trust his wives and mistresses. He did not trust his children. And he always turned out to be right.
>
> He had trusted one person, one only, in a life filled with mistrust ... [a man who] had turned around and offered Stalin his friendship. And Stalin had trusted him. That man was Adolf Hitler.

Solzyhenitsyn's compassion for people who tread water in a sea of corruption glows throughout his works. In *One Day in the Life of Ivan Denisovich*, he repeatedly evokes the plight of prison guards whose life differs little from that of the prisoners. Although *August 1914* criticizes the ineffectiveness of the General Staff and the unpreparedness of the Russian military, it is also a lament for the millions of lives valiantly lost in defense of Mother Russia. The enemy understood the Russians' weaknesses better than the Russians did themselves. "When fighting the Russians, one may allow oneself to make maneuvers which would be impermissible against any other enemy" (from German War Manual, *August 1914*). The Russian army of 1914 had nothing it needed with which to defeat the Germans except men willing to die for their country. "In the Russian army of 1914, rear guards did not save themselves by surrendering. Rear guards died" (*August 1914*). Solzhenitsyn portrays General Samsonov, a scapegoat for the army's first major defeat of the war, as a decent man struggling against impossible obstacles while trying to do the right thing. In the end, in his untenable position, there was no right thing to do.

Solzhenitsyn's own imprisonment in the Gulag and expulsion from Russia developed his spiritual sensibilities. Sentenced to a decade in the Soviet Gulag for criticizing Stalin in a private letter to a friend, Solzhenitsyn cherished his internment as the turning point in his life. "Bless you, prison, for being in my life" (*The Gulag Archipelago*). So evocative is his portrayal of the Soviet prison system that he introduced the term Gulag into the English language.

Such revelation helped Solzhenitsyn to concentrate his fiction on moral choice, the pivotal essence of the individual living soul. In a Soviet context such moral decisions involved arrest, torture, imprisonment, years of internal exile and often death. (A woman with whom Solzhenitsyn had left his manuscript for *The Gulag Archipelago*,

broken down by 120 hours of interrogation without sleep, told secret
police where she had hidden it. Then she committed suicide.) Yet
Solzhenitsyn looks *inwardly* to the source of evil, even to explain the
existence of Stalinist oppression. "We didn't love freedom enough,
we purely and simply deserved everything that happened afterward"
(*The Gulag Archipelago*). For Solzhenitsyn, human beings' inability
to love one another has made us fallen creatures who live without
God, for only God can redeem. "There is nothing more precious than
the development of a man's own soul; it is more important than the
well-being of countless future generations" (*August 1914*). Solzhenitsyn is equally certain that a well-tended soul will lead to the discovery of—not the creation of—justice, "but again not our own
invented justice, which we have simply thought up to fit our convenient earthly paradise. There is a justice which existed before us,
without us and for its own sake. And our task is to *divine* what it
is!" (*August 1914*).

Knowledge of the soul—religious ecstasy—is gained through
suffering and renunciation:

> Yes, the taiga and the tundra awaited them, the record cold of
> Oymyakon and the copper excavations of Dzhezhazgan; pick and
> barrow; starvation rations of soggy bread; the hospital; death. The
> very worst. But there was peace in their hearts. They were filled
> with the fearlessness of those who have lost everything, the fearless-
> ness which is not easy to come by but which endures [*The First Cir-
> cle*].

Solzhenitsyn encourages us to become "Interstellar Wanderers" (*The
Gulag Archipelago*) so that whatever our life circumstances may be
our souls are free. Solzhenitsyn's guide in the spiritual quest for
wholeness comes from trust in either our own innate conscience or
that of our ancestors (which explains Solzhenitsyn's interest in Russian history). For example, Volodin, a zek in *The First Circle*, gains
such guidance from the diaries of his deceased mother who states,
"Pity is the first action of a good soul."

With compassion and insight Solzhenitsyn uncovers the
hypocrisy of the Russian intelligentsia from Czarist times to our own
day. While those in power talked of the peasantry and the proletariat
in abstract terms, they neither associated with, understood nor cared
about the fate of the masses. Solzhenitsyn does care, deeply, and he
assumes the burden of speaking for the tens of millions of his silenced
countrymen and women, comrades who were slaughtered, imprisoned and forgotten by their rulers.

1970

"—for the ethical force with which he has pursued the indispensable traditions of Russian literature—"

© The Nobel Foundation, 1970

Just as that puzzled savage who has picked up — a strange cast-up from the ocean?— something unearthed from the sands?— or an obscure object fallen down form the sky?— intricate in curves, it gleams first dully and then with a bright thrust of light. Just as he turns it this way and that, turns it over, trying to discover what to do with it, trying to discover some mundane function within his own grasp, never dreaming of its higher function.

So also we, holding Art in our hands, confidently consider ourselves to be its masters; boldly we direct it, we renew, reform and manifest it; we sell it for money, use it to please those in power; turn to it at one moment for amusement — right down to popular songs and night-clubs, and at another — grabbing the nearest weapon, cork or cudgel — for the passing needs of politics and for the narrow-minded social ends. But art is not defiled by our efforts, neither does it thereby depart from its true nature, but on each occasion and in each application it gives to us a part of its secret inner light.

…Our artist sees himself as the creator of an independent spiritual world; he hoists onto his shoulders the task of creating this world, of peopling it and of bearing the all-embracing responsibility for it; but he crumples beneath it, for a mortal genius is not capable of bearing such a burden. Just as man in general, having declared himself the center of existence, has not succeeded in creating a balanced spiritual system. And if misfortune overtake him, he casts the blame upon the age-long disharmony of the world, upon the complexity of today's ruptured soul, or upon the stupidity of the public.

Another artist, recognizing a higher power above, gladly works as a humble apprentice beneath God's heaven; then, however, his responsibility for everything that is written or drawn, for the souls which perceive his work, is more exacting than ever. But, in return, it is not he who has created this world, not he who directs it, there is no doubt as to its foundations; the artist has merely to be more keenly aware than others of the harmony of the world, of the beauty and ugliness of the human contribution to it, and to communicate this acutely to his fellow-men. And in misfortune, and even at the depths of existence — in destitution, in prison, in sickness — his sense of stable harmony never deserts him.

But all the irrationality of art, its dazzling turns, its unpredictable discoveries, its shattering influence on human beings — they are too full of magic to be exhausted by this artist's vision of the world, by this artistic conception or by the work of his unworthy fingers.

Archaeologists have not discovered stages of human existence so early that they were without art. Right back in the early morning twilights of mankind we received it from Hands which we were too slow to discern. And we were too slow to ask: FOR WHAT PURPOSE have we been given this gift? What are we to do with it?

...Like that little looking-glass from the fairy-tales: look into it and you will see — not yourself — but for one second, the Inaccessible, whither no man can ride, no man fly. And only the soul gives a groan....

One day Dostoyevsky threw out the enigmatic remark: "Beauty will save the world." What sort of a statement is that? For a long time I considered it mere words. How could that be possible? When in bloodthirsty history did beauty ever save anyone from anything? Ennobled, uplifted, yes — but whom has it saved?

There is, however, a certain peculiarity in the essence of beauty, a peculiarity in the status of art: namely, the convincingness of a true work of art is completely irrefutable and it forces even an opposing heart to surrender. It is possible to compose an outwardly smooth and elegant political speech, a headstrong article, a social program, or a philosophical system on the basis of both a mistake and a lie. What is hidden, what distorted, will not immediately become obvious.

...But a work of art bears within itself its own verification: conceptions which are devised or stretched do not stand being portrayed in images, they all come crashing down, appear sickly and pale, convince no one. But those works of art which have scooped up the truth and presented it to us as a living force — they take hold of us, compel us, and nobody ever, not even in ages to come, will appear to refute them.

So perhaps that ancient trinity to Truth, Goodness and Beauty is not simply an empty, faded formula as we thought in the day of our self-confident, materialistic youth? If the tops of these three trees converge, as the scholars maintained, but the too blatant, too direct stems of Truth and Goodness are crushed, cut down, not allowed through — then perhaps the fantastic, unpredictable, unexpected stems of Beauty will push through and soar TO THAT VERY SAME PLACE, and in so doing will fulfill the work of all three?

In that case Dostoyevsky's remark, "Beauty will save the world," was not a careless phrase but a prophecy? After all HE was granted to see much, a man of fantastic illumination.

...From time immemorial man has been made in such a way that his vision of the world, so long as it has not been instilled under hypnosis, his motivations and scale of values, his actions and intention are determined by his personal and group experience of life. As the Russian saying goes, "Do not believe your brother, believe your own crooked eye." ... In the various parts of the world men apply their own hard-earned values to events, and they judge stubbornly, confidently, only according to their own scales of value and never according to any others. The divergent scales of values scream in discordance, they dazzle and daze us, and in order that it might not be painful we steer clear of all other values, as though from insanity, as though from illusion, and we confidently judge the whole world according to our home values.... Yet we cannot reproach human vision for [its] duality, for this dumbfounded incomprehension of another man's distant grief, man is just made that way.

...Who will create for mankind one system of interpretation, valid for good and evil deeds, for the unbearable and the bearable, as they are differentiated today? Who will make clear to mankind what is really heavy and intolerable and what only grazes the skin locally? Who will direct the anger to that which is most terrible and not to that which is nearer? Who might succeed in transferring such an understanding beyond the limits of his own human experience? Who might succeed in impressing upon a bigoted, stubborn human creature the distant joy and grief of others, an understanding of dimensions and deceptions which he himself has never experienced? Propaganda, constraint, scientific proof—are all useless. But fortunately there does exist such a means in our world! That means is art. That means is literature.

They can perform a miracle: They can overcome man's detrimental peculiarity of learning only from personal experience so that the experience of other people passes him by in vain. From man to man, as he completes his brief spell on Earth, art transfers the whole weight of an unfamiliar, lifelong experience with all its burdens, its colors, its sap of life; it recreates in the flesh an unknown experience and allows us to possess it as our own.

...And literature conveys irrefutable condensed experience in yet another invaluable direction; namely, from generation to generation. Thus it becomes the living memory of the nation.... And literature, as one of the most sensitive, responsive instruments possessed by the human creature,

has been one of the first to adopt, to assimilate, to catch hold of this feeling of a growing unity of mankind. And so I turn with confidence to the
world literature of today — to hundreds of friends whom I have never met
in the flesh and whom I may never see.

17. Heinrich Böll

I knew then that the war would never be over, never, as long as
somewhere a wound it had inflicted was still bleeding.

—"Breaking the News" in *The Stories of Heinrich Böll*

All of Germany wanted to forget the Nazis, World War II, tens
of millions dead, concentration camps and defeat. The German establishment conspired to inflate balloons labeled plans for a prosperous
future to obscure the past. Heinrich Böll (1917–1985) burst those balloons. "If our era deserves a name, it would have to be called the era
of prostitution. People are becoming accustomed to the vocabulary
of whores" (*The Clown*). Böll rebelled against an opportunistic morality that became, after the Second World War, "the German economic
miracle" which ignored the sins of the past. "The idiocy of our Western luxury-oriented society — and that of its victims, the criminals
who want to share in it — consists in taking luxury as an absolute"
("The Captive World" in *Missing Persons and Other Essays*). Compassion, inspired by sincere spirituality, was Böll's gauge of morality:

> He had wanted to erect a monument of dust and rubble for those
> who had not [had] historical monuments and whom no one had
> thought to spare... "a monument for the lambs no one had fed,"
> Robert Faehmel thinks to himself. "I won't come to the consecra-
> tion," thought Robert, "for I'm not reconciled" [*Billiards at Half-
> Past Nine*].

Böll peeled away clichés with a precise ear for the simple phrase.
In *Group Portrait with Lady*, the Mother Superior of a convent sums
up her resentment of a recently dead and transcendentally spiritual
nun, Sister Rahel. "Now at least she can't pester us any more about
her tiresome cigarette rations." After Sister Rahel's burial, roses bloom
above her grave in winter; the Catholic Church tries time and again

119

to kill the miraculous flowers, even resorting to cremating Rahel's remains. All attempts fail. Rather than accept God's grace in the form of this miracle, the Church (Böll's church) concocts a lie about a mysterious hot spring to explain the flowers. Then the Church poisons the ground of the miracle and markets the area to tourists as a resort spa. Much of Böll's anger toward his church is embedded here: hypocrisy, lies, denial of the idiosyncratic humanity and commercialized spirituality. He never forgave the Roman Catholic Church for the Vatican Concordant with Hitler which accorded the Nazis their first major international recognition. "And if you can't understand that we weren't born to be happy, you will at least understand that we weren't born to forget" (*A Soldier's Legacy*).

Böll's heroes are not winners by conventional standards, but Böll's point is that they are not losers either. They are moral men and women, twisted and turned by forces beyond their control. "The damage caused by Lev, to the total [German] economy is almost beyond computation" (*Group Portrait with a Lady*). In fact, Lev is a lazy garbage man, nothing more. The assumption that the values of the establishment should overwhelm all other values galled Böll. A psychiatrist diagnoses Lev to be suffering, from "xenophilogy," defined as the "desire to learn the language of foreigners," a so-called disease. Lev is further diagnosed with "normality-simulation — hysterically directed compensation concealing a strong latent homosexual tendency beneath extreme heterosexual activity." Heterosexuality is twisted into an aberration by the minions of established authority attempting to destroy an individual with the effrontery to challenge their values with values of his own.

Böll's most sympathetic characters are cranks: a soldier who awarded himself medals and a pension for wounds never inflicted, in battles never fought, and for disabilities never suffered; a whore who blushes to death; a sheep-lady prophetess who perfumes her underwear with sheep turds; and a woman whose abiding passion is coloring in an enormous outline of the cones and rods of a human retina. He also concocts outrageous groups. The "Academy of Military Memoirs" (*Adam, Where Art Thou?*) is proposed as a place "where every soldier from major upward may write his reminiscences, while a few healthy girls from the people are to sweeten the evening of the retired heroes." The preposterousness of the "Academy" is typical of Böll's satire: common soldiers are forgotten, and women do not matter anymore than does the cause these soldiers served.

Böll's war stories have no soldier heroes. The perversion of an entire society in the interests of war incites Böll's wrath: farms become observation posts, schools are transformed into hospitals and furniture vans transport Jews to concentration camps. When Lenie's husband and brother—both soldiers—are caught operating in the black market, they are sentenced to the firing squad. Her husband's last words before his execution are, "Shit on Germany" (*Group Portrait with Lady*).

While Böll's stories are told against the panorama of war, they are intimate tales speaking in multiple voices. Typically, the events occur over only the course of a day while the characters and their histories stretch back to childhood. The stubborn individual opposing the state machinery is a character of love for Böll. In *Billiards at Half-Past Nine*, Grandmother, on a one-day leave from an insane asylum, shoots a soldier who represents Hindenburg, thereby restoring her family to wholeness. In "At the Bridge" (*The Stories of Heinrich Böll*) cautious rebellion triumphs as the "counter" refuses to count the woman who catches his eye each time she crosses the bridge. "My little darling had passed by, and never in my life will I let this pretty child be transported into the future perfect; this little darling of mine is not to be multiplied and divided and turned into a negligible percentabel." The authorities do not suspect the subversives among them, but Heinrich Böll will not let them forget.

Heinrich Böll provides the reader with a social history of Germany from the First World War up to post–World War II reconstruction. He offers more. His characters, particularly in his novels, exhibit a whimsical eccentricity tinged with both love and compassion for their fellow humans. "I suffer not only from depression, headaches, laziness, and the mystical ability to detect smells through the telephone, the most terrible affliction of all is my disposition to monogamy" (*The Clown*). Böll understood that we all suffer from minor self-imposed wounds that require love to heal. He insisted that the Christian Church, to be worthy of its calling, should be a source of solace. His message is clear: Love is the rational calling of man, nothing else.

1972

"—for his writing which through its combination of a broad perspective on his time and a sensitive skill in characterization has contributed to a renewal of German literature—"

© The Nobel Foundation, 1972

An Essay on the Reason of Poetry

It is said by those who ought to know ... that in matters which to all appearances are rational, calculable ... there remain a few millimeters or centimeters of incalculability. Should we also call this almost incalculable element irony, poetry, God, resistance or fiction? How can we cope without it? Not to mention love. No one will ever know how many novels, poems, analyses, confessions, sufferings and joys have been piled up on this continent called Love, without it ever having turned out to be totally investigated.

...Writing is — at least for me — movement forward, the conquest of a body that I do not know at all, away from something to something that I do not yet know; I never know what will happen — and here "happen" is not intended as plot resolution, in the sense of classical dramaturgy, but in the sense of a complicated and complex experiment that with given imaginary, spiritual, intellectual and sensual materials in interaction strives — on paper to boot! — toward incarnation. In this respect there can be no successful literature, nor would there be any successful music or painting, because no one can already have seen the object it is striving to become, and in this respect everything that is superficially called modern, but which is better named living art, is experiment and discovery — and transient, can be estimated and measured only in its historical relativity, and it appears to me irrelevant to speak of eternal values, or to seek them. How will we survive without this gap, this remainder, which can be called irony, be called poetry, be called God, fiction, or resistance?

Countries, too, are always only approaching what they claim to be, and there can be no state which does not leave this gap between the verbal expression of its constitution and its realization, a space that remains, where poetry and resistance grow — and hopefully flourish. And there exists no form of literature which can succeed without this gap.... Politicians, ideologists, theologians and philosophers try time and again to provide solutions with nothing remaining, prefab solved problems. That is their duty — and it is ours, the writers' — since we know that we are not able to solve anything without remainders or resistance — to penetrate into the gaps. There are too many unexplained and inexplicable remainders, entire provinces of waste.

...Did, or does, the tragedy of our churches perhaps indeed consist, not of what the Enlightenment might have designated as unreasonable matters, but in the despairing and desperately failed attempt to pursue or even overtake a reason that has never been and never can be merged with something so irrational as the incarnated God? Regulations, law texts, approval of experts, a figure-laden forest of numbered regulations, and the production of prejudices that have been hammered into us and set out along the tracks of history teaching, in order to make people ever more estranged from one another.... How many provinces of disparagement and disdain has history bequeathed to us?... Entire populations remained strangers to one another, supposedly speaking the same language. Where marriage in the Western manner was prescribed as creating order, people ignored the fact that it was a privilege: unattainable, unachievable for those who worked the land, the people called farm hands and milk maids, who simply didn't have the money even to buy a pair of sheets, and if they had saved up or stolen the money, wouldn't have had the bed to put the sheets on. And so they were left untouched in their illegitimacy; they produced kids anyway! From above and from the outside, everything seemed completely settled. Clear answers, clear questions, clear regulations, catechism as delusion. And just think of everything passed off, foisted off on God, this much-abused and pitiable authority: everything, yes, everything that was a problem: all the guides for inescapable misery in social, economic or sexual form pointed to him, everything despicable, contemptible, was palmed off on God, all the leftover "remainders," and yet at the same time he was being preached about as the Incarnate, without considering that one cannot place the burden of man on God, nor the burden of God on man, if he is to be considered incarnate.... This madness of ours, this arrogance "in itself" again and again buries both: the incarnate Deity, who is called God become Man, and the vision set in its place, that of the future of the entirety of mankind. We who so easily humiliate others, we are lacking in something: humility — which is not to be confused with subordination or obedience, let alone submission.

I have got a bit away from the building of bridges, baking of rolls and writing of novels, and hinted at gaps, ironies, fictive areas, remnants, divinities, mystifications and resistance of other regions — they appeared to me worse, in greater need of illumination than the slight, unilluminated corners in which not our traditional reason, but the reason of poetry — as in for example a novel — lies hidden.... May I not dare expect that people do not merely trust in, but strengthen the reason of poetry, not by leaving it in peace, but by absorbing a bit of its calmness and the pride of its humbleness, which can only be a humbleness towards those below, and never a humbleness towards those above. Regard for others, politeness and justice reside therein, and the wish to recognize and be recognized.

I do not wish to provide new missionary starting-points and vehicles, but I do believe that in the sense of poetic humbleness, politeness and justice I must say that I see considerable similarity, I see possibilities for rapprochement between the stranger à la Camus, the strangeness of the Kafkaesque official and the incarnated God, who after all remains a stranger and — if one neglects a few outbursts of temper — is polite and literal in a remarkable way. Why else has the Catholic Church long — I don't know exactly how long — blocked direct access to the literal nature of the texts they declare holy, or else kept it hidden in Latin and Greek, available only to the initiated? I imagine it is in order to keep out the dangers they sensed in the poetry of the incarnated word, and to protect the reason of their power from the dangerous reason of poetry. And after all it is not accidental that the most important consequence of the Reformation was the discovery of languages and their corporeality. And what empire ever could do without language imperialism, i.e., the diffusion of their own language and suppression of the languages of those ruled? In this — but in no other — connection I regard the for once not imperialistic, but supposedly anti-imperialistic attempts to denounce poetry, the sensuality of language, its incarnation and the power of the imagination (for language and the power of the imagination are one and the same), and to introduce the false dichotomy of information or poetry, as a new version of "divide et impera." It is the brand-new, but once again almost international arrogance of a New Reason, which may possibly permit the poetry of the Indians as an anti-ruling class force, but withholds its own poetry from the classes to be liberated in its own land. Poetry is not a class privilege, it has never been one. Much about this is papal: withholding incarnation and sensuality from others while developing new catechisms which speak of the only correct and the truly false possibilities of expression. One cannot separate the power of the message from the power of the expression in which the message occurs.

...No class can be liberated by first withholding something from them.... One may readily quarrel about the concept of beauty, develop new aesthetics — they are indeed overdue — but they must not begin by withholding matters, and they must not exclude one thing; the possibility of transferal that literature offers; it transfers us to South or North America, to Sweden, India, Africa. It can *also* transfer us to another class, another time, another religion and another race. It has — even in its bourgeois form — never been its goal to create strangeness, but to remove it.... No author can take over alleged or specious divisions and judgments, and to me it appears almost suicidal that we are even and still discussing the division into committed literature and other kinds. Not only do we, precisely when we think that it is the one, have to intervene for the other with all our might; no, it is precisely through this falsified alternative that we accept a bourgeois principle of divisions, one which turns us into strangers. It is not only the division of our potential strength, but also of our potential — and

I'll risk this without even blushing — incarnated beauty, since it too can liberate, just as the communicated thought can: It can be liberating in itself, or as the provocation that it may create. The strength of undivided literature is not the neutralization of directions, but the internationality of resistance, and to this resistance belong poetry, incarnation, sensuality, imaginative power and beauty.... No curse, no bitterness, not even the information about the desperate situation of a class is possible without poetry, and even to condemn it requires that it first must be recognized. Go and read Rosa Luxemburg carefully and note which statues Lenin ordered erected first: the first for Count Tolstoy, of whom he said that until this count began to write, Russian literature contained no peasants; the second for the "reactionary" Dostoyevsky.

Art is always a good hiding-place, not for dynamite, for intellectual explosive and social time bombs. Why would there otherwise have been the various Indices? And precisely in their despised and often even despicable beauty and lack of transparency lies the best hiding-place for the barb that brings about the sudden jerk or the sudden recognition.

18. Saul Bellow

> Art is the community's medicine for the worst disease of mind,
> the corruption of consciousness.
>
> *— Culture Now: Some Animadversions, Some Laughs*

Saul Bellow's (1915–) novels probe the loose ends of human
desire for wholeness in an era rife with distraction and fragmentation. From his first novel, *Dangling Man*, to his most recent, *Ravelstein,* his protagonists are acute cultural observers seeking solace, not
in hand-me-down ideologies, but in a vital connection to the core
of their expressive selves. "We are all drawn toward the same craters
of spirit — to know what we are, and what we are for, to know our
purpose, to seek grace" (*Dangling Man*). Arthur Sammler, Dean
Corde, Moses Herzog, Von Humboldt Fleisher, Augie March, and
Bellow's other imagined selves occupy front row seats in the theater
of the soul. And it is a challenging, not a depressing, place. "If life
is not intoxicating, it's nothing. Here it's burn or rot" (*Humboldt's
Gift*). Bellow often places a serious exploration of meaning in the
hands of a distracted and disorganized character such as Henderson,
The Rain King.

> I often looked into books to see whether I could find some helpful
> words, and one day I read, "The forgiveness of sins is perpetual and
> righteousness first is not required." This impressed me so deeply that
> I went around saying it to myself. But then I forgot which book it
> was.

Imagine Eugene Henderson, a middle-aged violin-playing mul-
timillionaire pig farmer, built like an over-the-hill defensive tackle,
haunted by Daniel's warning to King Nebuchadnezzar about
dwelling with the beasts of the field, suffering the recurring auditory

hallucination of a voice saying "I want, I want, I want" who, upon finding his cook dead in the kitchen, pins a note to her skirt saying "Do Not Disturb" and convinces a friend to allow him to become the third person on a honeymoon to Africa where he encounters a frog plague of biblical memory. With good intention he triggers a rain of frogs and a drought. Henderson then binds the frayed ends of his soul together while communing with lions in their den. Look what adventure awaits, Bellow implies, when we don't agree to the death of our souls. Henderson displays Bellow's comic power to draw characters who occupy a class by themselves, obsessed with issues beyond the call of reason.

Often classified as an author of "novels of ideas," Bellow censures intellectuals for deifying the soul's distractions. "We crave more than ever the radiant vividness of boundless love, and more and more the barren idols thwart this. A world of categories devoid of spirit waits for life to return" (*Humboldt's Gift*). Specialists and "reality instructors" who think they have all the answers and who would deny the value of any imaginative speculation incur Bellow's anger for having usurped the legitimacy and drained dry the pools of awe from broader forms of knowledge. These "specialists without spirit, sensualists without heart, this nullity imagines it has attained a level of civilization never before achieved" (*Mr. Sammler's Planet*). The academics' evisceration of fiction for careerist ambitions, "turning a cognitive profit on someone else's imaginative activities," earns Bellow's special ire (*Conversations*). As an alternative to the rationalists' devices of reduction and analysis, and the mistaken assumption of taking a small part for the mysterious whole, Bellow offers the uncertainty of a soulful quest. "About some paths of life either you guess or you never know, because you can't be told" (*The Adventures of Augie March*).

Art, believes Bellow, is a force that can deliver us from this malaise. "What really frees you from those insulting social and psychological fictions is the other fiction of art" (*Zetland: By a Character Witness*). Art quarries deeper than cognition into an area that may be beyond vocabulary, but not beyond experience, to unite the dispersed elements of the self, creating a vibrant relationship with the universe.

> You are drawn to feel and to penetrate further, as if you were being informed that what was spread over you had to do with your existence, down to the very blood and the crystal forms inside your bones. Rocks, trees, animals, men and women, these also drew you to penetrate further, under the distortions (comparable to the

atmospheric ones, shadows within shadows) to find their real being with your own [*The Dean's December*].

Bellow's novels parody the truth of the modernist and post-modernist creeds, locating the home of the spirit not in existential angst but in the fundamental questions of identity and relationship raised by serious novelists since Cervantes. "The writer asks himself, 'Why shall I write this next thing?' It is still possible, despite all theories to the contrary, to answer, 'Because it is necessary.' A book, any book, may easily be superfluous. But to manifest love — can that be superfluous? Is there so much of it about us? Not so much. It is still rare, still wonderful. It is still effective against distraction."[1] Profoundly out of touch with his times, Bellow invites us to awaken to the joy of being in all its complexity and seriousness. With a cosmic, comic sensibility and a colloquial vernacular, his characters struggle to overcome their personal limitations, push past the "reality instructors," and liberate their souls from bondage to received opinions, in the process breaking through to ecstasy.

1976

"—for the human understanding and subtle analysis of contemporary culture that are combined in his work—"

...Perhaps Joseph Conrad appealed to me because he was like an American — he was an uprooted Pole sailing exotic seas, speaking French and writing English with extraordinary power and beauty.... His views on art were simply stated in the preface to *The Nigger of the Narcissus*. There he said that art was an attempt to render the highest justice to the visible universe: that it tried to find in that universe, in matter as well as in the facts of life, what was fundamental, enduring, essential. The writer's method of attaining the essential was different from that of the thinker or the scientist. These, said Conrad, knew the world by systematic examination. To begin with the artist had only himself; he descended within himself and in the lonely regions to which he descended, he found "the terms of his appeal." Conrad appealed "to that part of our being which is a gift, not an acquisition, to the capacity for delight and wonder ... our sense of pity and pain, to the latent feeling of fellowship with all creation — and to the subtle but invincible conviction of solidarity that knits together the loneliness of innumerable hearts ... which binds together all humanity — the dead to the living and the living to the unborn."

...Hemingway's youthful readers were convinced that the horrors of the twentieth century had sickened and killed humanistic beliefs with their deadly radiations. I told myself, therefore, that Conrad's rhetoric must be resisted. But I never thought him mistaken. He spoke directly to me.

...I feel no need now to sprinkle Conrad's sentences with skeptical salt. But there are writers from whom the Conradian novel — all novels of that sort — are gone forever. Finished. There is, for instance, M. Alain Robbe-Grillet, one of the leaders of French literature, a spokesman for "thingism" — choseisme.... "The novel of characters," he says, "belongs entirely in the past [in Balzac's time].... It was something to have a face in a universe where personality represented both the means and the end of all exploration." But our world, he concludes, is more modest. It has renounced the omnipotence of the person.

...We all know what it is to be tired of "characters." Human types have become false and boring. D.H. Lawrence put it early in this century that we human beings, our instincts damaged by Puritanism, no longer care for, were physically repulsive to one another. "The sympathetic heart is broken," he said.... Then, too, the psychoanalytic conception of character is that it is an ugly rigid formation — something we must resign ourselves to, not a thing we can embrace with joy.

...The message of Robbe-Grillet is not new.... I myself am tired of obsolete notions and of mummies of all kinds but I never tire of reading the master novelists. And what is one to do about the characters in their books? Is it necessary to discontinue the investigation of character?... I suggest that it is not in the intrinsic interest of human beings but in these ideas and accounts that the problem lies. The staleness, the inadequacy of these [ideas] repels us. The fact that the death notice of character "has been signed by the most serious essayists" means only that another group of mummies, the most respectable leaders of the intellectual community, has laid down the law. It amuses me that these serious essayists should be allowed to sign the death notices of literary forms. Should art follow culture? Something has gone wrong.

There is no reason why a novelist should not drop "character" if the strategy stimulates him. But it is nonsense to do it on the theoretical ground that the period which marked the apogee of the individual, and so on, has ended. We must not makes bosses of our intellectuals. And we do them no good by letting them run the arts. Should they, when they read novels, find nothing in them but the endorsement of their own opinions? Are we here on earth to play such games?

...Every year we see scores of books and articles which tell the Americans what a state they are in — which make intelligent or simpleminded or extravagant or lurid or demented statements. All reflect the crises we are in while telling us what we must do about them; these analysts are produced by the very disorder and confusion they prescribe for. It is as a writer that I am considering their extreme moral sensitivity, their desire of perfection, their intolerance of the defects of society, the touching, the comical boundlessness of their demands, their anxiety, their irritability, their sensitivity, their tender-mindedness, their goodness, their convulsiveness, the recklessness with which they experiment with drugs and touch-therapies and bombs.

...And with this private disorder goes public bewilderment.

...But my purpose is not to get into debates I can't win but to direct your attention to the terrible predictions we have to live with, the background of disorder, the visions of ruin. We stand open to all anxieties. The decline and fall of everything is our daily dread, we are agitated in private life and tormented by public questions.

...And art and literature — what of them? Well, there is a violent uproar but we are not absolutely dominated by it. We are still able to think, to discriminate, and to feel. The purer, subtler, higher activities have not succumbed to fury or to nonsense. Not yet. Books continue to be written and read. It may be more difficult to reach the whirling mind of a modern reader but it is possible to cut through the noise and reach the quiet zone. In the quiet zone we may find that he is devoutly waiting for us. When complications increase, the desire for essentials increases too.

...Looking into Proust's *Time Regained* I find that he was clearly aware of it. Without art, he insists, shirking no personal or collective horrors, we do not know ourselves or anyone else. Only art penetrates what pride, passion, intelligence and habit erect on all sides — the seeming realities of this world. There is another reality, the genuine one, which we lose sight of. This other reality is always sending us hints, which, without art, we can't receive. Proust calls these hints our "true impressions."

...Proust was still able to keep a balance between art and destruction, insisting that art was a necessity of life, a great independent reality, a magical power. But for a long time art has not been connected, as it was in the past, with the main enterprise. The historian Edgar Wind tells us in *Art and Anarchy* that Hegel long ago observed that art no longer engaged the central energies of man. These energies were now engaged by science —

a "relentless spirit of rational inquiry." Art had moved to the margins.... Nor am I sure that at this moment, it is the spirit of rational inquiry in pure science that engages the central energies of man. The center seems (temporarily perhaps) to be filled up with the crises I have been describing.

...What would writers do today if it would occur to them that literature might once again engage those "central energies," if they were to recognize that an immense desire had arisen for a return from the periphery, for what was simple and true?

...We do not, we writers, represent mankind adequately.... There is in the intellectual community a sizable inventory of attitudes that have become respectable — notions about society, human nature, class, politics, sex, about mind, about the physical universe, the evolution of life. Few writers, even among the best, have taken the trouble to re-examine these attitudes or orthodoxies.... Literature has for nearly a century used the same stock of ideas, myths, strategies. "The most serious essayists of the last fifty years," says Robbe-Grillet. Yes, indeed. Essay after essay, book after book, confirm the most serious thoughts — Baudelairian, Nietzschean, Marxian, Psychoanalytic, etcetera, etcetera — of these most serious essayists. What Robbe-Grillet says about character can be said also about these ideas, maintaining all the usual things about mass society, dehumanization and the rest. How weary we are of them. How poorly they represent us. The pictures they offer no more resemble us than we resemble the reconstructed reptiles and other monsters in a museum of paleontology. We are much more limber, versatile, better articulated, there is much more to us, we all feel it.

...At such a time it is essential to lighten ourselves, to dump encumbrances, including the encumbrances of education and all organized platitudes, to make judgments of our own, to perform acts of our own. Conrad was right to appeal to that part of our being which is a gift. We must hunt for that under the wreckage of many systems. The failure of those systems may bring a blessed and necessary release from formulations, from an over-defined and misleading consciousness.... Our very vices, our mutilations, show how rich we are in thought and culture. How much we know. How much we even feel. The struggle that convulses us makes us want to simplify, to reconsider, to eliminate the tragic weakness which prevented writers — and readers — from being at once simple and true.

Writers are greatly respected. The intelligent public is wonderfully patient with them, continues to read them and endures disappointment after disappointment, waiting to hear from art what it does not hear from theology, philosophy, social theory, and what it cannot hear from pure science. Out of the struggle at the center has come an immense, painful longing for a broader, more flexible, fuller, more coherent, more comprehensive account of what we human beings are, who we are, and what this life is for. At the center humankind struggles with collective powers for its freedom, the individual struggles with dehumanization for the possession of his soul. If writers do not come again into the center it will not be because the center is pre-empted. It is not. They are free to enter. If they so wish.

The essence of our real condition, the complexity, the confusion, the pain of it is shown to us in glimpses, in what Proust and Tolstoy thought of as "true impressions." This essence reveals, and then conceals itself. When it goes away it leaves us again in doubt. But we never seem to lose our connection with the depths from which the glimpses comes. The sense of our real powers, powers we seem to derive from the universe itself, also comes and goes. We are reluctant to talk about this because there is nothing we can prove, because our language is inadequate and because few people are willing to risk talking about it. They would have to say, "There is a spirit" and that is taboo. So almost everyone keeps quiet about it, although almost everyone is aware of it.

The value of literature lies in these intermittent "true impressions." A novel moves back and forth between the world of objects, of actions, of appearances, and that other world from which these "true impressions" come and which moves us to believe that the good we hang onto so tenaciously — in the face of evil, so obstinately — is no illusion.

No one who has spent years in the writing of novels can be unaware of this. The novel can't be compared to the epic, or to the monuments of poetic drama. But it is the best we can do just now. It is a sort of latter-day lean-to, a hovel in which the spirit takes shelter. A novel is balanced between a few true impressions and the multitude of false ones that make up most of what we call life. It tells us that for every human being there is a diversity of existences, that the single existence is itself an illusion in part, that these many existences signify something, tend to something, fulfill something; it promises us meaning, harmony and even justice. What Conrad said was true, art attempts to find in the universe, in matter as well as in the facts of life, what is fundamental, enduring, essential.

19. Isaac Bashevis Singer

Every writer must write on his own topics, which are connected with his main passions, with the things he is pondering about, or brooding over. This is the part what gives a writer his charm and makes him genuine.

—Conversations with Isaac Bashevis Singer

"The Ten Commandments lacked all preciseness," Isaac Singer (1904–1991) writes in *The Family Moskat*, but he broadened the complaint later saying, "The Ten Commandments are commandments against human nature" (*Conversations with Isaac Bashevis Singer*). The figures in Singer's stories poignantly illustrate his point, being both unable to live without the rules and simultaneously open to every temptation of the flesh. Singer claims, "There isn't any explanation for human behavior — there are only patterns" ("The Mentor" in *A Friend of Kafka*). In spite of the eccentrics among "his people," he denies inventing them. "Experts at fingerprints do not create fingerprints. They learn how to read them. In the same way the writer reads human characters" (*Conversations with Isaac Bashevis Singer*).

Singer exaggerates what lies in each of us. The effect is both funny and sad. After a redemptive visit to the synagogue, "Yasha remembered that while praying he had made all sorts of resolutions and had sworn the most exacting vows, but in the few minutes he had been standing here, all their substance had vanished" (*The Magician of Lublin*). Singer's wry view of human nature creates the structure of nearly all his works:

> One day all people will realize there is not a single idea that can really be called true — that everything is a game — nationalism, internationalism, religion, atheism, spiritualism, materialism, even suicide....

135

> Since we are sure of nothing and there is even no evidence that the
> sun will rise tomorrow, play is the very essence of human endeavor,
> perhaps even the thing-in-itself. God is a player, the cosmos a play-
> ground [*Shosha*].

His novels and short stories beguile with their insight, humor,
pathos and sheer earthiness of the characters.

> I was not born. My father, a yeshiva student, sinned as did Onan,
> and from his seed I was created — half spirit, half demon, half air,
> half shade, horned like a buck and winged like a bat, with the mind
> of a scholar and the heart of a highwayman ["Diary of One Not
> Born" in *Gimpel the Fool*].

Singer ironically attributes to imps, demons and dybbuks the
troubles that people bring on themselves. These agents of the Devil
bear an uncomfortable resemblance to us all. "Yawning, I considered my next step. Should I seduce a rabbi's daughter? deprive a
bridegroom of his manhood? plug up the synagogue chimney? turn
the Sabbath wine into vinegar? ... An imp never lacks for things to
do" ("The Mirror" in *An Isaac Bashevis Singer Reader*). With deadpan reporting he renders his version of the murder of a village woman
without a hint of malice toward the killer or awareness of the origin
of the crime:

> On the night of Hoshana Rabba a dreadful thing happened: A
> woman who had gone to fetch water was thrown by demons into the
> well, where she was found dead the next morning, head down and
> feet up. The evil spirits also molested the old night watchman, tear-
> ing off half his beard [*Satan in Goray*].

A Jewish woman, so consumed with stylish clothing that she converts to Catholicism, late in life, to avoid being buried in a common
shroud, adds another item to the catalogue of lusts in "The Primper"
(*A Friend of Kafka*). A practical joke turns lethal in "The Wager" (*A
Friend of Kafka*), killing two young men while ruining the lives of
those who planned it. But as Singer explains, they wanted to "play
a joke on Yosele that he would long remember.... Life was too good
to us; we had to ask for trouble." In Singer's world piety isn't natural to man, lust is. In *The Family Moskat*, Nyunie, sitting at his
dying wife's bedside thinks "that as soon as the prescribed thirty-
day period of mourning was over he would go to see the widow
Gritzhendler and have a direct talk with her." Singer's acceptance of
the irrational in man, free of categorical judgment, blossoms in the
many failures of sanctioned love in this novel. Entangled in loveless

marriages, the major characters enjoy passionate love affairs. But true to the restlessness of human nature, when these couples divorce and marry their lovers, happiness eludes them still.

"Every artist must have an address," Singer said in *The Magician of West 86th Street*. Singer's own address is the Jewish section of a small Polish village prior to World War II. His characters grow like trees with deep roots of ancestry, religion, culture and history anchoring them to the earth. Even the wanderers, decades after they leave their childhood homes, are marked by their roots.

One of the hallmarks of a Singer story is his devout reverence for nature (God): "God's hand was evident everywhere. One could almost hear the roots sucking the earth, the stalks growing, the underground streams trickling" (*The Magician of Lublin*). His stories read effortlessly. He summed up his impatience with intellectualized notions of literature by listing ten of the reasons he wrote children's books:

1. Children read books, not reviews. They don't give a hoot about the critics.

2. They don't read to find their identity.

3. They don't read to free themselves of guilt, to quench the thirst for rebellion, or to get rid of alienation.

4. They have no use for psychology.

5. They detest sociology.

6. They don't try to understand Kafka or *Finnegans Wake*.

7. They still believe in God, the family, angels, devils, and witches.

8. They love interesting stories, not commentary, guide or footnotes.

9. When a book is boring, they yawn openly without any shame or fear of authority.

10. They don't expect their beloved writer to redeem humanity. Young as they are, they know that it is not in his power. Only adults have such childish delusions.[1]

Isaac Bashevis Singer considered himself to be an entertainer. He saw our weaknesses, along with his own weakness, and laughed at us and with us. With a light touch he portrayed the age old problems of good and evil, sanctity and lust, duty and desire. For Singer all humankind, including the small segment with which he identified (Eastern European Jews), were driven by passions they neither understood nor controlled. He called Jews, "a people who can't sleep themselves and won't let anybody else sleep" (*The Family Moskat*). Only

the pious avoid the pitfalls of the world, and they too struggle might-
ily against their own natures to achieve and retain their piety. Singer
recorded the passion and hypocrisy of our species with a bemused
smile, like a wise and forgiving uncle, making each of us a bit richer
for having read him.

1978

*"—for his impassioned narrative art which, with roots in a Polish-Jew-
ish cultural tradition, brings universal human conditions to life—"*

The storyteller and poet of our time, as in any other time, must be
an entertainer of the spirit in the full sense of the word, not just a preacher
of social or political ideals. There is no paradise for bored readers and no
excuse for tedious literature that does not intrigue the reader, uplift him,
give him the joy and the escape that true art always grants. Nevertheless,
it is also true that the serious writer of our time must be deeply concerned
about the problems of his generation. He cannot but see that the power
of religion, especially belief in revelation, is weaker today than it was in
any other epoch in human history. More and more children grow up without faith in God, without belief in reward and punishment, in the immortality of the soul and even in the validity of ethics. The genuine writer
cannot ignore the fact that the family is losing its spiritual foundation. All
the dismal prophecies of Oswald Spengler have become realities since the
Second World War. No technological achievements can mitigate the disappointment of modern man, his loneliness, his feeling of inferiority, and
his fear of war, revolution and terror. Not only has our generation lost
faith in Providence but also in man himself, in his institutions and often
in those who are nearest to him.

In their despair a number of those who no longer have confidence in
the leadership of our society look up to the writer, the master of words.
They hope against hope that the man of talent and sensitivity can perhaps
rescue civilization. Maybe there is a spark of the prophet in the artist after
all.

As the son of a people who received the worst blows that human madness can inflict, I must brood about the forthcoming dangers. I have many
times resigned myself to never finding a true way out. But a new hope
always emerges telling me that it is not yet too late for all of us to take

stock and make a decision. I was brought up to believe in free will. Although I came to doubt all revelation, I can never accept the idea that the Universe is a physical or chemical accident, a result of blind evolution. Even though I learned to recognize the lies, the clichés and the idolatries of the human mind, I still cling to some truths which I think all of us might accept some day. There must be a way for man to attain all possible pleasures, all the powers and knowledge that nature can grant him, and still serve God — a God who speaks in deeds, not in words, and whose vocabulary is the Cosmos.

I am not ashamed to admit that I belong to those who fantasize that literature is capable of bringing new horizons and new perspectives — philosophical, religious, aesthetical and even social. In the history of old Jewish literature there was never any basic difference between the poet and the prophet. Our ancient poetry often became law and a way of life.

Some of my cronies in the cafeteria near the *Jewish Daily Forward* in New York call me a pessimist and a decadent, but there is always a background of faith behind resignation. I found comfort in such pessimists and decadents as Baudelaire, Verlaine, Edgar Allan Poe, and Strindberg. My interest in psychic research made me find solace in such mystics as your Swedenborg and in our own Rabbi Nachman Bratzlaver, as well as in a great poet of my time, my friend Aaron Zeitlin who died a few years ago and left a literary inheritance of high quality, most of it in Yiddish.

The pessimism of the creative person is not decadence but a mighty passion for the redemption of man. While the poet entertains he continues to search for eternal truths, for the essence of being. In his own fashion he tries to solve the riddle of time and change, to find an answer to suffering, to reveal love in the very abyss of cruelty and injustice. Strange as these words may sound I often play with the idea that when all the social theories collapse and wars and revolutions leave humanity in utter gloom, the poet — whom Plato banned from his Republic — may rise up to save us all.

The high honor bestowed upon me by the Swedish Academy is also a recognition of the Yiddish language — a language of exile, without a land, without frontiers, not supported by any government, a language which possesses no words for weapons, ammunition, military exercises, war tactics; a language that was despised by both gentiles and emancipated Jews. The truth is that what the great religions preached, the Yiddish-speaking people of the ghettos practiced day in and day out. They were the people of The Book in the truest sense of the word. They knew of no greater joy than the study of man and human relations, which they called Torah,

Talmud, Mussar, Bacala. The ghetto was not only a place of refuge for a persecuted minority but a great experiment in peace, in self-discipline and in humanism. As such it still exists and refuses to give up in spite of all the brutality that surrounds it. I was brought up among those people. My father's home on Krochmalna Street in Warsaw was a study house, a court of justice, a house of prayer, of storytelling, as well as a place for weddings and Chassidic banquets. As a child I had heard from my older brother and master, I.J. Singer, who later wrote *The Brothers Ashkenazi*, all the arguments that the rationalists from Spinoza to Max Nordau brought out against religion. I have heard from my father and mother all the answers that faith in God could offer to those who doubt and search for the truth. In our home and in many other homes the eternal questions were more actual than the latest news in the Yiddish newspaper. In spite of all the disenchantments and all my skepticism I believe that the nations can learn much from those Jews, their way of thinking, their way of bringing up children, their finding happiness where others see nothing but misery and humiliation. To me the Yiddish language and the conduct of those who spoke it are identical. One can find in the Yiddish tongue and in the Yiddish spirit expressions of pious joy, lust for life, longing for the Messiah, patience and deep appreciation of human individuality. There is a quiet humor in Yiddish and a gratitude for every day of life, every crumb of success, each encounter of love. The Yiddish mentality is not haughty. It does not take victory for granted. It does not demand and command but it meddles through, sneaks by, smuggles itself amidst the powers of destruction, knowing somewhere that God's plan for Creation is still at the very beginning.

There are some who call Yiddish a dead language, but so was Hebrew called for two thousand years. It has been revived in our time in a most remarkable, almost miraculous way. Aramaic was certainly a dead language for centuries but then it brought to light the Zohar, a work of mysticism of sublime value. It is a fact that the classics of Yiddish literature are also the classics of the modern Hebrew literature. Yiddish has not yet said its last word. It contains treasures that have not been revealed to the eyes of the world. It was the tongue of martyrs and saints, of dreamers and Cabalists — rich in humor and in memories that mankind may never forget. In a figurative way, Yiddish is the wise and humble language of us all, an idiom of [a] frightened and hopeful Humanity.

20. Czesław Miłosz

If I accomplished anything, it was only when I,
a pious boy, chased after the disguises of the lost Reality.
After the real presence of divinity in our flesh and blood
which are at the same time bread and wine.
Hearing the immense call of the Particular,
despite the earthly law that sentences memory to extinction.

—"Capri" in *Facing the River*

Cesław Miłosz (1911–) has swum against the prevailing currents of thought throughout his life. A Pole born in Lithuania, an opponent of communism and nihilism, a Christian poet spiritually estranged from the dominant "isms" of his times, he became a pre–Enlightenment rebel looking to the seventeenth century, not the twentieth, for wisdom.

"I had to learn to live like a pariah," he wrote, "in self-exile from the 'respectable society' of Western intellectuals, because I dared to offend their most hallowed assumptions, which I took to be a compilation of historical, geographical, and political ignorance" (*The Captive Mind*). He is a man apart: "Behold the enduring image of a poet, ill at ease in one place, ill at ease in the other — always and everywhere ill at ease" (*The Land of Ulro*).

Miłosz believes the Enlightenment dislodged man's sense of place in the cosmos. "The Enlightenment's fundamentally wrong decision [was] to put all of man's hopes in science and reason." He also regards the theory of Darwinism as misguided: "The differences among species are so clearly drawn that I can't believe in evolution. How do you get from the fox to the elephant?" (*Conversations with Cesław Miłosz*).

Miłosz's life can be viewed as one of giving testimony to the continual search for truth without compromise yet with a sense of

141

whimsy. "The world is so ungraspable that our relationship to the world is like that of a hamster to ballet music" (*Conversations with Czesław Miłosz*). He once described himself as an "angelic spirit in a bumptious skull, brilliance layered with mediocrity" (*Conversations with Czesław Miłosz*).

Cesław Miłosz frankly admits that the process of poetic creation mystifies him. "['A Nation'] was a poem written entirely outside my control, in the sense that something comes, grabs my hand, and orders me to write.... Something arises in me, but just how is a mystery" (*Conversations with Czesław Miłosz*). While the creative process confounds analysis, it demands a response on two levels. The poet is obliged to follow his calling (in spiritual obedience) and the poetry that results must resist the corruption of truth by expediency. Poets, he believes, must confront oppression and coercion by evoking and recording new ways of viewing man's relationship to space, freeing readers to retrieve obscure but vital reference points for the mind and imagination away from the clamor of the mainstream. Miłosz holds a pure view of the function of all literature:

> Of course literature should be edifying.... The word "edifying" is pronounced sarcastically today and that is sufficient proof that something is wrong with us. What great works of literature were not edifying? Homer perhaps? Or *The Divine Comedy*? or *Don Quixote*? or *Leaves of Grass*? [*Unattainable Earth*]

Miłosz thinks communism was founded upon three fundamental errors: underestimating individuality, the denial of God, and confusing symbols with reality. In *The Captive Mind* he analyzes the pervasive weight of omnipotent communist dogma on the psychology of the middle class, describing this corrosive dynamic as a "pill of Murti-Being; the swallowing of which allows one to feel relieved from any individual responsibility." The Ketman phenomenon, a side effect of Murti-Being, Miłosz describes as, "the art of secretly knowing the truth and, at the same time, publicly adhering to the official doctrine."

He chides communism and other elitist movements for creating hollow symbols of humanity and then dividing mankind into two categories, the initiated and the rest. As a devout Christian himself, Miłosz abrades the compromises made by Christian communists as untenable at the core, pointing out that Christianity is based on individual merit, or salvation, and communism is founded on (historical) group merit. "Only one language can do justice to the highest claim of the human imagination — that of Holy Writ" (*Conversations with Czesław Miłosz*).

Czesław Miłosz shuns the use of symbol and metaphor in literature. "By endowing masks and facades with a real existence, we find ourselves one day the victims of an illusion" (*The Captive Mind*). His stark aesthetics forbid him from accepting any compromise with his artistic ideals. "A thing improperly stated is a betrayal of that thing, then better to remain silent than to commit a betrayal" (*The Land of Ulro*).

Cleaving to this belief, Miłosz strives to describe each phenomenon with such particularity that it cannot be mistaken for another, similar thing. He does not merely depict an orange; he describes *this orange* so concretely that it cannot be mistaken for *that orange*.

To Miłosz explanation is falsehood. "Vulgarized knowledge characteristically gives birth to a feeling that everything is understandable and explained. It is like a system of bridges built over chasms. One can travel boldly ahead over these bridges, ignoring the chasms ... but that, alas, does not alter the fact that they exist" (*The Captive Mind*). Accurate description is the best we can expect from ourselves as we skate "on the incomprehensible borderline between mind and flesh" (*Unattainable Earth*).

Miłosz's literary recognition comes as a result of his willingness to sincerely grapple with dilemmas that can never—finally—be resolved. The mystery cannot be decoded, only commented upon and appreciated for its beauty.

1980

"—*who with uncompromising clear-sightedness voices man's exposed condition in a world of severe conflicts—*"

...One of the Nobel laureates whom I read in childhood influenced to a large extent, I believe, my notions of poetry. That was Selma Lagerlöf. Her *Wonderful Adventures of Nils*, a book I loved, places the hero in a double role. He is the one who flies above the Earth and looks at it from above but at the same time sees it in every detail. This double vision may be a metaphor of the poet's vocation. I found a similar metaphor in a Latin ode of a seventeenth-century poet, Maciej Sarbiewski, who was once known all over Europe under the pen-name of Casimire. He taught poetics at my university. In that ode he describes his voyage — on the back of Pegasus — from Vilno to Antwerp, where he is going to visit his poet-friends. Like Nils Holgersson he beholds under him rivers, lakes, forests, that is, a map, both distant and yet concrete. Hence, two attributes of the poet: avidity of the eye and the desire to describe that which he sees. Yet, whoever considers poetry as "to see and to describe" should be aware that he engages in a quarrel with modernity, fascinated as it is with innumerable theories of a specific poetic language.

Every poet depends upon generations who wrote in his native tongue; he inherits styles and forms elaborated by those who lived before him. At the same time, though, he feels that those old means of expression are not adequate to his own experience. When adapting himself, he hears an internal voice that warns him against mask and disguise. But when rebelling, he falls in turn into dependence upon his contemporaries, various movements of the avant-garde. Alas, it is enough for him to publish his first volume of poems, to find himself entrapped. For hardly has the print dried, when that work, which seemed to him the most personal, appears to be enmeshed in the style of another. The only way to counter an obscure remorse is to continue searching and to publish a new book, but then everything repeats itself, so there is no end to that chase. And it may happen that leaving books behind as if they were dry snake skins, in a constant escape forward from what has been done in the past, he receives the Nobel Prize.

What is this enigmatic impulse that does not allow one to settle down in the achieved, the finished? I think it is a quest for reality. I give to this word its naive and solemn meaning, a meaning having nothing to do with philosophical debates of the last few centuries. It is the Earth as seen by Nils from the back of the gander and by the author of the Latin ode from the back of Pegasus. Undoubtedly, the Earth *is* and her riches cannot be exhausted by any description. To make such an assertion means to reject in advance a question we often hear today: "What is reality?" for it is the same as the question of Pontius Pilate: "What is truth?" If among pairs of opposites which we use every day, the opposition of life and death has such an importance, no less importance should be ascribed to the oppositions of truth and falsehood, of reality and illusion.

Simone Weil, to whose writing I am profoundly indebted, says: "Distance is the soul of beauty." Yet sometimes keeping distance is nearly impossible. I am *A Child of Europe*, as the title of one of my poems admits, but that is a bitter, sarcastic admission. I am also the author of an autobiographical book which in the French translation bears the title *Une Autre Europe*. Undoubtedly, there exist two Europes and it happens that we, inhabitants of the second one, were destined to descend into "the heart of darkness" of the twentieth century. I wouldn't know how to speak about poetry in general. I must speak of poetry in its encounter with peculiar circumstances of time and place. Today, from a perspective, we are able to distinguish outlines of the events which by their death-bearing range surpassed all natural disasters known to us, but poetry, mine and my contemporaries', whether of inherited or avant-garde style, was not prepared to cope with those catastrophes. Like blind men we groped our way and were exposed to all the temptation the mind deluded itself with in our time.

It is not easy to distinguish reality from illusion, especially when one lives in a period of the great upheaval that began a couple of centuries ago on a small western peninsula of the Euro-Asiatic continent, only to encompass the whole planet during one man's lifetime with the uniform worship of science and technology. And it was particularly difficult to oppose multiple intellectual temptations in those areas of Europe where degenerate ideas of dominion over men, akin to the ideas of dominion over Nature, led to paroxysms of revolution and war at the expense of millions of human beings destroyed physically or spiritually. And yet perhaps our most precious acquisition is not an understanding of those ideas, which we touched in their most tangible shape, but respect and gratitude for certain things which protect people from internal disintegration and from yielding to tyranny. Precisely for that reason some ways of life, some institutions became a target for the fury of evil forces, above all, the bonds between people that exist organically, as if by themselves, sustained by family, religion, neighborhood, common heritage. In other words, all that disorderly, illogical humanity, so often branded as ridiculous because of its parochial attachments and loyalties.

...A patron saint of all poets in exile, who visit their towns and provinces only in remembrance, is always Dante. But how has the number of Florences increased! The exile of a poet is today a simple function of a relatively recent discovery: that whoever wields power is also able to control language and not only with the prohibitions of censorship, but also by changing the meaning of words. A peculiar phenomenon makes its appearance: The language of a captive community acquires certain durable habits; whole zones of reality cease to exist simply because they have no name. There is, it seems, a hidden link between theories of literature as

Écriture, of speech feeding on itself, and the growth of the totalitarian state. In any case, there is no reason why the state should not tolerate an activity that consists of creating "experimental" poems and prose, if these are conceived as autonomous systems of reference, enclosed within their own boundaries. Only if we assume that a poet constantly strives to liberate himself from borrowed styles in search for reality, is he dangerous. In a room where people unanimously maintain a conspiracy of silence, one word of truth sounds like a pistol shot. And, alas, a temptation to pronounce it, similar to an acute itching, becomes an obsession which doesn't allow one to think of anything else. That is why a poet chooses internal or external exile. It is not certain, however, that he is motivated exclusively by his concern with actuality. He may also desire to free himself from it and elsewhere, in other countries, on other shores, to recover, at least for short moments, his true vocation — which is to contemplate Being.

...We are surrounded today by fictions about the past, contrary to common sense and to an elementary perception of good and evil. As *The Los Angeles Times* recently stated, the number of books in various languages which deny that the Holocaust ever took place, that it was invented by Jewish propaganda, has exceeded one hundred. If such an insanity is possible, is a complete loss of memory as a permanent state of mind improbable? And would it not present a danger more grave than genetic engineering or poisoning of the natural environment?

For the poet of the "other Europe" the events embraced by the name of the Holocaust are a reality, so close in time that he cannot hope to liberate himself from their remembrance unless, perhaps, by translating the Psalms of David. He feels anxiety, though, when the meaning of the word Holocaust undergoes gradual modifications, so that the word begins to belong to the history of the Jews exclusively, as if among the victims there were not also millions of Poles, Russians, Ukrainians and prisoners of other nationalities. He feels anxiety, for he senses in this foreboding of a not distant future when history will be reduced to what appears on television, while the truth, as it is too complicated, will be buried in the archives, if not totally annihilated.

...I hope you forgive my laying bare a memory like a wound. This subject is not unconnected with my meditation on the word "reality," so often misused by always deserving esteem. Complaints of peoples, pacts more treacherous than those we read about in Thucydides, the shape of a maple leaf, sunrises and sunsets over the ocean, the whole fabric of causes and effects, whether we call it Nature or History, points towards, I believe, another hidden reality, impenetrable, though exerting a powerful attraction that is the central driving force of all art and science. There are moments when it seems to me that I decipher the meaning of afflictions which befell the nations of the "other Europe" and that meaning is to make them the bearers of memory — at the time when Europe, without an adjective, and America possess it less and less with every generation.

It is possible that there is no other memory than the memory of wounds. At least we are so taught by the Bible, a book of the tribulations of Israel. The book for a long time enabled European nations to preserve a sense of continuity — a word not to be mistaken for the fashionable term, historicity.

...Our century draws to its close.... I would not dare to curse it, for it has also been a century of faith and hope. A profound transformation, of which we are hardly aware, because we are a part of it, has been taking place, coming to the surface from time to time in phenomena that provoke general astonishment. That transformation has to do, and I use here words of Oscar Miłosz, with "the deepest secret of toiling masses, more than ever alive, vibrant and tormented." Their secret, an unavowed need of true values, finds no language to express itself and here not only the mass media but also intellectuals bear a heavy responsibility. But transformation has been going on, defying short term predictions, and it is probable that in spite of all horrors and perils, our time will be judged as a necessary phase of travail before mankind ascends to a new awareness. Then a new hierarchy of merits will emerge, and I am convinced that Simone Weil and Oscar Miłosz, writers in whose school I obediently studied, will receive their due.

21. Gabriel García Márquez

You don't know how much a dead man can weigh.

— *Gabriel García Márquez*[1]

From misunderstanding grows solitude. "To the Europeans, South America is a man with a mustache, a guitar, and a gun. They don't understand the problem," the doctor says in *No One Writes to the Colonel*. The vast geography of South America appears dreamlike or nightmarish from a European perspective. The Amazon River, containing 20 percent of the world's fresh water, measures a hundred miles across at the mouth. Rain forests are larger than European countries. The land is shaken by frequent violent earthquakes, devastated by hurricanes and deluged by unending rain for months. This is the reality of South America. To the European it is an exaggerated reality.

Interwoven with outsized geography is a variegated history of brutality, impotence, temporary triumph and frustrated expectations. Gabriel García Márquez (1928–) absorbs all these contradictions and reforms them with pulsating boundless humanity in his writing. While many "new novelists" consciously attempt to narrow and desiccate the human consciousness, Gabo, as he is affectionately known in South America, paints a panorama of the organic human experience in this immense reality. His tableau realistically portrays the interwoven fabric of climate, geography, history, and politics as felt in South America. If the fabric of daily life in Colombia seems magical to the European mind-set, it illustrates the continental differences. He describes himself as a "realist writer."[2] For Gabo, realism includes both objective reality and the response of ordinary people to those realities while swimming "in a sea of common catastrophes."[3]

149

Much of the "magical realism" attributed to his writing comes either from the folktales of the region or family stories he was told as a youth. To cite but one example, his grandfather, Colonel Nicolas Márquez, a veteran of the Thousand Days' War, reportedly sired a dozen illegitimate children while soldiering and spent his last years waiting for a government pension that never came. These facts were each reported in *One Hundred Years of Solitude* and *No One Writes to the Colonel*, respectively. South America is rich in the humanity of growth and decay, and García Márquez reflects that organic richness in his writing.

Gabo himself argues, "There is a tendency to underestimate literary culture, to believe in spontaneous invention. Actually literature is a science one has to learn and there are 10,000 years standing behind every short story that gets written. Ultimately you learn literature not in the university but from reading and rereading other writers."[4] He fully acknowledges his inheritance from dozens of great writers, among them: Faulkner, Hemingway, Woolf, Rabelais, France, and Kafka. "I understood that there existed in literature other possibilities besides the rational and academic ... and I found my true path as a writer,"[5] he responded after his first reading of Kafka's *Metamorphosis*.

What sets Gabo apart from many of his contemporaries is his stunning skill at depicting the life of common people with the subtlety of Dickens, the humor and pathos of Cervantes, all the while enlisting those sleepy priests, pool-hall souses, provincial wheeler-dealers, revengeful dentists, sweet whores, and tired revolutionaries in the profound struggle between good and evil, trust and cynicism, and corruption and truth. Deeply buried in many of his characters are what are often thought to be Nordic characteristics: perseverance, stoicism and passive resistance to ridiculous authority.

The courageous, often Quixote-like endurance of characters in Gabo's world is neither European nor Nordic. It's South American. Gabo's solitude grows in this misunderstanding. In the words of his Job-like colonel, responding to yet another challenge to his faith:

"It'll take centuries," his lawyer said.
"It doesn't matter. If you wait for the big things, you can wait for the little ones" [*No One Writes to the Colonel*].

1982

"—for his novels and short stories, in which the fantastic and the realistic are combined in a richly composed world of imagination, reflecting a continent's life and conflicts—"

The Solitude of Latin America

Antonio Pigafetta, a Florentine navigator who went with Magellan on the first voyage around the world, wrote, upon his passage through our southern lands of America, a strictly accurate account that nonetheless resembles a venture into fantasy. In it he recorded that he had seen hogs with navels on their haunches, clawless birds whose hens laid eggs on the backs of their mates, and others still, resembling tongueless pelicans, with beaks like spoons. He wrote of having seen a misbegotten creature with the head and ears of a mule, a camel's body, the legs of a deer and the whinny of a horse. He described how the first native encountered in Patagonia was confronted with a mirror, whereupon that impassioned giant lost his senses to the terror of his own image.

This short and fascinating book, which even then contained the seeds of our present-day novels, is by no means the most staggering account of our reality in that age. The chronicles of the Indies left us countless others. El Dorado, our so avidly sought and illusory land, appeared on numerous maps for many a long year, shifting its place and form to suit the fantasy of cartographers. In his search for the fountain of eternal youth, the mythical Alvar Núñez Cabeza de Vaca explored the north of Mexico for eight years, in a deluded expedition whose members devoured each other and only five of whom returned, of the six hundred who had undertaken it. One of the many unfathomed mysteries of that age is that of the eleven thousand mules, each loaded with one hundred pounds of gold, that left Cuzco one day to pay the ransom of Atahualpa and never reached their destination. Subsequently, in colonial times, hens were sold in Cartegena de Indias that had been raised on alluvial land and whose gizzards contained tiny lumps of gold. One founder's lust for gold beset us until recently. As late as the last century, a German mission appointed to study the construction of an interoceanic railroad across the Isthmus of Panama concluded that the project was feasible on one condition: that the rails not be made of iron, which was scarce in the region, but of gold.

Our independence from Spanish domination did not put us beyond the reach of madness. General Antonio López de Santana, three times dictator of Mexico, held a magnificent funeral for the right leg he had lost in the so-called Pastry War. General Gabriel García Moreno ruled Ecuador for sixteen years as an absolute monarch; at his wake, the corpse was seated on the presidential chair, decked out in full-dress uniform and a protective layer of medals. General Maximiliano Hernández Martínez, the theosophical despot of El Salvador who had thirty thousand peasants slaughtered in a savage massacre, invented a pendulum to detect poison in his food, and had street lamps draped in red paper to defeat an epidemic of scarlet fever. The statue to General Francisco Morazán erected in the main square of Tegucigalpa is actually one of Marshal Ney, purchased at a Paris warehouse of second-hand sculptures.

...I dare to think that it is this outsized reality, and not just its literary expression, that has deserved the attention of the Swedish Academy of Letters. A reality not of paper, but one that lives within us and determines each instant of our countless daily deaths, and that nourishes a source of insatiable creativity, full of sorrow and beauty, of which this roving and nostalgic Colombian is but one cipher more, singled out by fortune. Poets and beggars, musicians and prophets, warriors and scoundrels, all creatures of that unbridled reality, we have had to ask but little of imagination, for our crucial problem has been a lack of conventional means to render our lives believable. This, my friends, is the crux of our solitude.

And if these difficulties, whose essence we share, hinder us, it is understandable that the rational talents on this side of the world, exalted in the contemplation of their own cultures, should have found themselves without valid means to interpret us. It is only natural that they insist on measuring us with the yardstick that they use for themselves, forgetting that the ravages of life are not the same for all, and that the quest of our own identity is just as arduous and bloody for us as it was for them. The interpretation of our reality through patterns not our own serves only to make us ever more unknown, ever less free, ever more solitary. Venerable Europe would perhaps be more perceptive if it tried to see us in its own past. If only it recalled that London took three hundred years to build its first city wall, and three hundred years more to acquire a bishop; that Rome labored in a gloom of uncertainty for twenty centuries, until an Etruscan King anchored it in history; and that the peaceful Swiss of today, who feast us with their mild cheeses and apathetic watches, bloodied Europe as soldiers of fortune, as late as the Sixteenth Century. Even at the height of the Renaissance, twelve thousand lansquenets in the pay of the imperial armies sacked and devastated Rome and put eight thousand of its inhabitants to the sword.

...Latin America neither wants, nor has any reason, to be a pawn without a will of its own; nor is it merely wishful thinking that its quest for independence and originality should become a Western aspiration. However, the navigational advances that have narrowed such distances between our Americas and Europe seem, conversely, to have accentuated our cultural remoteness. Why is the originality so readily granted us in literature so mistrustfully denied us in our difficult attempts at social change?... This, my friends, is the very scale of our solitude.

...On a day like today, my master William Faulkner said, "I decline to accept the end of man." I would fall unworthy of standing in this place that was his, if I were not fully aware that the colossal tragedy he refused to recognize thirty-two years ago is now, for the first time since the beginning of humanity, nothing more that a simple scientific possibility. Faced with this awesome reality that must have seemed a mere utopia through all of human time, we, the inventors of tales, who will believe anything, feel entitled to believe that it is not yet too late to engage in the creation of the opposite utopia. A new and sweeping utopia of life, where no one will be able to decide for others how they die, where love will prove true and happiness be possible, and where the races condemned to one hundred years of solitude will have, at last and forever, a second opportunity on earth.

22. *William Golding*

In a world of enchantment glum intellect has nothing to say of
the fairy prince and the sleeping beauty but much to say of the
tower and the dungeon.... I say we have erected cages of iron
bars; and ape-like I seize those bars and shake them with a help-
less fury.
                    —"Belief and Creativity" in *A Moving Target*

One question threads throughout William Golding's (1911–
1993) works: "Who are we when we are stripped of our usual
restraints?" Mining the depths of free will, choice and responsibility, Golding scrapes the soul, searching for the essence of man. "The
themes close to my purpose, to my imagination have ... been themes
of man at an extremity, man tested like building material, taken into
the laboratory and used to destruction; man isolated, man obsessed,
man drowning in a literal sea or in the sea of his own ignorance"
("Belief and Creativity" in *A Moving Target*). Golding pulls his reader
so completely into each story that only after finishing the tale does
the reader gain a perspective on the work. Golding's writing leaves
an aftertaste like retsina, delicately created and slightly bitter.

He exposes the young to extreme tests because "Eighteen is a
good time for suffering. One has all the necessary strength, and no
defenses" (*The Pyramid*). Time and place matter not in Golding's
world, from the prehistoric world of *The Inheritors* to the modern
era of *Pincher Martin*, *Darkness Visible* and *Lord of the Flies*, his characters suffer or witness the dark night of the soul. Golding's novels
embody Jung's belief that we become conscious by making the darkness conscious, not by imagining angels. A sardonic view of his fellow creatures mitigates Golding's often dour appraisals. "In the
conflict between social propriety and sexual attraction there was
never much doubt which would win" (*The Pyramid*).

155

If William Golding's view of the basic nature of man is despairing, he also clears a path toward redemption. "Turn your face to God and he becomes light but turn your face away from him and he becomes darkness," he said, explaining the theme of *Pincher Martin* (*Conversations with William Golding*). Rid of sincere spirituality and freed from social constraint, we are, Golding believes, murderous, stupid, or both. In *The Inheritors* Homo sapiens, driven by fear, ignorance and ethnocentrism demonstrate their newly acquired skills with both weapons and facile brains by killing the Neanderthals. Edmund Talbot (*Rites of Passage, Close Quarters, Fire Down Below*), cannot bring himself to believe his own eyewitness experience when it contradicts conventional wisdom. It is, of course, the question of theory verses empiricism. After his ship comes within inches of being crushed by a gigantic iceberg, he allows a friend to convince him that icebergs don't exist in those waters, for it would be geographically impossible.

Lord of the Flies explores the drama of a dozen schoolboys marooned for several weeks on an island during the Second World War. Terror lurks in the background like a ravenous shark. Both humorous and hopeful episodes depict the reality of unsupervised juveniles with the accuracy of a schoolteacher, which Golding was. Ralph explains "beasties" away by claiming the island is too small; they only exist in big countries like Africa and India. Since the boys do not know any better, they are duped and comforted by this quasi-logic until they discover a beastie, along with evil in their hearts. Golding questions the assumptions of Western culture in *Lord of the Flies*. "I am astonished at the ease with which uninformed persons come to a settled, a passionate opinion when they have no grounds for judgment" (*Fire Down Below*). Are we, Golding asks, much different from the boys of that island who will believe anything to make themselves feel better?

Golding starkly challenges our comfortable notions of personal and moral worth in *Darkness Visible*, the story of Matty Windup, morally worthy and physically disfigured, "born from the sheer agony of a burning city [the London blitz]." Polar opposites to Matty are the Stanhope sisters, navigating social acceptance with beauty and depraved cruelty. In *Pincher Martin* we share an unstable mind, vacillating between flashbacks and reality, unable to tell one from the other. Dean Jocelin in *The Spire* hears the voice of God and responds in obedience, thereby ruining himself. What does it mean, Golding asks, to hear the voice of God and respond? Golding doesn't shrink from the sour reality he uncovers beneath the placid surface of social convention. "It is possible to live astonished for a long time; and it looks increasingly possible that you can die that way too. My epitaph must be 'He wondered'"("Belief and Creativity" in *A Moving Target*).

Speaking of the writer's craft Golding tells us, "The writer watches the greatest mystery of all. It is the moment of most vital awareness, the moment of most passionate and *unsupported* conviction. It shines or cries. There is the writer, trying to grab it as it passes, as it emerges impossibly and heads to be gone. It is that twist of behavior, that phrase, sentence, paragraph, that happening of which the writer would bet his whole fortune, stake his whole life as a *true* thing. Like God, he looks on his creation and knows what he has done" ("Belief and Creativity" in *A Moving Target*).

Not a panoramic writer, Golding examines with microscopic clarity a small number of characters living under intense stress. "The act of creation is a fierce, concentrated light that plays on a small area" ("Rough Magic" in *A Moving Target*). If Golding's rigorous analysis of humankind doesn't yield many comforting findings, he successfully penetrates the evil of our species without shrinking from what he finds. Golding practices what he called Grade One Thinking, the passionate inquiry into truth. "Sanity is the ability to appreciate reality" (*Pincher Martin*).

1983

"—for his novels which, with the perspicuity of realistic narrative art and the diversity and universality of myth, illuminate the human condition in the world of today—"

Those of you who have some knowledge of your present speaker as revealed by the loftier-minded section of the British Press will be resigning yourselves to a half hour of unrelieved gloom. Indeed, your first view of me, white bearded and ancient, may have turned that gloom into profound dark; dark, dark, dark, amid the blaze of noon, irrecoverably dark, total eclipse. But the case is not as hard as that.... Critics have dug into my books until they could come up with something that looked hopeless. I can't think why. I don't feel hopeless myself. Indeed I tried to reverse the process by explaining myself. Under some critical interrogation I named myself a universal pessimist but a cosmic optimist.... I meant, of course, that when I consider a universe which the scientist constructs by a set of rules which stipulate that this construct must be repeatable and identical, then I am a pessimist and bow down before the great god Entropy. I am optimistic when I consider the spiritual dimension which the scientist's discipline forces him to ignore.

...The truth is that though each of the subjects for which the prizes are awarded has its own and unique importance, none can exist wholly to itself. Even the novel, if it climbs into an ivory tower, will find no audience except those with ivory towers of their own. I used to think that the outlook for the novel was poor. Let me quote myself, I speak of boys growing up — not exceptional boy, but average boy.

> Boys do not evaluate a book. They divide books into categories. There are sexy books, war books, westerns, travel books, science fiction. A boy will accept anything from a section he knows rather than risk another sort. He has to have the label on the bottle to know it is the mixture as before. You must put his detective story in a green paperback or he may suffer the hardship of reading a book in which nobody is murdered at all — I am thinking of the plodders, the amiable majority of us, not particularly intelligent or gifted; well-disposed, but left high and dry among a mass of undigested facts with their scraps of saleable technology. What chance has literature of competing with the defined categories of entertainment which are laid on for them at every hour of the day? I do not see how literature is to be for them anything but simple, repetitive and a stop-gap for when there are no westerns on the telly. They will have a far less brutish life than their Nineteenth-century ancestors, no doubt. They will believe less and fear less. But just as bad money drives out good, so inferior culture drives out superior. With any capacity to make value judgments vitiated or underdeveloped, what mass future is there, then, for poetry, for belles-lettres, for real fearlessness in the theater, for the novel which tries to look at life anew — in a word, for intransigence?

I wrote that some twenty years ago, I believe, and the process as far as the novel is concerned has developed but not improved. The categories are more and more defined. Competition from other media is fiercer still. Well, after all the novel has no build — it claims on immortality.

"Story" of course is a different matter. We like to hear of succession of events and as an inspection of our press will demonstrate have only a marginal interest in whether the succession of events is minutely true or not. Like the late Mr. Sam Goldwyn who wanted a story which began with an earthquake and worked up to a climax, we like a good lead in but have most pleasure in a succession of events with a satisfactory end-point. Most simply and directly — when children holler and yell because of some infant tragedy or tedium, at once when we take them on our knee and begin shouting if necessary — "once upon a time" they fall silent and attentive. Story will always be with us. But story in a physical book, in a sentence what the West means by "a novel"—what of that? Certainly, if the form fails let it go. We have enough complication in life, in art, in literature without preserving dead forms fossilized, without cluttering ourselves with Byzantine sterilities. Yes, in that case, let the novel go. But what goes with it? Surely something of profound importance to the human spirit! A novel ensures that we can look before and after, take action at whatever pace we choose, read again and again, skip and go back. The story in a book is humble and serviceable, available, friendly, is not switched on and off but taken up and put down, lasts a lifetime.

Put simply the novel stands between us and the hardening concept of statistical man. There is no other medium in which we can live for so long and so intimately with a character. That is the service a novel renders. It performs no less an act than the rescue and the preservation of the individuality and dignity of the single being, be it man, woman or child. No other art, I claim, can so thread in and out a single mind and body, so live another life. It does ensure that at the very least a human being shall be seen to be more than just one billionth of one billion.

…Literature has words only, surely a tool as primitive as the flint ax or even the soft copper chisel with which man first carved his own likeness in stone. That tool makes a poor showing one would think among the products of the silicon chip. But remember Churchill. For despite the cynical critic, he got the Nobel Prize neither for poetry nor prose. He got if for about a single page of simple sentences which are neither poetry nor prose but for what, I repeat, has been called finely the poetry of the fact. He got if for those passionate utterances which were the very stuff of human courage and defiance. Those of us who lived through those times know that Churchill's poetry of the fact changed history.

Perhaps then the soft copper chisel is not so poor a tool after all. Words may, through the devotion, the skill, the passion, and the luck of writers prove to be the most powerful thing in the world. They may move men to speak to each other because some of those words somewhere express not just what the writer is thinking but what a huge segment of the world is thinking. They may allow man to speak to man, the man in the street to speak to his fellow until a ripple becomes a tide running through every nation—of commonsense, of simple healthy caution, a tide that rulers and negotiators cannot ignore so that nation does truly speak unto nation. Then there is hope that we may learn to be temperate, provident, taking no more from nature's treasury than is our due. It may be by books, stories, poetry, lectures we who have the ear of mankind can move man a little nearer the perilous safety of a warless and provident world.

23. Joseph Brodsky

The story to be told below is truthful.
Unfortunately, nowadays it's not
just lies alone but simple truth as well
that needs compelling argument and sound
corroboration. Isn't that a sign
of our arrival in a wholly new
but doleful world? In fact, a proven truth,
to be precise, is not a truth at all —
it's just the sum of proofs. But now
what's said is "I agree," not "I believe."

— "Homage to Yalta" in *A Part of Speech*

Joseph Brodsky (1940–1996) embodied the possibilities of "freedom to" as developed in Erich Fromm's *Escape from Freedom*[1] with passionate intensity, unwilling to accede to any pressure to conform. A high school dropout who fled from the limits and rationalizations of accepted dogma, he won the Nobel Prize for his highly tuned sensibility and the poetry which flows from it.

At fifteen Brodsky set his own curriculum of study. He taught himself English and Polish in order to translate the works of John Donne and Czesław Miłosz, ignoring Soviet authorities' opinion that his writing was not socially useful. Charged with social parasitism and imprisoned for refusing to take the authorities seriously, he was finally exiled.

Brodsky, a Jew, declined an invitation of asylum from Israel. He chose America instead where he spurned the easy (and potentially lucrative) role of a Soviet dissident. Brodsky, the autodidact, shrugged off both coercion and well-intentioned classification (Jew or refusnik) which would have limited him as a free agent, a poet, "because, for all its beauty, a distinct concept always means a shrinkage of meaning, cutting off loose ends. While the loose ends are

161

what matter most in the phenomenal world, for they interweave"
(*Less Than One*). He met the world fully equipped with the discipline and tradition of poetry to guide him, and for Brodsky it was
enough.

Joseph Brodsky's advice regarding unpleasant experiences,
informed by his own travails, hovers between peasant "common
sense" and whimsy:

> Therefore, steal, or still, the echo, so that you don't allow an event,
> however unpleasant or momentous, to claim any more time than it
> took for it to occur. What our foes do derives its significance or con-
> sequence from the way you react ["Speech at the Stadium" in *On
> Grief and Reason*].

He viewed the Communist regime of his homeland as evil, yet
not uniquely so. Brodsky also thought the myopic individualism of
the West has led to serious misinterpretation of the Soviets. He found
a humorous irony in the American attempt to make *individual*
demons out of many Communist leaders:

> The funniest thing of all, however, is the realization that any one of
> these men can become a tyrant... we are dealing not with the
> tyranny of an individual but with the tyranny of a party that simply
> has put the production of tyrants on an industrial footing ["On
> Tyranny" in *A Part of Speech*].

"Cripple think" was Brodsky's term for depicting Soviet threats
and American enticements intended to promote conformity. He
identified American materialism as "canned ecstasy claiming raw
flesh" ("In Praise of Boredom" in *On Grief and Reason*). He viewed
attempts by both governments to program individual behavior and
thought as "a mirror, for that is what human evil always is" ("Letter to a President" in *On Grief and Reason*).

Joseph Brodsky refused to allow his time in the Gulag Archipelago (which Solzhenitsyn made infamous) to taint his poetry. Using
the radically altered perspective of a prisoner under a long sentence,
Brodsky paints a laconic view of the world in "Lithuanian Nocturne"
(*To Urania*). A moralist, he knew that the source of evil in the world
lay within each human breast. With the insight of a poet and the
experience of an exile, he advised new graduates of an American university to eschew abstractions and pursue their uniqueness as a haven
from falsehood:

> The surest defense against Evil is extreme individualism, originality
> of thinking, whimsicality, even — if you will — eccentricity. That is,

something that can't be feigned, faked, imitated; something even a sea-soned impostor couldn't be happy with. Something, in other words, that can't be shared, like your own skin: not even by a minority. Evil is a sucker for solidity ["A Commencement Address" in *Less Than One*].

Brodsky embodied a humility that results from continual toil. For him the process of writing always skirted the goal of linking the writer's solitary imagination with the reader's yearning. "Seen from the outside, creativity is the object of fascination or envy; seen from within, it is an unending exercise in uncertainty and a tremendous school for insecurity" ("A Cat's Meow" in *On Grief and Reason*). Yet, he held aesthetics to be the highest moral system. "An individual's aesthetics give rise to his ethics and his sense of history — not the other way around."[2]

> *Gorbunov and Gorchakov*
> canto ten
>
> Silence in the future of the days
> that roll toward speech, with all we emphasize
> in it, as, in our greetings, silence pays
> respect to unavoidable goodbyes.
> Silence is the future of the words
> whose vowels have gobbled up internally
> the stuff of things, things with terror towards
> their corners: a wave that cloaks eternity.
> Silence is the future of our love;
> a space, not an impediment, a space
> depriving love's blood-throbbed falsetto of
> its echo, of its natural response.
> Silence is the present for the men
> who lived before us. And, procuress-like,
> silence gathers all together in
> itself, admitted by the speech-filled present. Life
> is but a conversation in the face
> of silence.
>
> [*To Urania*]

If Joseph Brodsky's perspective on life tended toward the melancholy, his belief in the redemptive power of language in general, and poetry in particular, was inspiring. He believed that the practice of poetry, both the reading and writing of it, was littered with blessings:

The way to develop good taste in literature is to read poetry.... A child of epitaph and epigram, conceived, it appears, as a shortcut to any conceivable subject matter, poetry is a great disciplinarian to prose. It teaches the latter not only the value of each work but also the mercurial mental patterns of the species ["How to Read a Book" in *On Grief and Reason*].

Brodsky proclaimed a deep commitment toward the poetic enterprise and an unshakable belief in its highest rewards. His poetry and prose provide ample evidence that his belief was not misplaced. From age fifteen to the end of his life, Joseph Brodsky revisioned man's place in the twentieth century in fervent words that incarnate a lone man's struggle against the rulers of orthodoxy from every sphere.

1987

"— for an all-embracing authorship, imbued with clarity of thought and poetic intensity—"

...If art teaches anything (to the artist, in the first place), it is the privateness of the human condition. Being the most ancient as well as the most literal form of private enterprise, it fosters in a man, knowingly or unwittingly, a sense of his uniqueness, of individuality, or separateness — thus turning him from a social animal into an autonomous "I." Lots of things can be shared: a bed, a piece of bread, convictions, a mistress, but not a poem by, say, Rainer Maria Rilke. A work of art, of literature especially, and a poem in particular, addresses a man tête-à-tête, entering with him into direct — free of any go-betweens — relations.

It is for this reason that art in general, literature especially, and poetry in particular, is not exactly favored by the champions of the common good, masters of the masses, heralds of historical necessity. For there, where art has stepped, where a poem has been read, they discover, in place of the anticipated consent and unanimity, indifference and polyphony; in place of the resolve to act, inattention and fastidiousness. In other words, into the little zeros with which the champions of the common good and the rulers of the masses tend to operate, art introduces a "period, period, comma, and a minus," transforming each zero into a tiny human, albeit not always pretty, face.

Language and, presumably, literature are things that are more ancient and inevitable, more durable than any form of social organization. The revulsion, irony, or indifference often expressed by literature towards the state is essentially a reaction of the permanent — better yet, the infinite — against the temporary, against the finite. To say the least, as long as the state permits itself to interfere with the affairs of literature, literature has the right to interfere with the affairs of the state. A political system, a form of social organization, as any system in general is by definition, a form of the past tense that aspires to impose itself upon the present (and often on the future as well); and a man whose profession is language is the last one who can afford to forget this. The real danger for a writer is not so much the possibility (and often the certainty) of persecution on the part of the state, as it is the possibility of finding oneself mesmerized by the state's features, which, whether monstrous or undergoing changes for the better, are always temporary.

...Regardless of whether one is a writer or a reader, one's task consists first of all in mastering a life that is one's own, not imposed or prescribed from without, no matter how noble its appearance may be. For each of us is issued but one life, and we know full well how it all ends. It would be regrettable to squander this one chance on someone else's appearance, someone else's experience, on a tautology — regrettable all the more because the heralds of historical necessity, at whose urging a man may be prepared to agree to this tautology, will not go to the grave with him or give him so much as a thank-you.

...Art is a recoilless weapon, and its development is determined not by the individuality of the artist, but by the dynamics and the logic of the material itself, by the previous fate of the means that each time demand (or suggest) a qualitatively new aesthetic solution. Possessing its own genealogy, dynamics, logic, and future, art is not synonymous with, but at best parallel to history; and the manner by which it exists is by continually creating a new aesthetic reality. That is why it is often found "ahead of progress," ahead of history, whose main instrument is — should we not, once more, improve upon Marx — precisely the cliché.

Nowadays, there exists a rather widely held view, postulating that in his work a writer, in particular a poet, should make use of the language of the street, the language of the crowd. For all its democratic appearance, and its palpable advantages for a writer, this assertion is quite absurd and represents an attempt to subordinate art, in this case, literature, to history. It is only if we have resolved that it is time for Homo sapiens to come to a halt in his development that literature should speak the language of the people. Otherwise, it is the people who should speak the language of literature.

...The more substantial an individual's aesthetic experience is, the sounder his taste, the sharper his moral focus, the freer — though not necessarily the happier — he is.

It is precisely in the applied, rather than Platonic, sense that we should understand Dostoevsky's remark that beauty will save the world, or Matthew Arnold's belief that we shall be saved by poetry. It is probably too late for the world, but for the individual man there always remains a chance. An aesthetic instinct develops in man rather rapidly, for, even without fully realizing who he is and what he actually requires, a person instinctively knows what he doesn't like and what doesn't suit him. In an anthropological respect, let me reiterate, a human being is an aesthetic creature before he is an ethical one. Therefore, it is not that art, particularly literature, is a by-product of our species' development, but just the reverse. If what distinguishes us from other members of the animal kingdom is speech, then literature — and poetry in particular, being the highest form of locution — is, to put it bluntly, the goal of our species.

Since there are no laws that can protect us from ourselves, no criminal code is capable of preventing a true crime against literature; though we can condemn the material suppression of literature — the persecution of writers, acts of censorship, the burning of books — we are powerless when it comes to its worst violation: that of not reading the books. For that crime, a person pays with his whole life; if the offender is a nation, it pays with its history.

To be sure, it is natural for a person to perceive himself not as an instrument of culture, but, on the contrary, as its creator and custodian. But if today I assert the opposite, it's not because toward the close of the twentieth century there is a certain charm in paraphrasing Plotinus, Lord Shaftesbury, Schelling, or Novalis, but because, unlike anyone else, a poet always knows that what in the vernacular is called the voice of the Muse is, in reality, the dictate of the language; that it's not that the language happens to be his instrument, but that he is language's means toward the continuation of its existence. Language, however, even if one imagines it as a certain animate creature (which would only be just), is not capable of ethical choice.

One who writes a poem, however, writes it not because he courts fame with posterity, although often he hopes that a poem will outlive him, at least briefly. One who writes a poem writes it because the language prompts, or simply dictates, the next line. Beginning a poem, the poet as a rule doesn't know the way it's going to come out, and at times he is very surprised by the way it turns out, since often it turns out better than he expected, often his thought carries further than he reckoned. And that is the moment when the future of language invades its present.

There are, as we know, three modes of cognition: analytical, intuitive, and the mode that was known to the biblical prophets, revelation.

What distinguished poetry from other forms of literature is that it uses all three of them at once (gravitating primarily toward the second and the third). For all three of them are given in the language; and there are times when, by means of a single word, a single rhyme, the writer of a poem manages to find himself where no one has ever been before him, further, perhaps, than he himself would have wished for. The one who writes a poem writes it above all because verse writing is an extraordinary accelerator of conscience, of thinking, of comprehending the universe. Having experienced this acceleration once, one is no longer capable of abandoning the chance to repeat this experience; one falls into dependency on this process, the way others fall into dependency on drugs or on alcohol. One who finds himself in this sort of dependency on language is, I guess, what they call a poet.

24. Naguib Mahfouz

The language to which the millions respond is still the language
of emotions and instincts; songs of nationalism and patriotism
and racism, stupid dreams and delusions. This is the universal
tragedy.

— Naguib Mahfouz[1]

Naguib Mahfouz (1911–) accomplishes a task reserved for the
best writers of any locale and literary tradition; he makes his place
so particular and so achingly human that it becomes universally rec-
ognizable. His place is Egypt, particularly Cairo. He chronicles the
turbulence of English occupation, war, revolution, and dethrone-
ment as experienced by members of a middle class Cairo family, the
al-Sayyids, in his best known works, known collectively as the Cairo
Trilogy. Mahfouz became a cultural hero in the process of becoming the most widely read contemporary author in the Islamic world.
Like a benevolent God viewing his faltering children, he mourns for
our inevitable folly.

In the Cairo Trilogy (*Palace Walk, Palace of Desire, Sugar Street*)
Mahfouz explores the themes of deviance and conformity, drunkenness and bliss, mythology and modernity, and the impact of
politics on the individual and family structure. The al-Sayyids (particularly the men) fiercely contend with the tensions of individuality. When Yasin, the son of Ahmad al-Sayyid, tries to seduce and
then rape Umm Hanafi, an old and ugly maid, he brings shame on
the family. Ironically, his father's philandering is a source of secret
family pride. Mahfouz asks, what makes one behavior so different
from the other? His style extends the tradition of Dickens, rendering the small details of Cairo so authentically that the reader can smell
the heat of the midday sun. Not content with a faultless rendering of
the milieu, Mahfouz threads the basic questions of human existence

169

throughout his novels. When is conformity to an oppressive system justified? When is rebellion moral?

Mahfouz alters his style and historical perspective in *Children of Gebelawi*, a fable portraying the sordid and glorious history of our species from Adam to the present. In simple fabulist language Mahfouz paints a reality rife with sins of the flesh in spite of the potency and guidance of gifted spiritual prophets. The people of this Cairo alley are so preoccupied with their momentary delights and woes that they seldom comprehend the lessons of their own history. "If our alley were not plagued with forgetfulness, good examples would not be wasted." A peculiarly Egyptian novel, *Children of Gebelawi* becomes a universal one by testing the effect of power, money, justice and forgiveness on the lives of the inhabitants. "All we see is men like Saadallah and Yussef, Aggaag and Santoury [all brutal chiefs], but all we hear about is Gebel, Rifaa and Kassem [prophets]." Mahfouz poses the question, are we capable of envisioning a rule of law different from that to which we have become accustomed?

Brutality and irresponsible sexuality are to Mahfouz inherent properties of our species. "The illustrious Gebelawi now had a granddaughter who is a whore and a grandson who is a murderer," says Idris, describing the Egyptian parallels to Adam and Eve. Only the grinding down of time, a theme throughout Mahfouz's works, seems to quell the irascible spirit of humanity. In *Respected Sir* time itself assumes the role of the protagonist, eroding the life of Othman Bayyumi as he single-mindedly pursues the director general's chair in a huge bureaucracy. Mahfouz is both a devout Moslem and a realist. "'Our religion is wonderful,' I said to myself in grief, 'but our life is pagan'" (*The Journey of Ibn Fattouma*).

Naguib Mahfouz employs varied techniques in many of his others stories. In *The Time and the Place and Other Stories*, the title story blends traces of nihilism with magical realism. When a murder victim reappears in "The Man and the Other Man," he teaches his killer that "the world is subject to many laws, not just one." Pure vengeance, another Mahfouz theme, has two objectives in "The Wasteland": to kill the man who humiliated the protagonist and to recover the woman stolen from him. But time works on a different scale than passion; when the moment for revenge finally comes, the villain has been dead for years and the woman is no longer desirable. The Theater of the Absurd guides the surrealistic tale "At the Bus Stop," examining a well behaved passivity in the face of a violent and irrational world. Mahfouz questions the notion of innocent bystanders who, while witnessing brutality, remain on the sidelines. At the end of the story the bystanders, too, are murdered for their passive complicity.

Mahfouz molds social and personal questions in his capable hands, forcing the impact of the story on the reader. What determines the evilness of evil? he asks. How can an individual firmly establish his identity in a world of shifting values? Such religious issues, Mahfouz believes, can only be raised within the family structure and cultural tradition. He poses his questions about our existence with a feeling for both the grand scheme and the minute detail. When Mahfouz pours his brew, the reader savors the aroma of Egypt.

1988

"— who, through works rich in nuance — now clear-sightedly realistic, now evocatively ambiguous — has formed an Arabian narrative art that applies to all mankind — "

© The Nobel Foundation, 1988

I was told by a foreign correspondent in Cairo that the moment my name was mentioned in connection with the prize silence fell, and many wondered who I was. Permit me, then, to present myself in as objective a manner as is humanely possible. I am the son to two civilizations that at a certain age in history have formed a happy marriage. The first of these, seven thousand years old, is the Pharaonic civilization; the second, one thousand four hundred years old, is the Islamic one.

As for Pharaonic civilization I will not talk of the conquests and the building of empires.... Nor will I talk about how it was guided for the first time to the existence of God and its ushering in the dawn of human conscience.... I will not even speak of this civilization's achievement in art and literature, and its renowned miracles: the Pyramids and the Sphinx and Karnak.... Let me, then, introduce Pharaonic civilization with what seems like a story since my personal circumstances have ordained that I become a storyteller. Hear, then, this recorded historical incident: Old papyri relate that Pharaoh had learned of the existence of a sinful relation between some women of the harem and men of his court. It was expected that he should finish them off in accordance with the spirit of his time. But he, instead, called to his presence the choice men of law and asked them to investigate what he has come to learn. He told them that he wanted the Truth so that he could pass his sentence with Justice.

This conduct, in my opinion, is greater than founding an empire or building the Pyramids. It is more telling of the superiority of that civilization than any riches or splendor. Gone now is that civilization — a mere story of the past. One day the great Pyramid will disappear too. But Truth and Justice will remain for as long as Mankind has a ruminative mind and a living conscience.

As for Islamic civilization I will not talk about its call for the establishment of a union between all Mankind under the guardianship of the Creator, based on freedom, equality and forgiveness. I will not talk of its conquests which have planted thousands of minarets calling for worship, devoutness and good throughout great expanses of land.... Nor will I talk of the fraternity between religion and races that has been achieved in its embrace in a spirit of tolerance unknown to Mankind neither before nor since. I will, instead, introduce that civilization in a moving dramatic situation summarizing one of its most conspicuous traits: In one victorious battle against Byzantium it has given back its prisoners of war in return for a number of books of the ancient Greek heritage in philosophy, medicine and mathematics. This is a testimony of value for the human spirit in its demand for knowledge, even though the demander was a believer in God and the demanded a fruit of pagan civilization.

Ladies and Gentlemen, You may be wondering: This man coming from the Third World, how did the man coming from the Third World find the peace of mind to write stories? ... I come from a world laboring under the burden of debts whose paying back exposes it to starvation or very close to it. Some of its people perish in Asia from floods, others do so in Africa from famine. In South Africa millions have been undone with rejection and with deprivation of all human rights in the age of human rights, as though they were not counted among humans. In the West Bank and Gaza there are people who are lost in spite of the fact that they are living on their own land; land of their fathers, grandfathers and great grandfathers.... Fortunately, art is generous and sympathetic. In the same way that it swells with the happy ones it does not desert the wretched. It offers both alike the convenient means for expressing what swells up in their bosom.

In this decisive moment in the history of civilization it is inconceivable and unacceptable that the moans of Mankind should die out in the void. There is no doubt that Mankind has at last come of age, and our era carries the expectation of entente between the Super Powers. The human mind now assumes the task of eliminating all causes of destruction and annihilation. And just as scientists exert themselves to cleanse the environment of industrial pollution, intellectuals ought to exert themselves to cleanse humanity of moral pollution. It is both our right and duty to demand of the big leaders in the countries of civilization as well as their economists to affect a real leap that would place them into the focus of the age.

In the olden times every leader worked for the good of his own nation alone. The others were considered adversaries, or subjects of exploitation. There was no regard to any value but that of superiority and personal glory. For the sake of this, many morals, ideals and values were wasted; many unethical means were justified; many uncounted souls were made to perish. Lies, deceit, treachery, cruelty reigned as the signs of sagacity and the proof of greatness. Today, this view needs to be changed from its very source. Today, the greatness of a civilized leader ought to be measured by the universality of his vision and his sense of responsibility towards all human-kind. The developed world and the Third World are but one family. Each human being bears responsibility towards it by the degree of what he has obtained of knowledge, wisdom, and civilization. I would not be exceeding the limits of my duty if I told them in the name of the Third World: Be not spectators to our miseries. You have to play therein a noble role befitting your status. From your position of superiority you are responsible for any misdirection of animal, or plant, to say nothing of Man, in any of the four corners of the world. We have had enough of words. Now is the time for action. It is time to end the age of brigands and usurers. We are in the age of leaders responsible for the whole globe. Save the enslaved in the African south! Save the famished in Africa! Save the Palestinians from the bullets and the torture! Nay, save the Israelis from profaning their great spiritual heritage! Save the ones in debt from the rigid laws of economy! Draw their attention to the fact that their responsibility to Mankind should precede their commitment to the laws of science that Time has perhaps overtaken.

I beg your pardon, ladies and gentlemen, I feel I may have somewhat troubled your calm. But what do you expect from one coming from the Third World? Is not every vessel colored by what it contains? Besides, where can the moans of Mankind find a place to resound if not in your oasis of civilization planted by its great founder for the service of science, literature and sublime human values? And as he did one day by consecrating his riches to the service of good, in hope of obtaining forgiveness, we, children of the Third World, demand of the able ones, the civilized one, to follow his example, to imbibe his conduct, to meditate upon his vision.

Ladies and Gentlemen, in spite of all what goes on around us I am committed to optimism until the end. I do not say with Kant that Good will be victorious in the other world. Good is achieving victory every day.

It may even be that Evil is weaker than we imagine. In front of us is an indelible proof: were it not for the fact that victory is always on the side of Good, hordes of wandering humans would not have been able in the face of beasts and insects, natural disasters, fear and egotism, to grow and multiply. They would not have been able to form nations, to excel in creativeness and invention, to conquer outer space, and to declare Human Rights. The truth of the matter is that Evil is a loud and boisterous debaucherer, and that Man remembers what hurts more than what pleases. Our great poet Abul-'Alaa' Al-Ma'ari was right when he said:

> A grief at the hour of death
> Is more than a hundred-fold
> Joy at the hour of birth.

25. *Nadine Gordimer*

> For it is instinct which dictates duty and intelligence which offers
> pretexts for avoiding it. But excuses do not count, the artist must
> at all times follow his instinct, which makes art the most real
> thing, the most austere school in life and the last true judgment.
>
> — *Conversations with Nadine Gordimer*

Nadine Gordimer (1923–) expresses a moralist's outrage at the
manifold schemes of social injustice (racism, sexism, ageism) in
which power is abused, denying the full humanity of each person.
Moral indignation by itself is not enough to sustain decades of successful fiction or gain worldwide influence. Gordimer brings to her
writing a psychologist's ear for the nuance of relationship, wedded
to the evocative sensuality of a courtesan, as well as an artist's eye
for telling detail. An "engaged" writer, she explores the impact of
political struggle on the lives of her characters. She juxtaposes tones
in "Some are Born to Sweet Delight" (*Jump and Other Stories*) by
quoting from William Blake's *Auguries of Innocence*: "Some are Born
to sweet delight/Some are born to endless night." Vera, the protagonist of the story, believes she is living out her own "true" love story
with Rad while he exploits her innocence for his own political ends.
He convinces Vera to meet his parents before they marry and puts
her on an airplane with a bomb secretly hidden in her luggage. The
bomb explodes, killing all the passengers. Gordimer believes that we
dehumanize others by making caricatures of them, denying them
their full human dignity: When people become characters, they cease
to be regarded as human; they are something to be pointed out, like
the orange tree that President Kruger planted, the statue in the park,
or the filling station that once was the first church hall ("The Last
Kiss" in *Friday's Footprint*).

The freshness of her eye gives Gordimer's work an overwhelming

175

sense of intimacy. She compares love to the experience of "opening a cupboard and burying a nose in the folds of a forgotten garment" (*A Sport of Nature*). Her stories are related with a sensuality and directness achieved by removing her narrative voice from the story. "He sat there before them sane, and was confronted by the madness" ("Jump" in *Jump and Other Stories*). A strong sense of the physical ebbs from her work. "Neglect of the body doesn't mean not washing or cutting toe-nails. It's a turning away from its powers. It's using it like a briefcase, to carry oneself around, instead of living through it" (*A Sport of Nature*).

Gordimer transforms the physical into pulsing description:

> To touch in women's token embrace against the live, night cheek of Marisa, seeing huge for a second the lake-flash of her eye, the lilac-pink of her inner lip against translucent-edged teeth, to enter for a moment the invisible magnetic field of the body of a beautiful creature and receive on oneself its imprint — breath misting and quickly fading on a glass pane — that was to immerse in another mode of perception [*Burger's Daughter*].

A master of the short story, Gordimer describes the impetus that drives a story on to the page with what she terms "a sublime lucidity":

> A short story *occurs*, in the imaginative sense. To write one is to express from a situation in the exterior or interior world the life-giving drop — sweat, tear, semen, saliva — that will spread an intensity on the page; burn a hole in it [Introduction to *Selected Stories*].

She believes that the paramount example of exploitation of human beings is racism. Gordimer takes an unequivocal stance: "I just know that any form of racism is wrong. I don't see how one can see both sides of this ugly question: there aren't two sides — there are people who have the right to be human" (*Conversations with Nadine Gordimer*). The corruption of racism seeps into her work like a poison polluting the water supply. "Six Feet of the Country" relates the story of a black family trying to bury a young relative after his body has undergone a mandatory autopsy. The family receives the wrong body back from town officials. The authorities think so little of him (another dead black boy) they cannot even find the body when they *try* to do so. Gordimer understands that in the quiet of conscience every white South African knows he or she would become a better person by opposing racism and the preferences based upon it. Explaining the recurrent nature of her themes, Gordimer says, "This is a theory I have about most writers, not only about myself. I think that in effect we all write one book, but we write it piecemeal and often from very different points of view throughout our lives" (*Conversations with Nadine Gordimer*).

Nadine Gordimer's influence extends far beyond South Africa. By exposing the use of language as a weapon to damage honest relationships, she discovered a universal theme: the political lie. She characterizes the human impact of those lies as "the fingerprint of flesh on history" ("Turning the Page"[1]). Employing a revolutionary's tactic, Gordimer undermines the foundations of social evil by exposing both the fallacy itself and the twisting of relationships that result from trying to accommodate falsehoods:

> It's necessary to demystify, always demystify. Controlled violence is a sanitized term for killing. Killing anyone who gets in the way of your symbolic target. Including your own people, if a bomb blows up in their own hands. Yourself. Killing is killing. Violence is pain and death [*A Sport of Nature*].

Out of her steadfast opposition to injustice and her ultimate optimism, Nadine Gordimer crafts a legacy of liberating hope for a more humane world.

1991

"— who through her magnificent epic writing has — in the words of Alfred Nobel — been of very great benefit to humanity —"

© The Nobel Foundation, 1991

Writing and Being

In the beginning was the Word.

The Word was with God, signified God's Word, the word that was Creation. But over the centuries of human culture the word has taken on other meanings, secular as well as religious. To have the word has come to be synonymous with ultimate authority, with prestige, with awesome, sometimes dangerous persuasion, to have Prime Time, a TV talk show, to have the gift of gab as well as that of speaking in tongues. The word flies through space, it is bounced from satellites, now nearer than it has ever been to heaven from which it was believed to have come. But its most significant transformation occurred for me and my kind long ago, when it

was first scratched on a stone tablet or traced on papyrus, when it mate-
rialized from sound to spectacle, from being heard to being read as a series
of signs, and then a script; and traveled through time from parchment to
Gutenberg. For this is a genesis story of the writer. It is the story that *wrote*
her or him into being.

It was, strangely, a double process, creating at the same time both the
writer and the very purpose of the writer as a mutation in the agency of
human culture. It was both ontogenesis as the origin and development of
an individual being, and the adaptation, in the nature of that individual,
of *the* individual being. For we writers are evolved for that task. Like the
prisoners incarcerated with the jaguar in the Borges story, "The God's
Script," who was trying to read, in a ray of light which fell only once, a
day, the meaning of being from the marking on the creature's pelt, we spend
our lives attempting to interpret through the word the readings we take
in the societies, the world of which we are part. It is in this sense, this
inextricable, ineffable participation, that writing is always and at once an
exploration of self and of the world; of individual and collective being.

...Since humans became self-regarding they have sought, as well,
explanations for the common phenomena of procreation, death, the cycle
of the seasons, the earth, sea, wind and stars, sun and moon, plenty and
disaster. With myth, the writer's ancestors, the oral story-tellers, began to
feel out and formulate these mysteries, using the elements of daily life —
observable reality — and the faculty of the imagination — the power of projection into the hidden — to make stories.

...Roland Barthes asks, "What is characteristic of myth?" And
answers: "To transform a meaning into form." Myths are stories that medi-
ate in this way between the known and unknown. Claude Levi-Strauss
wittily de-mythologizes myth as a genre between a fairy tale and a detec-
tive story. Being here; we don't know who-dun-it. But something satis-
fying, if not the answer, can be invented. Myth was the mystery plus the
fantasy — gods, anthropomorphized animals and birds, chimera, phantas-
magorical creatures — that posits out of the imagination some sort of explanation for the mystery. Humans and their fellow creatures were the
materiality of the story, but as Nikos Kazantzakis once wrote, "Art is the
representation not of the body but of the forces which created the body."

...Perhaps there is no other way of reaching some understanding of
being than through art? Writers themselves don't analyze what they do; to
analyze would be to look down while crossing a canyon on a tightrope.
To say this is not to mystify the process of writing but to make an image
out of the intense inner concentration the writer must have to cross the

chasms of the aleatory and make them the word's own, as an explorer plants a flag. Yeats' inner "lonely impulse of delight" in the pilot's solitary flight, and his "terrible beauty" born of mass uprising, both opposed and conjoined; E.M. Forster's modest "only connect"; Joyce's chosen, wily "silence, cunning and exile"; more contemporary, Gabriel García Márquez's labyrinth in which power over others, in the person of Simón Bolívar, is led to the thrall of the only unassailable power, death — these are some examples of the writer's endlessly varied ways of approaching the state of being through the word. Any writer of any worth at all hopes to play only a pocket-torch of light — and rarely, through genius, a sudden flambeau — into the bloody yet beautiful labyrinth of human experience, of being.

...The question of for whom do we write nevertheless plagues the writer, a tin can attached to the tail of every work published. Principally it jangles the inference of tendentiousness as praise or denigration. In this context, Camus dealt with the question best. He said that he liked individuals who take sides more than literatures that do. "One either serves the whole of man or one does not serve him at all. And if man needs bread and justice, and if what has to be done must be done to serve this need, he also needs pure beauty, which is the bread of his heart." So Camus called for "courage in one's life and talent in one's work." And Márquez redefined tendenz fiction thus: "The best way a writer can serve a revolution is to write as well as he can."

I believe that these two statements might be the credo for all of us who write. They do not resolve the conflicts that have come, and will continue to come, to contemporary writers. But they state plainly an honest possibility of doing so, they turn the face of the writer squarely to her and his existence, the reason to be, as a writer, and the reason to be, as a responsible human, acting, like any other, within a social context.

Being here: in a particular time and place. That is the existential position with particular implication for literature. Czesław Miłosz once wrote the cry: "What is poetry which does not serve nations or people?" and Brecht wrote of a time when "to speak of trees is almost a crime." Many of us have had such despairing thoughts while living and writing through such times, in such places, and Sartre's solution — there are times when a writer should cease to write, and act upon being only in another way — makes no sense in a world where writers were — and still are — censored and forbidden to write, where, far from abandoning the world, lives were and are at risk in smuggling it, on scraps of paper, out of prisons. The state of being whose ontogenesis we explore has overwhelmingly included such experiences. Our approaches, in Nikos Kazantzakis' words, have to "make the decision which harmonizes with the fearsome rhythm of our time."

Some of us have seen our book lie for years unread in our own countries, banned, and we have gone on writing. Many writers have been imprisoned.... Many of the greats, from Thomas Mann to Chinua Achebe, cast out by political conflict and oppression in different countries, have endured the trauma of exile, from which some never recover as writers, and some do not survive at all. I think of the South Africans, Can Themba, Alex La Guma, Nat Nakasa, Todd Matshikiza. And some writers, over half a century from Joseph Roth to Milan Kundera, have had to publish new works first in the word that is not their own, a foreign language.

Then in 1988 the fearsome rhythm of our time quickened in an unprecedented frenzy to which the writer was summoned to submit the word. In the broad span of modern times since the Enlightenment writers have suffered opprobrium, bannings and even exile for other than political reasons. Flaubert dragged into court for indecency, over *Madame Bovary*, Strindberg arraigned for blasphemy, over *Marrying*, Lawrence's *Lady Chatterley's Lover* banned — there have been many examples of so-called offense against hypocritical bourgeois mores, just as there have been of treason against political dictatorships. But in a period when it would be unheard of for countries such as France, Sweden and Britain to bring such charges against freedom of expression, there has risen a force that takes its appalling authority from something far more widespread than social mores, and far more powerful than the power of any single political regime. The edict of a world religion has sentenced a writer to death.

For more than three years, now, however he is hidden, wherever he might go, Salman Rushdie has existed under the Muslim pronouncement upon him of the *fatwa*. There is no asylum for him anywhere. Every morning when this writer sits down to write, he does not know if he will live through the day; he does not know whether the page will ever be filled.... With dictatorships apparently vanquished, this murderous new dictate invoking the power of international terrorism in the name of a great and respected religion should and can be dealt with only by democratic governments and the United Nations, as an offense against humanity.

...I return from the horrific singular threat to those that have been general for writers of this century now in its final, summing-up decade. In repressive regimes anywhere — whether in what was the Soviet bloc, Latin America, Africa, China — most imprisoned writers have been shut away for their activities as citizens striving for liberation against the oppression of the general society to which they belong. Others have been condemned by repressive regimes for serving society by writing as well as they can; for this aesthetic venture of ours becomes subversive when the shameful secrets of our times are explored deeply, with the artist's rebellious integrity to the state of being manifest in life around her or him; then the writer's themes and character inevitably are formed by the pressures and distortions of the society as the life of the fisherman is determined by the power of the sea.

There is a paradox. In retaining this integrity, the writer sometimes must risk both the state's indictment of treason, and the liberation forces' complaint of lack of blind commitment. As a human being, no writer can stoop to the lie of Manichean 'balance.' The devil always has lead in his shoes, when placed on his side of the scale. Yet, to paraphrase coarsely Márquez's dictum given by him both as a writer and a fighter for justice, the writer must take the right to explore, warts and all, both the enemy and the beloved comrade in arms, since only a try for the truth makes sense of being, only a try for the truth edges towards justice just ahead of Yeats' beast slouching to be born.

...The writer is of service to humankind only insofar as the writer uses the word even against his or her own loyalties, trusts the state of being, as it is revealed, to hold somewhere in its complexity filaments of the cord of truth, able to be bound together, here and there, in art: trusts the state of being to hold somewhere fragmentary phrases of truth, which is the final word of words, never changed by our stumbling efforts to spell it out and write it down, never changed by lies, by semantic sophistry, by the dirtying of the word for the purposes of racism, sexism, prejudice, domination, the glorification of destruction, the curses and the praise-songs.

26. Derek Walcott

> Their first sound should be like their last, the cry. The voice must grovel in search of itself, until gesture and sound fuse and the blaze of their flesh astonishes them. The children of slaves must sear their memory with a torch.
>
> —*Dream on Monkey Mountain and Other Plays*

Derek Walcott (1930–), like the poet-playwright William Butler Yeats, founds regional theater companies, writes poems and plays based on regional themes and focuses on dividedness of the psyche as a major theme. On the most feral level Yeats and Walcott share a conviction that the cure for a diseased consciousness lies in a return to the deepest memories of man. "For imagination and body to move with original instinct, we must begin again from the bush. That return journey, with all its horror of rediscovery, means the annihilation of what is known" (*Dream on Monkey Mountain*). And so Walcott chips away at the rational, like a sculptor chiseling rough stone, to liberate what lies beneath the surface on a mythic and pre-linguistic level.

Walcott takes care to point out that the Caribbean experience is one of diversity, encompassing many influences — not only African but also Lebanese, Indian and Chinese among others. He celebrates his multicultural and polyphonic inheritance. He freely acknowledges his debt to dozens of great writers he studied during his apprenticeship, disparaging vaunted notions of originality. "It's everybody's voice that makes that one song."[1] He feels no need to establish his blackness nor his credentials as a black writer. But as Joseph Brodsky said, "It has been hard for the world to acknowledge that the great poet of the English language is a black man."[2]

Walcott's personal poetry is a diary of estrangement, longing and sorrow. "It could not lift the heavy agonies I felt/for the fatherless

183

wanderings of my own sons/but some sorrows are like stones, and they never melt" (*Omeros*). In "Early Pompeian" (in *The Fortunate Traveller*) he extracts the pain of losing a child so hauntingly that we cannot help but believe the poem to be anything but a lament for his own child (lost late in pregnancy):

> In your noble, flickering gaze there was that which repeated
> to the stone you carried
> "The hardest times are the noblest, my dead child,"
> and the torch passed its flame to your tongue.
>
> Child, wherever you are,
> I am still your father;
> let your small, dead star
> rock in my heart's black salt,
> this sacrificial basin where I weep;
> you passed from a sleep to a sleep
> with no pilot, without a light.

Walcott annihilates the consciousness dictated by the Caribbean's colonial past, "something always being missed/ between the floating shadow and the pelican."[3] He replaces that phony "quaint" self-image — handed down by oppressors — with a reformed view of himself. "I start here," he says. Walcott's "here" unites the past and embraces the present, while redefining both in primal and authentic terms. Beyond the superficial and temporal resides an inseparable bond connecting man to man, woman to man and parent to child which binds the spirit of the living to that of their ancestors and descendants:

> In the archipelago particularly, nature, the elements if you want, are so new, so overpowering in their presence that awe is deeper than articulation of awe. To name is to contradict. The awe of God or of the universe is the unnamable, and this has nothing to do with literacy. It is better for us to be a race of illiterates who retain this awe than to be godless, without mystery.[4]

Walcott's rage at departed colonial masters whose world view relegated the former colonies to a now impoverished third world existence burns with the incandescence of cane fields set alight:

> All those who promise free and just debate,
> then blow up radicals to save the state,
> who allow, in democracy's defense,
> a parliament of spiked heads on a fence,
> all you go bawl out, "Spoils, things ain't so bad."
> This ain't the Dark Age, is just Trinidad."
>   ["The Spoiler's Return" in *The Fortunate Traveller*]

Walcott's Caribbean, awash in the colonial view of its history, gives his fierce attacks a tone of anguish: "These dead, these derelicts/the alphabet of the emaciated" (*Omeros*).

Walcott's pain isn't limited to his West Indian home. A hollow loss, summoning like a funeral bell in *The Fortunate Traveller*, tolls for the barbarism of World War II, for the pitilessness in modern man, for what cannot be atoned. Inspired by what he calls an illegitimate situation in the Caribbean, Walcott scrapes away the forgery, restoring the mythic and organic unity hidden beneath:

> Once the New World black had tried to prove that he was as good as his master, when he should have proven not his equality but his difference. It was this distance that could command attention without pleading for respect. My generation had looked at life with black skins and blue eyes, but only our own painful, strenuous looking, the learning of looking, could find meaning in the life around us, only our own strenuous hearing, the hearing of our hearing, could make sense of the sounds we made. And without comparisons. Without any startling access of "self-respect" ["An Overture" in *What the Twilight Says*].

For Walcott, legitimate human beings have no reason to look outside themselves for identity; identity comes from within and not by comparison to what lies without. Neither is identity based on the achievements of the past. Walcott's sense of the new Caribbean man and woman is far from Henri Rousseau's noble savage. Rather, he has formed a sophisticated view of Caribbean people which incorporates the tides, a history of colonialism, trade winds, tourism and the myriad of strains that meld together to form the Caribbean of today. In defiance of all that has gone before, especially in contrast to a Western view of the Caribbean, Walcott reiterates, "I start here." Polyglot and mixed race, I am here, acknowledge me.

1992

"— for a poetic oeuvre of great luminosity, sustained by a historical vision, the outcome of a multicultural commitment—"

The Antilles: Fragments of Epic Memory

…Break a vase, and the love that reassembles the fragments is stronger than that love which took its symmetry for granted when it was whole.

The glue that fits the pieces is the sealing of its original shape. It is such a love that reassembles our African and Asiatic fragments, the cracked heirloom whose restoration shows its white scars. This gathering of broken pieces is the care and pain of the Antilles, and if the pieces are disparate, ill-fitting, they contain more pain than their original sculpture, those icons and sacred vessels taken for granted in their ancestral places. Antillean art is this restoration of our shattered histories, our shards of vocabulary, our archipelago becoming a synonym for pieces broken off from the original continent.

And this is the exact process of the making of poetry, or what should be called not its "making" but its remaking, the fragmented memory, the armature that frames the god, even the rite that surrenders it to a final pyre; the god assembled cane by cane, reed by weaving reed, line by plaited line, as the artisans of Felicity would erect his holy echo.

Poetry, which is perfection's sweat but which must seem as fresh as the raindrops on a statue's brow, combines the natural and the marmoreal; it conjugates both tenses simultaneously; the past and the present, if the past is the sculpture and the present the beads of dew or rain on the forehead of the past. There is the buried language and there is the individual vocabulary, and the process of poetry is one of excavation and of self-discovery. Tonally the individual voice is a dialect; it shapes its own accent, its own vocabulary and melody in defiance of an imperial concept of language, the language of Ozymandias, libraries and dictionaries, law courts and critics, and churches, universities, political dogma, the diction of institutions. Poetry is an island that breaks away from the main. The dialects of my archipelago seem as fresh to me as those raindrops on the statue's forehead, not the sweat made from the classic exertion of frowning marble, but the condensations of a refreshing element, rain and salt.

...Here there are not enough books, one says, no theaters, no museums, simply not enough to do. Yet, deprived of books, a man must fall back on thought, and out of thought, if he can learn to order it, will come the urge to record, and in extremity, if he has no means of recording, recitation, the ordering of memory which leads to metre, to commemoration. There can be virtues in deprivation, and certainly one virtue is salvation from a cascade of high mediocrity, since books are now not so much created as remade. Cities create a culture, and all we have are the magnified market towns, so what are the proportions of the ideal Caribbean city? A surrounding, accessible countryside with leafy suburbs, and if the city is lucky, behind it, spacious plains. Behind it, fine mountains; before it, an indigo sea. Spires would pin its center and around them would be leafy, shadowy parks. Pigeons would cross its sky in alphabetic patterns, carrying with them memories of a belief in augury, and at the heart of the city there would be horses, yes, horses, those animals last seen at the end of the nineteenth century drawing broughams and carriages with top-hatted citizens, horses that live in the present tense without elegiac echoes from their hooves, emerging from paddocks at the Queen's Park Savannah at sunrise, when mist is unthreading from the cool mountains above the roofs, and at the center of the city seasonally there would be races, so that citizens would roar at the speed and grace of these nineteenth-century animals. Its docks, not obscured by smoke or defined by too much machinery, and above all, it would be so racially various that the cultures of the world — the Asiatic, the Mediterranean, the European, the African — would be represented in it, its humane variety more exciting than Joyce's Dublin. Its citizens would intermarry as they chose, from instinct, not tradition, until their children find it increasingly futile to trace their genealogy. It would not have too many avenues difficult or dangerous for pedestrians, its mercantile area would be a cacophony of accents, fragments of the old language that would be silenced immediately at five o'clock, its docks resolutely vacant on Sundays.

This is Port of Spain to me, a city ideal in its commercial and human proportions, where a citizen is a walker and not a pedestrian, and this is how Athens may have been before it became a cultural echo.

...I mean, by "the Antilles," the reality of light, of work, of survival. I mean a house on the side of a country road, I mean the Caribbean Sea, whose smell is the smell of refreshing possibility as well as survival. Survival is the triumph of stubbornness, the spiritual stubbornness, a sublime stupidity, is what makes the occupation of poetry endure, when there are so many things that should make it futile. Those things added together can go under one collective noun: "the world."

...For every poet it is always morning in the world. History a forgotten, insomniac night; History and elemental awe are always our early beginning, because the fate of poetry is to fall in love with the world, in spite of History.

There is a force of exultation, a celebration of luck, when a writer finds himself a witness to the early morning of a culture that is defining itself, branch by branch, leaf by leaf, in that self-defining dawn, which is why, especially at the edge of the sea, it is good to make a ritual of the sunrise. Then the noun, the "Antilles" ripples like brightening water, and the sounds of leaves, palm fronds, and birds are the sounds of a fresh dialect, the native tongue. The personal vocabulary, the individual melody whose meter is one's biography, joins in that sound, with any luck, and the body moves like a walking, a waking island.

This is the benediction that is celebrated, a fresh language and a fresh people, and this is the frightening duty owed.

...The Caribbean is not an idyll, not to its natives. They draw their working strength from it organically, like trees, like the sea almond or the spice laurel of the heights. Its peasantry and its fishermen are not there to be loved or even photographed; they are trees who sweat, and whose bark is filmed with salt.... They are here again, they recur, the faces, corruptible angels, smooth black skins and white eyes huge with an alarming joy, like those of the Asian children of Felicity at *Ramleela*; two different religions, two different continents, both filling the heart with the pain that is joy.

But what is joy without fear? The fear of selfishness that, here on this podium with the world paying attention not to them but to me, I should like to keep these simple joys inviolate, not because they are innocent, but because they are true. They are as true as when, in the grace of this gift, Perse [Alexis Saint-Léger] heard the fragments of his own epic of Asia Minor in the rustling of cabbage palms, the inner Asia of the soul through which imagination wanders, if there is such a thing as imagination as opposed to the collective memory of our entire race, as true as the delight of that warrior-child who flew a bamboo arrow over the flags in the field at Felicity; and now as grateful a joy and a blessed fear as when a boy opened an exercise book and, within the discipline of its margins, framed stanzas that might contain the light of the hills on an island blest by obscurity, cherishing our insignificance.

27. Toni Morrison

> The ability of writers to imagine what is not the self, to famil-
> iarize the strange and mystify the familiar, is the test of their
> power.
>
> —*Playing in the Dark*

Memory, imagination and rhythm bind Toni Morrison's (1931–) stories in a taut evocation of the past. A believer in knowledge deeper than the senses and wisdom beyond explanation, she probes the real and imagined memory of her people, the grandchildren of slaves. Her charge as a writer is much like that assumed by Isaac Bashevis Singer: reconstructing a vanished world for the benefit of its descendants. Toni Morrison's literary address is located primarily in black communities of midwest America, between 1915 and 1930. Buried deep in the background with ancestor slaves, memories of slave times haunt the present while the foreground blazes in testimony to the endurance of their offspring. She exposes the tensions of impoverished communities formed by the descendants of slaves and pays tribute to their splendid tactics for turning loss into victory. "Being a minority in both caste and class, we moved about anyway on the hem of life, struggling to consolidate our weaknesses and hang on, or to creep singly up into the major folds of the garment" (*The Bluest Eye*).

A master of dialogue that thumps like a drum expressing the cadence and fluidity of the spoken word, Morrison's work reads as if she were a Studs Terkel of the imagination, recording the oral history of her people. Her faithfulness to the oral tradition gives her novels their distinctive flavor. A young girl, Pilate, explains in lyric rhythm her shocking discovery that she was expected to have a navel:

> It was just like the thing her brother had on his stomach. He had one.
> She did not. He peed standing up. She squatting down. He had a penis

189

like a horse did. She had a vagina like the mare. He had a flat chest with two nipples. She had teats like the cow. He had a corkscrew in his stomach. She did not. She thought it was one more way in which male and females were different. The boy she went to bed with had one too. But until now she had never seen another woman's stomach. And from the horror on the older woman's face she knew there was something wrong with not having it [*Song of Solomon*].

Over a century ago Walt Whitman cogently summarized the gift Morrison powerfully employs: "Great writers penetrate the idioms of their races, and use them with simplicity and power."[1] The following passage (Milkman's reverie of what his grandfather, Macon Dead, might have said to him) with its pounding tom-tom-tom cadence vibrates both as a sermon and a lusty march at the same time.

Stop picking around the edges of the world. Take advantage, and if you can't take advantage, take disadvantage. We live here. On this planet, in this nation, in this country right here. Nowhere else! We got a home in this rock, don't you see! Nobody starving in my home, nobody crying in my home, and if I got a home you got one too! Grab it. Grab this land! Take it, hold it, my brothers, make it, my brothers, shake it, squeeze it, dig it, plow it, seed it, reap it, rent it, buy it, sell it, own it, build it, multiply it, and pass it on — can you hear me? Pass it on! [*Song of Solomon*]

Morrison delights in the tenacity of her people to battle overwhelming obstacles, win, and not merely win but overcome on their own terms:

"What's the world for if you can't make it up the way you want it?
"The way I want it?"
"Yeah, The way you want it. Don't you want it to be something more than what it is?"
"What's the point? I can't change it."
"That's the point. If you don't, it will change you and it'll be your fault cause you let it. I let it. And messed up my life."
"Messed it up how?"
"Forgot it."
"Forgot?"
"Forgot it was mine. My life. I just ran up and down the streets wishing I was somebody else" [*Jazz*].

A "normal" community has both geographic location and duration based on land ownership, a gradation from poverty to wealth, a scale of education from unlettered to professional, as well as relations with its neighboring communities and acceptance by the outside world. Morrison's communities lack these basic qualities. They form and cohere solely on the response of people to one another and the memory of their ancestors. And yet they endure. The irony — that these black towns embodied the same "self reliance" ethic that white communities championed but didn't practice, at least in relation to black towns — isn't lost on Morrison:

> What was taken by outsiders to be slackness, slovenliness or even generosity was in fact in full recognition of the legitimacy of forces other than good ones. They did not believe doctors could heal — for them, none ever had done so. They did not believe death was accidental — life might be, but death was deliberate. They did not believe Nature was ever askew — only inconvenient. Plague and drought were as "natural" as springtime. If milk could curdle, God knows robins could fall. The purpose of evil was to survive it and they determined (without ever knowing they had made up their minds to do it) to survive floods, white people, tuberculosis, famine and ignorance. They knew anger well but not despair, and they didn't stone sinners for the same reasons they didn't commit suicide — it was beneath them [*Sula*].

Morrison assumes the arduous task of explaining behavior that in "normal" communities is seen as disgusting, if not criminal. She shows mothers killing their children, pedophilia, self-mutilation, child killing child, rape and incest from the perspective of both the perpetrator and the community. Sula and Nel drown a young boy, Chicken Little (*Sula*), while *Jazz* opens with Joe Trace, a middle-aged man, shooting his teenaged lover, Dorcas, and Joe's wife, Violet (sometimes known as Violent), slashing the dead girl's face as she lies in her coffin. It is a testament to Morrison's skill as a storyteller that by the end of her novels we come to understand most of the violence we have seen. It would be easy for white Americans to view Morrison as a mere apologist for the black communities she chronicles. She's much more than that, and she does not apologize. Her compulsion is to communicate the strength of those communities and evoke its sources. In the face of all their pain and loss:

> They laughed too, even Rose Dear shook her head and smiled, and suddenly the world was right side up. Violet learned then what she had forgotten until this moment; that laughter is serious. More complicated, more serious than tears [*Jazz*].

Morrison takes special care throughout her works to champion the role of men in these communities. Her men are beset with pressures from all sides, and yet they endure. Some even triumph. The following passage highlights Morrison's dedication to exposing the pressure-cooker world of black men:

Look. It's the condition our condition is in. Everybody want the life of a black man. Everybody. White men want us dead or quiet — which is the same thing as dead. White women, same thing. They want us, you know, "universal," human, no "race consciousness." Tame, except in bed. They like a little racial loincloth in the bed. But outside the bed they want us to be individuals. You tell them, "But they lynched my papa," and they say, "Yeah, but you're better than the lynchers are, so forget it." And black women, they want your whole self. Love, they call it, and understanding. "Why don't you *understand* me?" What they mean is, "Don't love anything on earth except me." They say, "Be responsible," but what they mean is, "Don't go anywhere where I ain't...." They want your full attention [*Song of Solomon*].

Morrison also celebrates the bonds of heart, stronger and more pliable than steel, that tie black women to one another. In *Sula* she explores the depths and outer borders of the meaning of that shared womanhood. Although Sula becomes evil — and perhaps was always evil — she and Nel had grown up together, and Sula (on her deathbed) remembered "the days when we were two throats and one eye and we had no price." She remembered cutting off the tip of her finger to protect Nel from a group of rowdy boys. Now Sula is dying, and Nel doesn't understand that the evil is not about trying to hurt Nel or possess her husband Jude; it is Sula's own. Sula's last thoughts are of Nel:

She was not breathing because she didn't have to. Her body did not need oxygen. She was dead. Sula felt her face smiling. "Well, I'll be damned," she thought, "it didn't even hurt. Wait'll I tell Nel."

After Sula's death Nel feels the full dimension of the loss of an abiding female friend, more sharply than she ever feels the loss of her husband Jude:

"All that time, all that time, I thought I was missing Jude." And the loss pressed down on her chest and came up into her throat. "We was girls together," she said as though explaining something. "O Lord, Sula," she cried, "girl, girl, girlgirlgirl." It was a fine cry — loud and long — but it had no bottom and it had no top, just circles and circles of sorrow.

Toni Morrison exposes, for the enrichment of all who read her works, the depth of her sorrow and the core of joy which infects African Americans in a manner particular to their heritage. In reminding each of us that our inheritance binds us to this world in a distinct way she became a writer of universal human tragedy, transcendence and belonging.

1993

"— who in novels characterized by visionary force and poetic import, gives life to an essential aspect of American reality—"

© The Nobel Foundation, 1993

"Once upon a time there was an old woman. Blind but wise." Or was it an old man? A guru, perhaps. Or a griot soothing restless children. I have heard this story, or one exactly like it, in the lore of several cultures.

"Once upon a time there was an old woman. Blind. Wise."

In the version I know the woman is the daughter of slaves, black, American, and lives alone in a small house outside of town. Her reputation for wisdom is without peer and without question. Among her people she is both the law and its transgression. The honor she is paid and the awe in which she is held reach beyond her neighborhood to places far away; to the city where the intelligence of rural prophets is the source of much amusement.

One day the woman is visited by some young people who seem to be bent on disproving her clairvoyance and showing her up for the fraud they believe she is. Their plan is simple: they enter her house and ask the one question the answer to which rides solely on her difference from them, a difference they regard as a profound disability: her blindness. They stand before her, and one of them says, "Old woman, I hold in my hand a bird. Tell me whether it is living or dead."

She does not answer, and the question is repeated. "Is the bird I am holding living or dead?"

Still she doesn't answer. She is blind and cannot see her visitors, let alone what is in their hands. She does not know their color, gender or homeland. She only knows their motive.

The old woman's silence is so long, the young people have trouble holding their laughter.

Finally she speaks and her voice is soft but stern. "I don't know," she says. "I don't know whether the bird you are holding is dead or alive, but what I do know is that it is in your hands. It is in your hands."

Her answer can be taken to mean: if it is dead, you have either found it that way or you have killed it. If it is alive, you can still kill it. Whether it is to stay alive, it is your decision. Whatever the case, it is your responsibility.

For parading their power and her helplessness, the young visitors are reprimanded, told they are responsible not only for the act of mockery but also for the small bundle of life sacrificed to achieve its aims. The blind woman shifts attention away from assertions of power to the instrument through which that power is exercised.

Speculation on what (other than its own frail body) that bird-in-the-hand might signify has always been attractive to me, but especially so now, thinking as I have been, about the work I do that has brought me to this company. So I choose to read the bird as language and the woman as a practiced writer. She is worried about how the language she dreams in, given to her at birth, is handled, put into service, even withheld from her for certain nefarious purposes. Being a writer she thinks of language partly as a system, partly as a living thing over which one has control, but mostly as agency — as an act with consequences. So the question the children put to her: "Is it living or dead?" is not unreal because she thinks of language as susceptible to death, erasure; certainly imperiled and salvageable only by an effort of the will. She believes that if the bird in the hands of her visitors is dead the custodians are responsible for the corpse. For her a dead language is not only one no longer spoken or written, it is unyielding language content to admire its own paralysis.

She is convinced that when language dies, out of carelessness, disuse, and absence of esteem, indifference or killed by fiat, not only she herself, but all users and makers are accountable for its demise. In her country children have bitten their tongues off and use bullets instead to iterate the voice of speechlessness, of disabled and disabling language, of language adults have abandoned altogether as a device for grappling with meaning, providing guidance, or expressing love. But she knows tongue-suicide is not only the choice of children. It is common among the infantile heads of state and power merchants whose evacuated language leaves them with no access to what is left of their human instincts for they speak only to those who obey, or in order to force obedience.

The systematic looting of language can be recognized by the tendency of its users to forgo its nuanced, complex, mid-wifery properties for menace and subjugation. Oppressive language does more than represent violence; it is violence; does more than represent the limits of knowledge; it limits knowledge. Whether it is obscuring state language or the faux-language of mindless media; whether it is the proud but calcified language of the academy or the commodity driven language of science; whether it is the malign language of law-without-ethics, or language designed for the estrangement of minorities, hiding its racist plunder in its literary cheek — it must be rejected, altered and exposed. It is the language that drinks blood, laps vulnerabilities, tucks its fascist boots under crinolines of respectability and patriotism as it moves relentlessly toward the bottom line and the bottomed-out mind. Sexist language, racist language, theistic language — all are typical of the policing languages of mastery, and cannot, do not permit new knowledge or encourage the mutual exchange of ideas.

...There is and will be rousing language to keep citizens armed and arming; slaughtered and slaughtering in the malls, courthouses, post offices, playgrounds, bedrooms and boulevards; stirring, memorializing language to mask the pity and waste of needless death. There will be more diplomatic language to countenance rape, torture, assassination. There is and will be more seductive, mutant language designed to throttle women, to pack their throats like pate-producing geese with their own unsayable, transgressive words; there will be more of the language of surveillance disguised as research; of politics and history calculated to render the suffering of millions mute; language glamorized to thrill the dissatisfied and bereft into assaulting their neighbors; arrogant pseudo-empirical language crafted to lock creative people into cages of inferiority and hopelessness.

Underneath the eloquence, the glamour, the scholarly associations, however, stirring or seductive, the heart of such language is languishing, or perhaps not beating at all — if the bird is already dead.

...The vitality of language lies in its ability to limn the actual, imagined and possible lives of its speakers, readers, writers. Although its poise is sometimes in displacing experience it is not a substitute for it. It arcs toward the place where meaning may lie. When a president of the United States thought about the graveyard his country had become, and said, "The world will little note nor long remember what we say here. But it will never forget what they did here." His simple words are exhilarating in their life-sustaining properties because they refused to encapsulate the reality of 600,000 dead men in a cataclysmic race war. Refusing to monumentalize, disdaining the "final word," the precise "summing up," acknowledging their "poor power to add or detract," his words signal deference to the uncapturability of the life it mourns. It is the deference that moves her, that recognition that language can never live up to life once and for all. Nor should it. Language can never "pin down" slavery, genocide, war. Nor should it yearn for the arrogance to be able to do so. Its force, its felicity is in its reach toward the ineffable.

...Word-work is sublime, she thinks, because it is generative; it makes meaning that secures our difference, our human difference — the way in which we are like no other life.

We die. That may be the meaning of life. But we do language. That may be the measure of our lives.

...Think of our lives and tell us your particularized world (our readers say). Make up a story. Narrative is radical, creating us at the very moment it is being created. We will not blame you if your reach exceeds your grasp; if love so ignites your word they go down in flames and nothing is left but their scald. Or if, with the reticence of a surgeon's hands, your words suture only the places where blood might flow. We know you can never do it properly — once and for all. Passion is never enough; neither is skill. But try.

28. Kenzaburō Ōe

> Normally, I begin to imagine my novels from the doomed corner — the lacerated edge. Then I create that horizontal line to the other world.
>
> — Kenzaburō Ōe[1]

Kenzaburō Ōe (1935–) inhabits an intensely personal literary world where events leap by, giving the reader only one quick glance with each passing while leaving an indelible trail to be interpreted and disputed at length. The constants in his literary world are enigmatic, and they are repeated in several of his novels: a deformed baby, the forest, a storehouse, the loss of sight in one eye, underwater goggles, suicide and a fraudulent history distorted into family or national myth.

Ōe decries the misbegotten identity of the Japanese and their society, a society and a people so far off the true path that they cannot name their fathers except as "a certain party" and name themselves only by function, "the acting executor of the will" (*The Day He Himself Shall Wipe My Tears Away*). A society that cannot name its forebears is built on sand.

His world abounds with meaningless and unnecessary cruelty, a world where irrationality obscures meaning: "It was a nasty, stupid incident: one morning, as I was walking along the street, a group of primary school children in a fit of hysterical fear and anger flung a chunk of stone at me. Struck in the eye, I lay where I fell on the sidewalk" (*A Personal Matter*).

A young father, Bird, leaves the arms of his mistress to be present at the birth of his first child. In a conversation after the birth, the attending doctor tells the father about his firstborn son in the most callous of terms:

"As I said, I'm in obstetrics, but I consider myself fortunate to have run across a case of brain hernia — I hope to be present at the autopsy. You will consent to an autopsy, won't you?" [*A Personal Matter*]

The physician further encourages the young man to endorse a medical regime of "benign neglect" of the newborn to hasten the child's death. Ōe's own first child, a son, was born retarded with a brain tumor.

Bitter distortion in relationships between men and women expresses itself in defective sexual relations. "Sexual peculiarities aren't very important in the long run; they're only one distortion caused by something grotesque and really frightening coiled up in the depths of the personality" (*The Silent Cry*). Rape, murder and incest all punctuate the contortions of relationship in *The Silent Cry*. Mitsu pronounces his judgment on his wife. "She was nothing but a drunken slut in a deep sleep." Human sexual relations, brutalized by a defilement so primal that the human animal can no longer reproduce itself, forecasts doom for the species and recurs throughout Ōe's works.

In Kenzaburō Ōe's world the echoes of an event may be more significant than the event itself. A retarded, inarticulate son suggests more than our own inability to produce healthy offspring, he also represents us. "The fat man began to function as a window in his son's mind, permitting the light from the outside to penetrate to the dark interior which trembled with pain not adequately understood" (*Teach Us to Outgrow Our Madness*). The isolation of the retarded child reflects our own inability to communicate:

But with some personal experiences that lead you way into a cave all by yourself, you must eventually come to a side tunnel or something that opens on a truth that concerns not just yourself but everyone.... But what I'm experiencing personally now is like digging a vertical mine shaft in isolation; it goes straight down to a hopeless depth and never opens on anybody else's world [*A Personal Matter*].

Ōe achieves his dour world by degrading the abstract or mythic ideal into a grotesque and finite reality. Juxtaposing faulty myth with brutal fact, he forces us to reevaluate both our individual myths and those of our nations. He maintains that the ideals and mores of traditional Japanese society must be abandoned because they no longer serve as a healthy anchor for Japanese people. The maintenance of these inert myths creates self-inflicted wounds in the present. "I'm descended from a line of traitors," Takashi wails in *The Silent Cry*, when the facts are far different. Restoring the vitality to any crucial relationship requires the abolition of false belief. Obviating falsehood is Ōe's theme.

More than other great writers, Ōe's works are variations of the same story, carrying the same message of attack on traditional Japanese ideology. The more of Ōe one reads, the more powerful the assault becomes. Suicide is ridiculed in *The Silent Cry* when Mitsu's friend defiles his own body prior to hanging himself. Escape from individual responsibility, projected outward as veneration of the Emperor, is a mere charade masking lack of courage in the same novel. Ōe satirizes the conception of family honor, turning it into a dark farce in *The Day He Himself Shall Wipe My Tears Away*. In order to maintain the image of family honor, the patriarch of the family contracts to have his son murdered before word gets out that the son has dishonored the family while the hero ancestor, venerated in family and village legend, turns out to have been a coward who sat by silently as his followers were slaughtered.

Kenzaburō Ōe believes passionately in the function of politically committed literature and the role of the committed writer. Yet such literature shares little in common with propaganda. Ōe's technique is to erode the basic assumptions underpinning complacent yet false political and social beliefs. "Japan has lost the power to connect the principle or theory and reality. I think literature's value is in making those connections. That's the mission of literature. Morals are significant."[2] A highly controversial figure in Japanese literature, Kenzaburō Ōe refused Japan's highest cultural honor because he "would not recognize any authority, any value, higher than democracy." (The award was in the name of the Emperor.)

Kenzaburō Ōe goes beyond debunking the popular culture of Japan with jarring imagery and savage honesty. An intense longing for soulful connection between people seeps through the irrationality he depicts. In Ōe's work mourning for the lost and displaced has the vibrancy of new love. In his reverence for these memories, Ōe speaks for all who have faced significant loss of a loved one:

> You're still young, probably you haven't lost sight of anything in this world that you can never forget, that's so dear to you you're aware of its absence all the time. Probably the sky a hundred years or so above your head is still nothing more than sky to you. But all that means is that the storehouse happens to be empty at the moment.... That's why I haven't been living in present time ever since that incident with the baby, so I could stop that spreading. Since I'm not living in our time, I can't discover anything new, but I don't lose sight of anything, either — the state of my sky never changes ["Aghwee the Sky Monster"].

1994

"— who with poetic force creates an imagined world, where life and myth condense to form a disconcerting picture of the human predicament today—"

Japan, the Ambiguous, and Myself

During the last catastrophic World War, I was a little boy and lived in a remote wooded valley on Shikoku Island in the Japanese Archipelago, thousands of miles away from here. At that time there were two books by which I was really fascinated: *The Adventures of Huckleberry Finn* and *The Wonderful Adventures of Nils*. The whole world was then engulfed by waves of horror. By reading *Huckleberry Finn* I felt I was able to justify my act of going into the mountain forest at night and sleeping among the trees with a sense of security which I could never find indoors. The protagonist of *The Adventures of Nils* is transformed into a little creature, understands bird's language and makes an adventurous journey. I derived from the story sensuous pleasures of various kinds. Firstly, living as I was in a deep wood on the Island of Shikoku just as my ancestors had done long ago, I had a revelation that this world and this way of life there were truly liberating. Secondly, I felt sympathetic and identified myself with Nils, a naughty little boy, who, while traversing Sweden, collaborating with and fighting for the wild geese, transforms himself into a boy, still innocent, yet full of confidence as well as modesty. On coming home at last, Nils speaks to his parents. I think that the pleasure I derived from the story at its highest level lies in the language, because I felt purified and uplifted by speaking along with Nils. His words run as follows: "Mother and Father!" he cried. "I'm a big boy. I'm a human being again!"

I was fascinated by the phrase "I'm a human being again!" in particular. As I grew up, I was continually to suffer hardships in different realms of life — in my family, in my relationship to Japanese society and in my way of living at large in the latter half of the twentieth century. I have survived by representing these sufferings of mine in the form of the novel. In that process I have found myself repeating, almost sighing, "I'm a human being again!" Speaking like this as regards myself is perhaps inappropriate to this place and to this occasion. However, please allow me to say that the fundamental style of my writing has been to start from my personal matters and then to link it up with society, the state and the world. I hope you will forgive me for talking about my personal matters a little further.

Half a century ago, while living in the depth of that forest, I read *The Adventures of Nils* and felt within it two prophecies. One was that I might one day become able to understand the language of birds. The other was that I might one day fly off with my beloved wild geese — preferably to Scandinavia.

After I got married, the first child born to us was mentally handicapped. We named him *Hikari*, meaning "Light" in Japanese. As a baby he responded only to the chirps of wild birds and never to human voices. One summer when he was six years old we were staying at our country cottage. He heard a pair of water rails (*Rallus aquaticus*) warbling from the lake beyond a grove, and he said with the voice of a commentator on a recording of wild birds: "They are water rails." This was the first moment my son ever uttered human words. It was from then on that my wife and I began having verbal communication with our son.

Hikari now works at a vocational training center for the handicapped, an institution based on ideas we learned from Sweden. In the meantime he has been composing works of music. Birds were the originators that occasioned and mediated his composition of human music. On my behalf Hikari has thus accomplished the prophecy that I might one day understand the language of birds. I must say also that my life would have been impossible but for my wife with her abundant female force and wisdom. She has been the very incarnation of Akka, the leader of Nils' wild geese. Together with her I have flown to Stockholm and the second of the prophecies has also, to my utmost delight, now been realized.

...To tell you the truth, rather than with Kawabata my compatriot who stood here twenty-six years ago, I feel more spiritual affinity with the Irish poet William Butler Yeats, who was awarded a Nobel Prize for Literature seventy-one years ago when he was at about the same age as me. Of course I would not presume to rank myself with the poetic genius Yeats. I am merely a humble follower living in a country far removed from his. As William Blake, whose work Yeats revalued and restored to the high place it holds in this century, once wrote: "Across Europe & Asia to China & Japan like lightnings."

During the last few years I have been engaged in writing a trilogy which I wish to be the culmination of my literary activities. So far the first two parts have been published and I have recently finished writing the third and final part. It is entitled in Japanese *A Flaming Green Tree*. I am indebted for this title to a stanza from Yeats' poem "Vacillation":

> A tree there is that from its topmost bough
> Is half all glittering flame and half all green
> Abounding foliage moistened with the dew…

In fact my trilogy is soaked in the overflowing influence of Yeats' poems as a whole…. Yeats is the writer in whose wake I would like to follow. I would like to do so for the sake of another nation that has now been "accepted into the comity of nations" but rather on account of the technology in electrical engineering and its manufacture of automobiles. Also I would like to do so as a citizen of such a nation which was stampeded into "insanity in enthusiasm for destruction" both on its own soil and on that of the neighboring nations.

…My observation is that after one hundred and twenty years of its modernization since the opening of the country, present-day Japan is split between two opposite poles of ambiguity. I too am living as a writer with this polarization imprinted on me like a deep scar.

In the history of modern Japanese literature the writers most sincere and aware of their mission were those "post-war writers" who came onto the literary scene immediately after the last War, deeply wounded by the catastrophe yet full of hope for a rebirth. They tried with great pains to make up for the inhuman atrocities committed by Japanese military forces in Asian countries, as well as to bridge the profound gaps that existed not only between the developed countries of the West and Japan but also between African and Latin American countries and Japan. Only by doing so did they think that they could seek with some humility reconciliation with the rest of the world. It has always been my aspiration to cling to the very end of the line to that literary tradition inherited from those writers.

I am one of the writers who wish to create serious works of literature which dissociate themselves from those novels which are mere reflection of the vast consumer cultures of Tokyo and the subcultures of the world at large. What kind of identity as a Japanese should I seek? W.H. Auden once defined the novelist as follows:

> …among the Just
> Be just, among the Filthy filthy too,
> And in his own weak person, if he can,
> Must suffer dully all the wrongs of Man [*The Novelist*].

This is what has become my "habit of life" (in Flannery O'Connor's words) through being a writer as my profession.

To define a desirable Japanese identity I would like to pick out the word "decent" which is among the adjectives that George Orwell often used, along with words like "humane," "sane" and "comely," for the character types that he favored. This deceptively simple epithet may starkly set off and contrast with the word "ambiguous" used for my identification in "Japan, the Ambiguous, and Myself." There is a wide and ironical discrepancy between what the Japanese seem like when viewed from outside and what they wish to look like.

I hope Orwell would not raise an objection if I used the word "decent" as a synonym of "humanist" or "humaniste" in French, because both words share in common qualities such as tolerance and humanity. Among our ancestors were some pioneers who made painstaking efforts to build up the Japanese identity as "decent" or "humanist."

One such person was the late Professor Kazuo Watanabe, a scholar of French Renaissance literature and thought. Surrounded by the insane ardor of patriotism on the eve and in the middle of the Second World War, Watanabe had a lonely dream of grafting the humanist view of man onto the traditional Japanese sense of beauty and sensitivity to Nature, which fortunately had not been entirely eradicated. I must hasten to add that Professor Watanabe had a conception of beauty and Nature different from that conceived of by Kawabata in his "Japan, the Beautiful, and Myself."

The way Japan had tried to build up a modern state modeled on the West was cataclysmic. In ways different from, yet partly corresponding to, that process Japanese intellectuals had tried to bridge the gap between the West and their own country at its deepest level. It must have been a laborious task or *travail* but it was also one that brimmed with joy. Professor Watanabe's study of François Rabelais was thus one of the most distinguished and rewarding scholarly achievements of the Japanese intellectual world.

…In both my life and writing I have been a pupil of Professor Watanabe's. I was influenced by him in two crucial ways. One was in my method of writing novels. I learned concretely from his translation of Rabelais what Mikhail Bakhtin formulated as "the image system of grotesque realism or the culture of popular laughter"; the importance of material and physical principles; the correspondence between the cosmic, social and physical elements; the overlapping of death and passions for rebirth; and the laughter that subverts hierarchical relationships.

…Another way in which Professor Watanabe has influenced me is in his idea of humanism. I take it to be the quintessence of Europe as a living totality. It is an idea which is also perceptible in Milan Kundera's definition of the spirit of the novel. Based on his accurate reading of historical sources Watanabe wrote critical biographies, with Rabelais at the center, of people from Erasmus to Sébastien Castellion, and of women connected with Henri IV from Queen Marguerite to Gabrielle Destre. By doing so Wantanabe intended to teach the Japanese about humanism, about the importance of tolerance, about man's vulnerability to his preconceptions or machines of his own making. His sincerity led him to quote the remark by the Danish philologist Kristoffer Nyrop: "Those who do not protest against war are accomplices of war." In his attempt to transplant into Japan humanism as the very basis of Western thought Watanabe was bravely venturing on both "l'entreprise inouïe" and the "belle entreprise Pantgruelique."

As someone influenced by Watanabe's humanism I wish my task as a novelist to enable both those who express themselves with words and their readers to recover from their own sufferings and the sufferings of their time, and to cure their souls of the wounds. I have said I am split between the opposite poles of ambiguity characteristic of the Japanese. I have been making efforts to be cured of and restored from those pains and wounds by means of literature. I have made my efforts also to pray for the cure and recovery of my fellow Japanese.

If you will allow me to mention him again, my mentally handicapped son Hikari was awakened by the voices of birds to the music of Bach and Mozart, eventually composing his own works. The little pieces that he first composed were full of fresh splendor and delight. They seemed like dew glittering on grass leaves. The word *innocence* is composed of *in*–"not" and *nocere*–"hurt," that is, "not to hurt." Hikari's music was in this sense a natural effusion of the composer's own innocence.

As Hikari went on to compose more works, I could not but hear in his music also "the voice of a crying and dark soul." Mentally handicapped as he was, his strenuous effort furnished his act of composing or his "habit of life" with the growth of compositional techniques and a deepening of his conception. That in turn enabled him to discover in the depth of his heart a mass of dark sorrow which he had hitherto been unable to identify with words.

"The voice of a crying and dark soul" is beautiful, and his act of expressing it in music cures him of his dark sorrow in an act of recovery. Furthermore, his music has been accepted as one that cures and restores his contemporary listeners as well. Herein I find the ground for believing in the exquisite healing power of art.

This belief of mine has not been fully proved. "Weak person" though I am, with the aid of this unverifiable belief, I would like to "suffer dully all the wrongs" accumulated throughout the twentieth century as a result of the monstrous development of technology and transport. As one with a peripheral, marginal and off-center existence in the world I would like to seek how — with what I hope is a modest decent and humanist contribution — I can be of some use in a cure and reconciliation of mankind.

29. Dario Fo

Privilege and power irritate and mortify him. It is better to start out afresh, for freedom of spirit is worth more than a king's throne!

— *Tricks of the Trade* [Fo's description of Pulcinella, a stock character of medieval theater]

The irony of a Marxist satirist like Fo (1926–) winning the most prestigious award in literature from a royally chartered institution, funded with old capitalist money, reads like a Dario Fo farce. Centuries of public theatrical protest, blended with whimsy and absurdist scoffs, are Fo's recipe for drama. In his plays he inveighs against the government, disputes Catholic dogma, defames the Pope, vulgarizes the Gospels and ridicules Christ. He also castigates the Italian Communist Party, as well as the Communist regimes of Europe, for their feudalism. A political writer, engaged in polemics, he avoids becoming a mere propagandist by peeling back labels pasted over events by those who would limit interest and restrict the terms of discussion.

The *giullare*, a clown who mocks his oppressors, is Fo's prototype. With slapstick humor Fo drags this vulgar, scatological, irreligious, rebellious character (the wandering gagster with a social message) into our age.

The sketch "The Origin of the Giullare" in *Mistero Buffo* tells the story of a hardworking peasant wronged and destroyed by political and religious oppression, on the verge of suicide before Christ intervenes. Jesus performs a miracle, giving the peasant "a new language" which destroys the pretensions and self-serving mythology of the ruling class.

The next sketch, the "Origin of the Underling," a traditional *giullare* tale, claims the peasantry was born of the fart of a donkey, after Adam refused to give up another rib. Born ignobly, then yoked to a life of servile labor and insecurity by the sanctions of Church and State, the working class is ill served by those in power. The message is clear: something must be done.

A populist, Fo stages plays more often at jails, mental hospitals, and sit-ins than in theaters. Fo ignores two major twentieth century theatrical streams: one, a channel of abstract intellectual concepts; the other, a delta of amusement and commerce. His is not the theater of the well-fed, and well-read, but rather of the semiliterate. Pulsing with irreverence and frolic, his drama has more in common with stand-up comedy than it does with stylized production and elaborate sets. Referring back several centuries, he claims, "The theater was the people's spoken, dramatized newspaper."[1] Revitalizing that function of the theater is Fo's goal.

Unlike most current dramatists, the focus of Fo's work is not the individual but a class of people, the working class. None of the characters are memorable for their individuality. Rather, each represents a member of a class placed in a particular situation. Fo avoids deep psychological portraits and spiritual exploration of his characters to reflect instead on social and political restraints.

Fo, with his wife and co-author, Franca Rame, sketches Everyman characters, performed with sparse sets and minimal costuming, to create free working space for the imagination of his audience. His goal is always political, not individual:

> We don't want to liberate the indignation of the people who come along. We want them to keep their anger inside them, and not to be freed of it, so that they can take action on events, and get involved in the struggle.[2]

Imagine an arrogant and corrupt pope, Boniface VIII, meeting Christ (*Mistero Buffo*). Imagine a policeman, while investigating a store looting, revealing his secret Communist sympathy with the looters (*We Can't Pay? We Won't Pay!*). Imagine that the most powerful industrialist in Italy is rescued from a kidnapping by a leftist worker, and, unrecognized and incapacitated, he remains with the worker for weeks while the nation searches for him (*Trumpets and Raspberries*).

Fo's "target" audience governs his tools and techniques. Together, Fo and Rame explore many strands of the web of class repression — sexual, religious, and political — that limit the freedom of contemporary workers. Relying on a theatrical tradition going back more than five hundred years in Europe, Fo reinvents the divine fool, a man so oblivious to social pressure that he tells the truth. Fo cites Il Ruzzante, Angelo Beolco (1502–1542), and Molière (1622–1673) in his Nobel speech as his mentors:

> Above all, they were despised for bringing onto the stage the everyday life, joys and desperation of the common people; the hypocrisy and the arrogance of the high and mighty; and the incessant injustice. And their major, unforgivable fault was this: in telling these things, they made people laugh. Laughter does not please the mighty.[3]

The "Comic Mysteries," a portion of (and the literal translation of the title of his most famous and controversial play) *Mistero Buffo*, shreds the halo surrounding biblical tales, reminiscent of Pär Lagerkvist's *Barabbas* and Nikos Kazantzakis' *The Last Temptation of Christ*. The Vatican criticized the televised version of *Mistero Buffo* as "the most blasphemous show in the history of television."[4] Fo uses the comedy of human limitation on a small scale to revitalize these stories. In "The Resurrection of Lazarus," a critical crowd jostles for a good view, and a vendor of rental seats functions as a "miracle critic." At "The Marriage at Cana," Christ not only turns water to wine, he encourages everyone — including the Madonna — to get drunk and have a good time. Fo's relations with the Vatican were not improved when a psychotic pope, phobic of children, shoots down kids with a sacred bow in *The Pope and the Witch*.

A ten year old Jesus resorts to performing miracles to get the other kids to play with him in *The First Miracle of the Boy Jesus*. Joseph and Mary forbid the practice due to the danger that Herod will discover the boy's divine origin. Mary, in the way of all mothers, discovers Jesus' tricks — bringing clay birds to life and smiting a nasty rich boy to death — and makes the reluctant Jesus revive the young sinner. Jesus decides to complain to his *real* Father. This irreverent dialogue typifies Fo's satire and explains the Catholic Church's animus to his work. It begins with the boy Jesus crying to "Dad":

> "Sob, sob, sob…. That boy's naughty, he broke all the little clay things that we made to play with. He scrunched them all up with his horse. Sob, sob, sob, sob…."
> [He cries, sobbing.]
> "Look, son, was it really necessary to give your father a fright for such a silly thing? I was all the way on the other side of the universe, and I had to come tearing across…. I punctured twelve clouds, not

to mention running down a dozen cherubim, and my halo's all over
the place — it'll take an eternity to get it right again!"

"Yes, but he's been naughty. He's the rich man's son. He's got
everything! He's got all sorts of toys, but when he saw that we were
enjoying ourselves, he ... sob, sob, sob ... he broke everything....
Waaaah.... And I tried so hard..."

"Speak up, son."

"And I tried so hard to do the miracle, to get the birds to fly, so's I
could have some friends to play with.... And it was nice, because we
all made friends ... but now I'm all on my own again like before. All
my friends have run away. ... Waaah! I'm ever so unhappy, Dad,
ever so.... Waaaaah!"

"You're right. I have to say that smashing up children's games,
destroying their dreams, really is the worst of violence.... But he's
just a kid, son.... What do you expect me to do, eh?"

[JESUS lets out a long, thoughtful, weeping sigh, and then says,
in a very matter-of-fact tone:]

"Kill him!" [He smiles, looking heavenwards, naughtily.]

"Eh?" [He mimes smiles and little shrugs aimed at convincing his
father.]

"But Son, I sent you down from heaven specially to teach peace
between men, and to speak to them of love. The first time someone
upsets you, you want to kill them?! That's not a very good start, is
it, eh?!"

"Is that asking too much? Well, all right then, cripple him....
Blind him, eh? Or blind him and cripple him!"

"No, you can't do that sort of thing, son. You can't just go being
violent to people."

"You can't eh? What you mean is, *you* can't? Can I kill him,
then?"

"Alright then, do what you like. I can see there's no point my
talking to you. But don't go round telling people it was me that did
it."

Audience interplay is integral to Fo's theatrical process. Fo's
plays aren't packaged and presented to audiences as if the texts were
a box of cornflakes taken from the shelf. Much like a stand-up come-
dian, Fo warms up each audience to gauge their probable reactions
to his material. Then he improvises. As a result, none of his plays
has a "final form." Explaining the function of improvisation, Fo
states that his purpose is:

> To weave and shape a script with words, with gestures and off-the-
> cuff situations, but above all to rid actors of the false and dangerous
> notion that theater is no more than literature that happens to be
> staged, acted and adapted, rather than simply read.[5]

Fo's sense of improvisation parallels that of jazz musicians in a
jam session. In both cases, the result appears to be free-form to the

audience, yet it is firmly grounded in the shared knowledge of structure and technique among the performers. Just as musicians use keys and riffs to play off of each other, actors use mime, gestures, body language, stock characters, gags, and routines carefully polished over decades of practice.

Grammelot, a babel of sound conveying the impression of speech (like scatting in jazz), employs the voice as a musical instrument. It is a technique borrowed from medieval *giullare*, interspersing a few real words in a rapid patter of noises intoned and inflected in the native language of the character. It "indicates the onomatopoeic flow of a speech, articulated without rhyme or reason, but capable of transmitting with the aid of particular gestures, rhythms and sounds, an entire rounded speech" (*The Tricks of the Trade*). Simultaneously, grammelot ridicules the "buzz words" of the speaker as meaningless and denigrates the supporting arguments as nonsense. Relying on allusion rather than denotation, this nonsense language foils any attempt at censorship. Fo extends the technique in the twentieth century with dramatic punch.

This Italian clown jostles the gatekeepers of power with grotesque and obscene humor. He wants his audiences to engage their imaginations to dismantle the carefully tended fences restricting their rights as citizens:

> Authorities, any authorities, fear above all other things laughter, derision or even the smile, because laughter denotes a critical awareness; it signifies imagination, intelligence and a rejection of all fanaticism. In the scale of human evolution, we have first *Homo faber*, then *Homo sapiens* and finally *Homo ridens*, and this last is always the most difficult to subdue or make conform [*The Tricks of the Trade*].

Fo's laughing man, Homo ridens, is aware of his own folly and isn't easily fooled by the pretensions of the powerful.

The easiest way to understand this unconventional exponent of the wacky is to think of him as a modern day Italian Mark Twain. Both writers boldly assail the aristocracy; Twain called them "slave holders under another name."[6] Each lampoons the policies of their national government with biting sarcasm. Twain challenged foreign missionaries and the Christian Science Church, while Fo pokes fun at the Pope and Catholic dogma. They share an abiding faith in the intelligence of the common people, once their imagination is stimulated. Twain once explained his approach to the haughty: "Irreverence is the champion of liberty and its only sure defense."[7] Dario Fo has become a champion of liberty, molding serious scholarship into bawdy defenses of the rights of the common people.

1997

"— who emulated the jester of the Middle Ages in scourging authority and upholding the dignity of the downtrodden —"

Contra Jogulatores Obloquentes

["Against jesters who defame and insult," Law issued by Emperor Frederick II (Messina 1221), declaring that anyone may commit violence against jesters without incurring punishment of sanction.]

Ladies and gentlemen, the title I've selected for this little chat is "contra jogulatores obloquentes," which you all recognize as Latin, mediaeval Latin to be precise. It's the title of a law issued in Sicily in 1221 by Emperor Frederick II of Swabia, an emperor "anointed by God," who we were taught in school to regard a sovereign of extraordinary enlightenment, a liberal. "Jogulatores obloquentes" means "jesters who defame and insult." The law in question allowed any and all citizens to insult jesters, to beat them and even — if they were in that mood — to kill them, without running any risk of being brought to trial and condemned. I hasten to assure you that this law no longer is in vigor, so I can safely continue.

Friends of mine, noted men of letters, have in various radio and television interviews declared: "The highest prize should no doubt be awarded to the members of the Swedish Academy, for having had the courage this year to award the Nobel Prize to a jester." I agree. Yours is an act of courage that borders on provocation.

It's enough to take stock of the uproar it has caused: sublime poets and writers who normally occupy the loftiest of spheres, and who rarely take interest in those who live and toil on humbler planes, are suddenly bowled over by some kind of whirlwind.

...These poets had already ascended to the Parnassian heights when you, through your insolence, sent them toppling to earth, where they fell face and belly down in the mire of normality.

...Also the higher clergy have suffered their moments of madness. Sundry potentates — great electors of the Pope, bishops, cardinals and prelates of Opus Dei — have all gone through the ceiling, to the point that they've even petitioned for the reinstatement of the law that allowed jesters to be burned at the stake. Over a slow fire.

On the other hand I can tell you there is an extraordinary number of people who rejoice with me over your choice. And so I bring you the most festive thanks, in the name of a multitude of mummers, jesters, clowns, tumblers and storytellers.

And speaking of storytellers, I mustn't forget those of the small town on Lago Maggiore where I was born and raised, a town with a rich oral tradition. They were the old storytellers, the master glass blowers who taught me and other children the craftsmanship, the art, of spinning fantastic yarns. We would listen to them, bursting with laughter—laughter that would stick in our throats as the tragic allusion that surmounted each sarcasm would dawn on us.

I repeat, I owe much to these master glass blowers of mine, and they—I assure you—are immensely grateful to you, members of this Academy, for rewarding one of their disciples. And they express their gratitude with explosive exuberance. In my home town, people swear that on the night the news arrived that one of their own storytellers was to be awarded the Nobel Prize, a kiln that had been standing cold for some fifty years suddenly erupted in a broadside of flames, spraying high into the air—like a fireworks *finale*—a myriad splinters of colored glass, which then showered down on the surface of the lake, releasing an impressive cloud of steam.

…Above all others, this evening you're due the loud and solemn thanks of an extraordinary master of the stage, little-known not only to you and to people in France, Norway, Finland … but also to the people of Italy. Yet he was, until Shakespeare, doubtless the greatest playwright of Renaissance Europe. I'm referring to Ruzzante Beolco, my greatest master along with Molière: both actor-playwrights, both mocked by the leading men of letters of their times. Above all, they were despised for bringing onto the stage the everyday life, joys and desperation of the common people; the hypocrisy and the arrogance of the high and mighty; and the incessant injustice. And their major, unforgivable fault was this: in telling these things, they made people laugh. Laughter does not please the mighty.

Ruzzante, the true father of the *Commedia dell'Arte*, also constructed a language of his own, a language of and for the theater, based on a variety of tongues: the dialects of the Po Valley, expressions in Latin, Spanish, even German, all mixed with onomatopoeic sounds of his own invention. It is from him, from Beolco Ruzzante, that I've learned to free myself from conventional literary writing and to express myself with words that you can chew, with unusual sounds, with various techniques of rhythm and breathing, even with the rambling nonsense-speech of the *grammelot*. Allow me to dedicate a part of this prestigious prize to Ruzzante.

A few days ago, a young actor of great talent said to me: "Maestro, you should try to project your energy, your enthusiasm, to young people.

You have to give them this charge of yours. You have to share your professional knowledge and experience with them." Franca [Rame]—that's my wife—and I looked at each other and said: "He's right." But when we teach others our art, and share this charge of fantasy, what end will it serve? Where will it lead?

...Let me share this medal with Franca. Franca Rame, my companion in life and in art who you, the members of the Academy, acknowledge in your motivation of the prize as actress and author, who has had a hand in many of the texts of our theater.... Without her at my side, where she has been for a lifetime, I would never have accomplished the work you have seen fit to honor. Together we've staged and recited thousands of performances, in theaters, occupied factories, at university sit-ins, even in deconsecrated churches, in prisons and city parks, in sunshine and pouring rain, always together. We've had to endure abuse, assaults by the police, insults from the right-thinking and violence. And it is Franca who has had to suffer the most atrocious aggression. She has had to pay more dearly than any one of us, with her neck and limb in the balance, for the solidarity with the humble and the beaten that has been our premise.

In the past couple of months, Franca and I have visited a number of university campuses to hold workshops and seminars before young audiences. It has been surprising—not to say disturbing—to discover their ignorance about the time we live in ... thousands of students listened to us. The looks in their faces spoke of their astonishment and incredulity.... We told them about the proceeding now in course in Turkey against the accused culprits of the massacre in Sivas. Thirty-seven of the country's foremost democratic intellectuals, meeting in the Anatolian town to celebrate the memory of a famous mediaeval jester of the Ottoman period, were burned alive in the dark of the night, trapped inside their hotel. The fire was the handiwork of a group of fanatical fundamentalists that enjoyed protection from elements within the Government itself.... At another university we spoofed the project—alas well under way—to manipulate genetic material, or more specifically, the proposal by the European Parliament to allow patent rights on living organisms.... They're trying to get the approval of a directive which (and get this!) would authorize industries to take patents on living beings, or on parts of them, created with techniques of genetic manipulation that seem taken straight out of "The Sorcerer's Apprentice."

...So, we enacted these criminal farces to the kids at the universities, and they laughed their heads off. They would say of Franca and me: "They're a riot, they come up with the most fantastic stories." Not for a moment, not even with an inkling in their spines, did they grasp that the stories we told were true.... The terribly difficult thing is that in order to talk about what is happening today, I have to start with what happened thirty years ago and then work my way forward. It's not enough to speak about the present. And pay attention, this isn't just about Italy: the same thing happens everywhere, all over Europe.

...Salvini, a noted Italian democrat, was right on the mark when he observed: "The widespread ignorance of events is the main buttress of injustice." But this absent-mindedness on the part of the young has been conferred upon them by those who are charged to educate and inform them: among the absent-minded and uninformed, school teachers and other educators deserve first mention.

These encounters have strengthened us in our conviction that our job is — in keeping with the exhortation of the great Italian poet Savinio — "to tell our own story." Our task as intellectuals, as persons who mount the pulpit or the stage, and who, most importantly, address to young people, our task is not just to teach them method, like how to use the arms, how to control breathing, how to use the stomach, the voice, the falsetto, the *contracampo*. It's not enough to teach a technique or a style: we have to show them what is happening around us. They have to be able to tell their own story. A theater, a literature, an artistic expression that does not speak for its own time has no relevance.

The day it was announced that I was to be awarded the Nobel Prize I found myself in front of the theater on Via di Porta Romana in Milan where Franca, together with Giorgio Albertazzi, was performing *The Devil with Tits*. Suddenly I was surrounded by a throng of reporters, photographers and camera-wielding TV-crews. A passing tram stopped, unexpectedly, the driver stepped out to greet me, then all the passengers stepped out too, they applauded me, and everyone wanted to shake my hand and congratulate me ... when at a certain point they all stopped in their tracks and, as with a single voice, shouted "Where's Franca?" They began to holler "Francaaa" until, after a little while, she appeared. Discombobulated and moved to tears, she came down to embrace me. At that moment, as if out of nowhere, a band appeared, playing nothing but wind instruments and drums. It was made up of kids from all parts of the city and, as it happened, they were playing together for the first time. They struck up "Porta Romana bella, Porta Romana" in a samba beat. I've never heard anything played so out of tune, but it was the most beautiful music Franca and I had ever heard. Believe me, this prize belongs to both of us. Thank you.

30. José Saramago

There is no lack, there never has been, of those who affirm that
poets are truly superfluous, but I wonder what would become of
us if poetry were not there to help us understand how little clarity there is in the things we call clear.

— The Stone Raft

The fragile nature of modern myths, absorbed without thought
like the air we breathe, nurtures the imagination of the Portuguese
writer José Saramago (1922–). A myth in his hands is pure belief,
not necessarily from God — not even necessarily true — but accepted
as indisputable. He ponders the impact of the smallest basic unit of
any reality — words — on our image of the universe we inhabit. Only
once in his novels (available in English) does he directly speak of his
concern:

> We can only conclude that a word, once spoken, lasts longer that the
> sound and sounds that formed it, the word remains, invisible and
> inaudible, in order to be able to keep its own secret, a kind of hid-
> den seed below the surface of the earth that germinates out of sight
> until suddenly it pushes the soil aside and emerges into the light, a
> coiled stem, a crumpled leaf slowly unfolding [*The Stone Raft*].

If Saramago has an agenda, it is to instill in his readers the
courage to crack the molds of accepted dogma and burst into the
irrational realm where meaning can be found. The life of the imagination and dreams are the fertile grounds in which individual meaning grows. "Besides the conversation of women, it is dreams that
keep the world in orbit" (*Baltasar and Blimunda*). It can be a doleful or a joyful place. The doctor's wife in *Blindness* reflects to herself that "blindness is also this, to live in a world where all hope
is gone." In spite of the pessimistic tone of many of his stories,
the characters are often saved by their budding dreams. In his

introduction to *The Stone Raft,* Saramago clearly defines his concern: "The possibility of the impossible, dreams and illusions, are the subject of my novels."

A highly literary writer, Saramago obliquely alludes to other writers through a variety of devices: titles, names, descriptions, characters, and incidents. Baltasar Setei-Sois, like Miguel Cervantes, loses his hand in battle and is dismissed from the army. The tongue-in-cheek references to holy relics in Lisbon reflect Twain's *Innocents Abroad.* The title of Anatole France's *Penguin Island* might have been *The Stone Raft,* and his view of the treatment of history would slide comfortably into *The History of the Siege of Lisbon. The Gospel According to Jesus Christ* treats the humanness of Christ much as Kazantzakis does in *The Last Temptation of Christ,* echoing Dostoyevsky's torment over the fate of innocent children in *The Brothers Karamazov.*

The spiraling mind of Jorge Borges particularly intrigues Saramago. Veiled and open emulations of that elusive link between reality and literature (which characterizes much of Borges' work) pop up like exposed roots pushing their way through a concrete sidewalk. In *The Year of the Death of Ricardo Reis,* Saramago has the protagonist, Reis, carry with him throughout the novel *The God of the Labyrinth*, a book by Herbert Quain; both the author and the novel were creations of Borges in a story titled "An Examination of the Work of Herbert Quain."[1] Reis was a heteronym (a distinct literary personality, not merely a pen name) of the Portuguese poet, Fernando Pessoa. It is typical of both Borges and Saramago to pass back and forth from fiction to history without marking boundaries.

Saramago's concern for the welfare of the common people, suffering under the oppression of unjust or inept authority, shines through his literary devices and allusions. One of the dominating authorities of Portugal is the Catholic Church. By inverting the usual statements of God, Christ and the Church, Saramago tries to shake us free to review accepted Christian dogma. The debauched musing of the Bishop of Lisbon as he dons the robes of his office identify a corrupt and aristocratic Church:

> Kneel, kneel, for the sacred monstrance is about to pass and I am passing, and Christ the King is inside the monstrance, and inside me is the grace of being king on earth, the king made flesh, in order to feel; for you well know how nuns are regarded as the spouses of Christ, and that is the holy truth, for they receive me in their beds as they receive the Lord, and it is because I am their lord that they sigh in ecstasy, clutching their rosary in one hand [*Baltasar and Blimunda*].

Saramago goes further than merely attacking the Catholic Church as an imperfect instrument of God's love in the world. The problem of suffering haunts him. *The Gospel According to Jesus Christ* pivots on the question of how a just, omniscient and omnipotent God can allow the suffering of innocents. Both Joseph and Jesus are tormented in this novel by the nightmare of Herod's slaughter of babies. What could justify God's acceptance of murdering innocents?

> If people in those days were already familiar with the expression God never sleeps, we now know that the reason He never sleeps is that He made a mistake which no man would be forgiven. With every child begotten by Joseph, God raised His head a little higher, but He will never raise it fully, because twenty-seven infants were massacred in Bethlehem [*The Gospel According to Jesus Christ*].

Saramago also challenges the assumptions of Portuguese nationhood both modern (*Baltasar and Blimunda*) and historic (*The Year of the Death of Ricardo Reis, The History of the Siege of Lisbon, The Stone Raft, Blindness*). In *The Year of the Death of Ricardo Reis*, Fascist Portugal of the mid 1930s seems oblivious to the second-rate ideology and witless stupidity of its right-wing leaders. Saramago's satirical ire foams to the surface when quoting "free" press references to the governing dictatorship:

> ...the Portuguese nation and the statesmen who guide her are quoted worldwide, the political doctrine we pursue here is being studied abroad, and one can confidently say that other nations regard us with envy.

In *The Stone Raft* the Iberian Peninsula suffers a geological fault and floats free of Europe in the twentieth century. "Ah, who will write the history of what might have been?" the author asks the reader. The cast of this imagined reality are a small band of characters who cause the earth to tremble and split by such mundane acts as drawing a line in the dirt with an elm branch and throwing a stone in the ocean. The government attempts to solve the meta-geologic problem with sandbox technology before abandoning the masses to their fate. These Cervantes-like characters, abandoned to their own devices, trek the new island looking for a haven with only their abiding compassion for one another and a mystical dog to lead them.

In the vivid love story *Baltasar and Blimunda,* the protagonists pursue their separate dreams (Blimunda's of love, Baltasar's of manned flight) awash in the cauldron of medieval Portugal. Sabistina Maria de Jesus, Blimunda's mother, like Joan of Arc, hears the voice of God and enjoys spiritual visions for which she is flogged in the public square and sent into exile by the authorities of the Inquisition. Yet no one dares interfere with the young prince, Infante Dom Francisco, as he shoots sailors from the rigging of ships for target practice. Padre Bartolomeu Lourenco wants to float among the birds and angels in his flying machine, the *Passarola,* while Scarlatti composes masterpieces, each character pursuing a different reality. The sincerity of yearning shields the innocent and exposes the vile to the depravity of their time and place. Saramago characterizes Portugal as a vulgar and bloodthirsty nation of thieves, run by hypocrites and ruled by a sensualist monarchy. The King, on a whim, builds a monastery at Mafra as eternal evidence to his piety, power and glory, but it is built upon the backs of slaves. Look behind the surface of every edifice to explore its human foundations, Saramago advises, to uncover its real meaning.

Saramago provides clues to where redemption may be found. "I don't think we did go blind, I think we are blind, Blind but seeing, Blind people who can see, but do not see" (*Blindness*). The key for Saramago is to see actively, creatively, with the entire intelligence of which we are capable. "I've ... educated myself ... discovering the difference between looking and seeing, between seeing and observing" (*The History of the Siege of Lisbon*). By observing superficial reality, each of us is capable of seeing a deeper reality beyond appearances. We can use that vision to reform ourselves into people vibrantly tethered to one another through our dreams:

> In this life everyone has something to build ... once everything is assembled and ready we shall take off, for men are angels born without wings. Nothing could be nicer than to be born without wings and to make them grow. This is what we've achieved with our minds, and if we've succeeded in making our minds grow, we'll grow wings, too [*Baltasar and Blimunda*].

1998

"— who with parables sustained by imagination, compassion and irony continually enables us once again to apprehend an elusory reality —"

How Characters Became the Masters and the Author Their Apprentice

The wisest man I ever knew in my whole life could not read or write. At four o'clock in the morning, when the promise of a new day still lingered over French lands, he got up from his pallet and left for the fields, taking to pasture the half-dozen pigs whose fertility nourished him and his wife…. In winter when the cold of the night grew to the point of freezing the water in the pots inside the house, they [he and his wife] went to the sty and fetched the weaklings among the piglets, taking them to their bed. Under the coarse blankets, the warmth from the humans saved the little animals from freezing and rescued them from certain death….

Many times, in secret, dodging from the men guarding the cornfields, I went with my grandmother, also at dawn, armed with rakes, sacking and cord, to glean the stubble, the loose straw that would then serve as litter for livestock. And sometimes, on hot summer nights, after supper, my grandfather would tell me: "José, tonight we're going to sleep, both of us, under the fig tree." There were two other fig trees, but that one, certainly because it was the biggest, because it was the oldest, and timeless, was, for everybody in the house, the fig tree….

With sleep delayed, night was peopled with the stories and the cases my grandfather told and told: legends, apparitions, terrors, unique episodes, old deaths, scuffles with sticks and stones, the words of our forefathers, an untiring rumor of memories that would keep me awake while at the same time gently lulling me. I could never know if he was silent when he realized that I had fallen asleep or if he kept on talking so as not to leave half-unanswered the question I invariably asked into the most delayed pauses he placed on purpose within the account: "And what happened next?" Maybe he repeated the stories for himself, so as not to forget them, or else to enrich them with new detail.

When at first light the singing of birds woke me up, he was not there any longer, had gone to the field with his animals, letting me sleep on. Then I would get up, fold the coarse blanket and barefoot — in the village I always walked barefoot till I was fourteen — and with straws still stuck in my hair, I went from the cultivated part of the yard to the other part, where the sties were, by the house. My grandmother, already afoot before my grandfather, set in front of me a big bowl of coffee with pieces of bread in and asked me if I had slept well. If I told her some bad dream, born of my grandfather's stories, she always reassured me: "Don't make much of it, in dreams there's nothing solid."

It was only many years after, when my grandfather had departed from this world and I was a grown man, I finally came to realize that my grandmother, after all, also believed in dreams. There could have been no other reason why, sitting one evening at the door of her cottage where she now lived alone, staring at the biggest and smallest stars overhead, she said these words: "The world is so beautiful and it is such a pity that I have to die."

She didn't say she was afraid of dying, but that it was a pity to die, as if her hard life of unrelenting work was, in that almost final moment, receiving the grace of a supreme and last farewell, the consolation of beauty revealed. She was sitting at the door of a house like none other I can imagine in all the world, because in it lived people who could sleep with piglets as if they were their own children, people who were sorry to leave life just because the world was beautiful; and this Jerónimo, my grandfather, swineherd and story-teller, feeling death about to arrive and take him, went and said good-bye to the trees in the yard, one by one, embracing them and crying because he knew he wouldn't see them again.

Many years later, writing for the first time about my grandfather Jerónimo and my grandmother Josefa (I haven't said so far that she was, according to many who knew her when young, a woman of uncommon beauty), I was finally aware I was transforming the ordinary people they were into literary characters: this was, probably, my way of not forgetting them, drawing and redrawing their faces with the pencil that ever changes memory, coloring and illuminating the monotony of a dull and horizonless daily routine as if creating, over the unstable map of memory, the supernatural unreality of the country where one has decided to spend one's life.

The same attitude of mind that, after evoking the fascinating and enigmatic figure of a certain Berber grandfather, would lead me to describe more or less in these words an old photo (now almost eighty years old) showing my parents "both standing, beautiful and young, facing the photographer, showing in their faces an expression of solemn seriousness, maybe fright in front of the camera at the very instant when the lens is about to capture the image they will never have again, because the following day will be, implacably, another day.... My father has his arm round my mother's back, his callused hand showing over her shoulder, like a wing. They are standing, shy, on a carpet patterned with branches. The canvas forming the fake background of the picture shows diffuse and incongruous neo-classic architecture." And I ended, "The day will come when I will tell these things. Nothing of this matters except to me. A Berber grandfather from North Africa, another grandfather a swineherd, a wonderfully beautiful grandmother; serious and handsome parents, a flower in a picture — what other genealogy would I care for? And what better tree would I lean against?"

I wrote these words almost thirty years ago, having no other purpose than to rebuild and register instants of the lives of those people who engendered and were closest to my being, thinking that nothing else would need explaining for people to know where I came from and what materials the person I am was made of, and what I have become little by little. But after all I was wrong, biology doesn't determine everything and as for genetics, very mysterious must have been its paths to make its voyages so long....

Now I can clearly see those who were my life-masters, those who most intensively taught me the hard work of living, those dozens of characters from my novel and plays that right now I see marching past before my eyes, those men and women of paper and ink, those people I believed I was guiding as I the narrator chose according to my whim, obedient to my will as an author, like articulated puppets whose actions could have no more effect on me than the burden and the tension of the string I moved them with. Of those masters, the first was, undoubtedly, a mediocre portrait-painter, whom I called simply H, the main character of a story that I feel may reasonably be called a double initiation (his own, but also in a manner of speaking the author's) entitled *Manual of Painting and Calligraphy*, who taught me the simple honesty of acknowledging and observing, without resentment or frustration, my own limitations: as I could not and did not aspire to venture beyond my little plot of cultivated land, all I had left was the possibility of digging down, underneath, towards the roots....

Then came the men and women of Alentejo, the same brotherhood of the condemned of the earth where belonged my grandfather Jerónimo and my grandmother Josefa, primitive peasants obliged to hire out the strength of their arms for a wage and working conditions that deserved only to be called infamous, getting for less than nothing a life which the cultivated and civilized beings we are proud to be are pleased to call — depending on the occasion — precious, sacred or sublime.... Three generations of a peasant family, the Badewathers, from the beginning of the century to the April Revolution of 1974 which toppled dictatorship, move through this novel, called *Risen from the Ground*, and it was with such men and women risen from the ground, real people first, figures of fiction later, that I learned how to be patient, to trust and to confide in time, that same time that simultaneously builds and destroys us in order to build and once more to destroy us....

What other lessons could I possibly receive from a Portuguese who lived in the sixteenth century, who composed the *Rimas* and the glories, the shipwrecks and the national disenchantments in the *Lusíadas*, who was an absolute poetical genius, the greatest in our Literature, no matter how much sorrow this causes to Fernando Pessoa, who proclaimed himself its Super Camões? No lesson would fit me, no lesson could I learn, except the simplest, which could have been offered to me by Luís Vaz de Camões in his pure humanity, for instance the proud humility of an author who goes knocking at every door looking for someone willing to publish the book he has written, thereby suffering the scorn of the ignoramuses of blood and race, the disdainful indifference of a king and of his powerful entourage, the mockery with which the world has always received the visits of poets, visionaries and fools. At least once in life, every author has been, or will have to be, Luís de Camões, even if they haven't written the poem *Sôbolos Rios*.... Among nobles, courtiers and censors from the Holy Inquisition, among the loves of yesteryear and the disillusionments of premature old age, between the pain of writing and the joy of having written, it was this ill man, returning poor from India where so many sailed just to get rich, it was this soldier blind in one eye, slashed in his soul, it was this seducer of no fortune who will never again flutter the hearts of the ladies in the royal court, whom I put on stage in a play called *What Shall I Do with This Book?*, whose ending repeats another question, the only truly important one, the one we will never know if it will ever have a sufficient answer: "What will you do with this book?" It was also proud humility to carry under his arm a masterpiece and to be unfairly rejected by the world. Proud humility also, and obstinate too — wanting to know what the purpose will be, tomorrow, of the books we are writing today, and immediately doubting whether they will last a long time (how long?) the reassuring reasons we are given or that are given us by ourselves. No one is better deceived than when he allows others to deceive him.

Here comes a man whose left hand was taken in war and a woman who came to this world with the mysterious power of seeing what lies beyond people's skin. His name is Baltasar Mateus and his nickname Seven-Suns; she is known as Blimunda and also, later, as Seven-Moons because it is written that where there is a sun there will have to be a moon and that only the conjoined and harmonious presence of the one and the other will, through love, make earth habitable... This is the story of *Baltasar and Blimunda*, a book where the apprentice author, thanks to what had long ago been taught to him in his grandparents' Jerónimo's and Josefa's time, managed to write some similar words not without poetry: "Besides women's talk, dreams are what hold the world in its orbit. But it is also dreams that crown it with moons, that's why the sky is the splendor in men's heads, unless men's heads are the one and only sky." So be it.

...It was at the Industrial School Library that *The Year of the Death of Ricardo Reis* started to be written.... There, one day the young mechanic (he was about seventeen) found a magazine entitled *Atena* containing poems signed with that name and ... he thought that there really was a Portuguese poet called Ricardo Reis. Very soon, though, he found that this poet was really one Fernando Nogueira Pessoa, who signed his works with the names of non-existent poets, born of his mind. He called them heteronyms, a word that did not exist in the dictionaries of the time which is why it was so hard for the apprentice to learn to know what it meant. He learned many of Ricardo Reis' poems by heart ... but ... he could not accept that a superior mind could really have conceived, without remorse the cruel line, "Wise is he who is satisfied with the spectacle of the world." Later, much later, the apprentice, already with gray hairs and a little wiser in his own wisdom, dared to write a novel to show this poet of the *Odes* something about the spectacle of the world of 1936.... It was his way of telling him: "Here is the spectacle of the world, my poet of serene bitterness and elegant skepticism. Enjoy, behold, since to be sitting is your wisdom...."

The Year of the Death of Ricardo Reis ended with the melancholy words: "Here, where the sea has ended and land awaits." So there would be no more discoveries by Portugal, fated to one infinite wait for futures not even imaginable; only the usual fado, the same old saudade and little more.... Then the apprentice imagined that there still might be a way of sending the ships back to the water, for instance, by moving the land and setting that out to sea.... The novel I then wrote — *The Stone Raft* — separated from the Continent the whole Iberian Peninsula and transformed it into a big floating island, moving of its own accord with no oars, no sails, no propellers, in a southerly direction, "a mass of stone and land, covered with cities, villages, rivers, woods, factories and bushes, arable land, with its people and animals" on its way to a new Utopia.... A vision twice Utopian would see this political fiction as a much more generous and human metaphor: that Europe, all of it, should move South to help balance the world, as compensation for its former and its present colonial abuses. That is, Europe at last as an ethical reference.

Then the apprentice recalled that at a remote time of his life he had worked as a proof-reader and that if, so to say, in *The Stone Raft* he had revised the future, now it might not be a bad thing to revise the past, inventing a novel to be called *History of the Siege of Lisbon*, where a proof-reader, checking a book with the same title but a real history book and tired of watching how "History" is less and less able to surprise, decides to substitute a "yes" for a "no," subverting the authority of "historical truth."... It is useless to add that the apprentice had learned, with Raimundo Silva, the lesson of doubt. It was about time.

Well, probably it was this learning of doubt that made him go through the writing of *The Gospel According to Jesus Christ....* This time it was not a matter of looking behind the pages of the New Testament searing for antitheses, but of illuminating their surfaces, like that of a painting, with a low light to heighten their relief, the traces of crossings, the shadows of depressions. That's how the apprentice read, now surrounded by evangelical characters, as if for the first time, the description of the massacre of the innocents and, having read, he couldn't understand. He couldn't understand why there were already martyrs in a religion that would have to wait thirty years more to listen to its founder pronouncing the first word about it, he could not understand why the only person that could have done so dared not save the lives of the children of Bethlehem, he could not understand Joseph's lack of a minimum feeling of responsibility, or remorse, of guilt, or even of curiosity, after returning with his family from Egypt.... The apprentice's Gospel is not, consequently, one more edifying legend of blessed beings and gods, but the story of a few human beings subjected to a power they fight but cannot defeat. Jesus, who will inherit the dusty sandals with which his father had walked so many country roads, will also inherit his tragic feeling of responsibility and guilt that will never abandon him, not even when he raises his voice from the top of the cross: "Men, forgive him because he knows not what he has done," referring certainly to the God who has sent him there, but perhaps also, if in that last agony he still remembers, his real father who has generated him humanly in flesh and blood....

Had Emperor Charlemagne not established a monastery in North Germany, had that monastery not been the origin of the city of Münster, had Münster not wished to celebrate its twelve-hundredth anniversary with an opera about the dreadful sixteenth-century war between Protestant Anabaptists and Catholics, the apprentice would not have written his play *In Nomine Dei*. Once more, with no other help than the tiny light of his reason, the apprentice had to penetrate the obscure labyrinth of religious beliefs, the beliefs that so easily make human beings kill and be killed. And what he saw was, once again, the hideous mask of intolerance, an intolerance that in Münster became an insane paroxysm, an intolerance that insulted the very cause that both parties claimed to defend. Because it was not a question of war in the name of two inimical gods, but of war in the name of a same god.... The terrible slaughter in Münster taught the apprentice that religions, despite all they promised, have never been used to bring men together and that the most absurd of all wars is a holy war, considering that God cannot, even if he wanted to, declare war on himself.

Blind. The apprentice thought, "we are blind," and he sat down and wrote *Blindness* to remind those who might read it that we pervert reason when we humiliate life, that human dignity is insulted every day by the powerful of our world, that the universal lie has replaced the plural truths, that man stopped respecting himself when he lost the respect due to his fellow-creatures. Then the apprentice, as if trying to exorcize the monsters generated by the blindness of reason, started writing the simplest of all stories: one person is looking for another, because he has realized that life has nothing more important to demand from a human being. The book is called *All the Names*. Unwritten, all our names are there. The names of the living and the names of the dead.

My genealogical tree (you will forgive the presumption of naming it this way, being so diminished in the substance of its sap) lacked not only some of those branches that time and life's successive encounters cause to burst from the main stem but also someone to help its roots penetrate the deepest subterranean layers, someone who could verify the consistency and flavor of its fruit, someone to extend and strengthen its top to make of it a shelter for birds of passage and a support for nests. When painting my parents and grandparents with the paints of literature, transforming them from common people of flesh and blood into characters, newly and in different ways builders of my life, I was, without noticing, tracing the path … [that] would make of me the person whom I nowadays recognize as myself: the creator of those characters but at the same time their own creation. In one sense it could even be said that, letter-by-letter, word-by-word, page-by-page, book after book, I have been successively implanting in the man I was the characters I created. I believe that without them I wouldn't be the person I am today; without them maybe my life wouldn't have succeeded in becoming more than an inexact sketch, a promise that like so many others remained only a promise, the existence of someone who maybe might have been but in the end could not manage to be.

I conclude. The voice that read these pages wished to be the echo of the conjoined voices of my characters. I don't have, as it were, more voice than the voices they had. Forgive me if what has seemed little to you, to me is all.

31. Günter Grass

A writer, children, is someone who writes against the passage of time.
— "What Shall We Tell Our Children?"
in *On Writing and Politics*

If Günter Grass (1927–) relied only on his crisp imagery and poetic ear to spin his tales of Germany astride the beast of Nazism, he would be a trenchant novelist, playwright and poet. He goes further, dragging the irrational into clear view. With an imagination that is at once ribald and somber, playful and sinister, he establishes a homestead in the reader's mind. Could the history of sexual politics from the Neolithic age to the present be explained by a mythical talking fish? Grass does just that in his bawdy romp, *The Flounder*. What would have happened if the great literary figures in seventeenth century Germany had met for a conference during the Thirty Years' War? *The Meeting at Telgte* gives us a seat at the discussion table. Imagine an innocent middle-aged couple trying to succor the wounds of a war-ravaged Germany duped by "the German economic miracle," and you will detect *The Call of the Toad*. Grass loads his stories with eccentrics and lards them with humor, plot counterpoint, litany, biblical phrasing and absurdist perspectives. Comical and deadly serious at the same time, political yet not propagandist, Grass presents a collage of individuality in an age of marketing and mass movements. Few writers match the density of ideas, imagery, themes and humor of his richly textured novels.

Grass excels at agile description. He sees rival politicians examining "each other with the passionate interest of coroners" (*From the Diary of a Snail*) while future lovers, "looked upon each other as money in the bank" (*The Call of the Toad*). Dorothea of Montau

229

had a smile that "froze the snot in children's noses to icicles" (*The Flounder*). Cuds of chewing tobacco spat out on the ground are rendered as "tar stained oysters that no frost could freeze" in *The Tin Drum*. A cat describes Mahlke's Adam's apple in *Cat and Mouse*; the feline mistakes the bouncing cartilage for a mouse, stalks patiently through the grass and pounces as the innocent teenager sleeps on his back.

Grass' main characters don't hide their narcissism; they flaunt it. They take little notice of the pain and suffering of others unless it affects them directly. The three foot tall demon, Oskar Matzerath, serves as the drum major for the parade of strangeness in *The Tin Drum*. Oskar, born alert and articulate, refuses to grow or change once he reaches the age of three. He competes with Jesus for disciples and for the love of a statue of the Virgin Mary, teaches the boy Jesus (another statue) to play the drum, and etches holes in storefront windows with his voice to turn righteous citizens into thieves. Oskar kills one of his fathers (he has two), Matzerath, by forcing Matzerath's Nazi lapel pin into his hand as Soviet troops storm their refuge. Matzerath, attempting to hide evidence of his Nazi connection, tries to swallow the open pin, and the Soviet soldiers finish off the choking man with machine guns (to Oskar's satisfaction). At his graveside Oskar, now twenty, decides to grow again. Earlier in the war Oskar and his *other* father, Jan Bronski, are trapped in the Polish Post Office building as Nazi Home Guards storm the building. The son reacts with typical Oskar aplomb:

> Oskar, concerned for his [own] comfort and safety, made up to two Home Guards who struck him as good-natured ... put on an imitation of pathetic sniveling, and pointed to Jan, his father, with accusing gestures which transformed the poor man into a villain ... and his expectations were not disappointed: the Home Guards kicked Jan in the small of the back and battered him with their rifle stocks, but left me both drums [*The Tin Drum*].

Grass' characters are not quietly eccentric or marginal personalities. They are brazenly individual at the core. Eddie Amsel (*Dog Years*), whose voice protects his friends from a Nebuchadnezzar-like inferno and whose singing makes "sparrows ashamed," invents stuffed artificial men. His brown shirts compare favorably with Hitler's. With little effort he creates scarecrow soldiers, automatons, that surpass the best efforts of the Fuhrer:

> ...functioning, marching calmly firmly resolutely forward onward across toward upon and past, first in march step, then in goose step, as

required in parades: all nine of them. And nine times the chin-strapped pig's bladders under SA visor caps snap almost simultaneously to the right; eyes right [*Dog Years*].

After the war Eddie transforms the manufacture of his hollow men into a corporate enterprise with an underground factory reminiscent of Dante's *Inferno*. The grinder, Amsel's friend, after being expelled from the SA for "conduct unbecoming a storm trooper" (*Dog Years*), launches a revenge quest, reads divine messages of retribution off the walls of public urinals and confessionals, and starts (and later ends) the clap epidemic in postwar Germany. His father, the miller Matern, can hear the conversations of meal worms in a hundred pound bag of flour, a gift that transforms him into an oracle. The raucous Fat Gret (*The Flounder*) fuddles the memory of an abbot by baking a spoonful of his excrement into spice cakes for Advent. The lush imagination of Grass stamps his creatures with a life force that is both peculiar and universal at the same time.

He underscores the illogic of his fellow creatures and challenges the status quo with humor. In *The Flounder* the fish ironically convinces Edek to trust him by confiding, "A man's word is his bond!" This from a fish. In Ferdinand Schmuch's nightclub, "The Onion Cellar," patrons, unmoved and dry-eyed through the Holocaust, are exposed to succulent onions to bring tears to their eyes again (*The Tin Drum*). In Grass' hands, and Oskar's voice, even wartime rape becomes an occasion for sketch humor:

> Instantly three of the rectangular uniforms turned their attentions to Lina Greff.... La Greff, who after her long widowhood and the lean years preceding it, had scarcely expected such sudden popularity, let out a few screams of surprise but soon re-accustomed herself to an occupation she had almost forgotten [*The Tin Drum*].

The omens of Nazi evil and postwar evasion of responsibility for the Holocaust seep, like foul swamp gas, through the details of Grass' Danzig Trilogy. He uses stark visual imagery to convey the haunting presence of the crematories of slaughter. In *Dog Years* Matern, while serving in the army, knows the source of noxious odors that continuously waft over his position. Stark chimneys bear the news:

> But the smell which hung over the battery ... was projected ... by a whitish mound blocked off by barbed wire and situated to the south of the battery. This mound stood in front of, and half hid, a brick-red factory, which from a squat chimney discharged self-involved smoke.... No one talked about the pile of bones. But everybody saw

smelled tasted it. Anyone who stepped out of a barracks whose doors
opened southward had the cone-shaped mound in his field of
vision.... Chimneys speak for themselves.

Grass defines the writer's responsibility to society as that of any
other citizen, not as that of a propagandist. In *The Plebeians Rehearse
the Uprising: A German Tragedy,* Boss, a writer, is impotent (as a
writer), but as a citizen he has duties (which he shirks). At the same
time Grass shows that a writer can use wit and imagination to crack
open the "givens" of his culture, altering our perceptions of reality:
"The novelist's watchword is 'classify, accumulate, rearrange, and
disarrange'" (*On Writing and Politics*). Using magical realism, Grass
steps around the alibis, logic and facades of authority, directing his
appeal to the heart of the reader and achieving a human centered
revision of German cultural history:

> It's time that makes terror habitual: time is what we must write
> against.... Before their crime, criminals figure out how long it will
> take for their crime to be forgotten, overlaid by the crimes of other
> criminals, reduced to marginal history ... time, the passage of time,
> benefit the criminals; for their victims time does not pass [*From the
> Diary of a Snail*].

Grass does not bind himself to a single architecture for his prose.
Some of his novels follow a simple narrative line (*Cat and Mouse,
The Meeting at Telgte*); in others he bounces back and forth from the
present to the past, changing names and voices without warning
(*The Diary of a Snail, The Flounder, The Tin Drum, My Century*). A
peculiar interlocutor is a common feature of Grass novels. Often the
narrator reports social events as if seen in a passing glance, through
the wrong end of a telescope, while combing through the trivia of
his own personal life like an anthropologist on a dig. By flaunting
the robust quirkiness of his characters, Grass denies attempts to
reduce the human experience to ideology through the use of arche-
types. At the same time the witless egotism of his creatures cedes
control of society to fanatical idealists. It is in this sense that these
zany characters are much like the rest of us: distracted and therefore
vulnerable. Anything is possible in the fictional world of Günter
Grass, except resisting self-absorption. A human, Grass shows us, will
expose his soul only in an offhand moment when his or her social
mask slips out of place. Miss Spollenhauer, Oskar's first teacher,
suffers a brief lapse from her usual pose: "For a moment she became
a not unpleasant old maid, who had forgotten her prescribed occu-
pational caricature and became human, that is, childlike, curious,
complex, and immoral" (*The Tin Drum*).

1999

"— whose frolicsome black fables portray the forgotten face of history — "

"To Be Continued..."

Honored Members of the Swedish Academy, Ladies and Gentlemen: Having made this announcement, nineteenth-century works of fiction would go on and on. Magazines and newspapers gave them all the space they wished: the serialized novel was in its heyday. While the early chapters appeared in quick succession, the core of the work was being written out by hand, and its conclusion was yet to be conceived. Nor was it only trivial horror stories or tearjerkers that thus held the reader in thrall. Many of Dickens' novels came out in serial form, in installments. Tolstoy's Anna Karenina was a serialized novel. Balzac's time, a tireless provider of mass-produced serializations, gave the still anonymous writer lessons in the technique of suspense, of building to a climax at the end of a column. And nearly all Fontane's novels appeared first in newspapers and magazines as serializations. Witness the publisher of the Vossisiche Zeitung, where Trials and Tribulations first saw print, who exclaimed in a rage, "Will this sluttish story never end!"

People have always told tales. Long before humanity learned to write and gradually became literate, everybody told tales to everybody else and everybody listened to everybody else's tales. Before long it became clear that some of the still illiterate storytellers told more and better tales than others, that is, they could make more people believe their lies. And there were those among them who found artful ways of stemming the peaceful flow of their tales and diverting it into a tributary, that, far from drying up, turned suddenly and amazingly into a broad bed, though now full of flotsam and jetsam, the stuff of sub-plots. And because these primordial storytellers — who were not dependent upon day or lamp light and could carry on perfectly well in the dark, who were in fact adept at exploiting dusk or darkness to add to the suspense — because they stopped at nothing, neither dry stretches nor thundering waterfalls, except perhaps to interrupt the course of action with a "To Be Continued..." if they sensed their audience's attention flagging, many of their listeners felt moved to start telling tales of their own.

What tales were told when no one could yet write and therefore no one wrote them down? From the days of Cain and Abel there were tales of murder and manslaughter. Feuds — blood feuds, in particular — were always good for a story. Genocide entered the picture quite early along with floods and droughts, fat years and lean years. Lengthy lists of cattle and slaves were perfectly acceptable, and no tale could be believable without detailed genealogies of who came before whom and who came after, heroic tales especially. Love triangles, popular even now, and tales of monsters — half man, half beast — who made their way through labyrinths or lay in wait in the bulrushes attracted mass audiences from the outset, to say nothing of legends of gods and idols and accounts of sea journeys, which were then handed down, polished, enlarged upon, modified, transmogrified into their opposites, and finally written down by a storyteller whose name was supposedly Homer or, in the case of the Bible, by a collective of storytellers. In China and Persia, in India and the Peruvian highlands, wherever writing flourished, storytellers — whether as groups or individuals, anonymously or by name — turned into literati.

Writing-fixated as we are, we nonetheless retain the memory of oral storytelling, the spoken origins of literature. And a good thing too, because if we were to forget that all storytelling comes through the lips — now inarticulate, hesitant, now swift, as if driven by fear, now in whisper, to keep the secrets revealed from reaching the wrong ears, now loudly and clearly, all the way from self-serving bluster to sniffing out the very essence of life — if our faith in writing were to make us forget all that, our storytelling would be bookish, dry as dust.

Yet how good too that we have so many books available to us and that whether we read them aloud or to ourselves they are permanent. They have been my inspiration. When I was young and malleable, masters like Melville and Döblin or Luther with his biblical German prompted me to read aloud as I wrote, to mix ink with spit. Nor have things changed much since. Well into my fifth decade of enduring, no, relishing the moil and toil called writing, I chew tough, stringy clauses into manageable mush, babble to myself in blissful isolation, and put pen to paper only when I hear the proper tone and pitch, resonance and reverberation.

Yes, I love my calling. It keeps me company, a company whose polyphonic chatter calls for literal transcription into my manuscripts. And there is nothing I like more than to meet books of mine — books that have long since flown the coop and been expropriated by readers — when I read out loud to an audience what now lies peacefully on the page. For both the young, weaned early from language, and the old, grizzled yet still rapacious, the written word becomes spoken, and the magic works again and again. It is the shaman in the author earning a bit on the side, writing against the current of time, lying his way to tenable truths. And everyone believes his tacit promise: To Be Continued...

...And so on and so forth. The publication of my first two novels, *The Tin Drum* and *Dog Years*, and the novella I stuck between them, *Cat and Mouse*, taught me early on, as a relatively young writer, that books can cause offense, stir up fury, even hatred, that what is undertaken out of love for one's country can be taken as soiling one's nest. From then on I have been controversial.

Which means that like writers banished to Siberia or suchlike places I am in good company. So I have no grounds to complain; on the contrary, writers should consider the condition of permanent controversiality to be invigorating, part of the risk involved in choosing the profession. It is a fact of life that writers have always and with due consideration and great pleasure spit in the soup of the high and mighty. That is what makes the history of literature analogous to the development and refinement of censorship.

I come from the land of book-burning. We know that the desire to destroy a hated book is still (or once more) part of the spirit of our times and that when necessary it finds appropriate telegenic expression and therefore a mass audience. What is much worse, however, is that the persecution of writers, including the threat of murder and murder itself, is on the rise throughout the world, so much so that the world has grown accustomed to the terror of it.

What makes books — and with them writers — so dangerous that church and state, politburos and the mass media feel the need to oppose them? Silencing and worse are seldom the result of direct attacks on the reigning ideology. Often all it takes is a literary allusion to the idea that truth exists only in the plural — that there is no such thing as a single truth but only a multitude of truths — to make the defenders of one or another truth sense danger, mortal danger. Then there is the problem that writers are by definition unable to leave the past in peace: they are quick to open closed wounds, peer behind closed doors, find skeletons in the cupboard, consume sacred cows or, as in the case of Jonathan Swift, offer up Irish children, "stewed, roasted, baked, or boiled," to the kitchens of the English nobility. In other words, nothing is sacred to them, not even capitalism, and that makes them offensive, even criminal. But worst of all they refuse to make common cause with the victors of history: they take pleasure milling about the fringes of the historical process with the losers, who have plenty to say but no platform to say it on. By giving them a voice, they call the victory into question, by associating with them, they join ranks with them.

Of course the powers-that-be, no matter what period costume they may be wearing, have nothing against literature as such. They enjoy it as an ornament and even promote it. At present its role is to entertain, to serve the fun culture, to de-emphasize the negative side of things and give people hope, a light in the darkness. What is basically called for, though not quite so explicitly as during the Communist years, is a "positive hero." In the jungle of the free market economy he is likely to pave his way to success Rambolike with corpses and a smile; he is an adventurer who is always up for a quick fuck between battles, a winner who leaves a trail of losers behind him, in short, the perfect role model for our globalized world. And the demand for the hard-boiled he-man who always lands on his feet is unfailingly met by the media: James Bond has spawned any number of Dolly-like children. Good will continue to prevail over evil as long as it assumes his cool-guy pose.

Does that make his opposite or enemy a negative hero? Not necessarily. I have my roots, as you will have noticed from your reading, in the Spanish or Moorish school of the picaresque novel. Tilting at windmills has remained a model for that school down through the ages, and the picaro's very existence derives from the comic nature of defeat. He pees on the pillars of power and saws away at the throne knowing full well he will make no dent in either: once he moves on, the exalted temple may look a bit shabby, the throne may wobble slightly, but that is all. His humor is part and parcel of his despair…. The reason Rabelais was constantly on the run from the secular police and the Holy Inquisition is that his larger-than-life Gargantua and Pantagruel had turned the world according to scholasticism on its head. The laughter they unleashed was positively infernal. When Gargantua stooped bare-arsed on the towers of Notre-Dame and pissed the length and breadth of Paris under water, everyone who did not drown guffawed. Or to go back to Swift: his modest culinary proposal for relieving the hunger in Ireland could be brought up to date if at the next economic summit the board set for the heads of state were groaning with lusciously prepared street children from Brazil or southern Sudan. Satire is the name of the art form I have in mind, and in satire everything is permitted, even tickling the funny bone with the grotesque.

…By the early fifties, when I had started writing consciously, Heinrich Böll was a well-known if not always well-received author. Post-war German literature, still young, was having a hard time with German, which had been corrupted by the Nazi regime. In addition, Böll's generation — but also the younger writers like myself— were stymied to a certain extent by a prohibition that came from Theodor Adorno: "It is barbaric to write a poem after Auschwitz, and that is why it has become impossible to write poetry today…"

In other words, no more "To Be Continued…" Though write we did. We wrote by bearing in mind, like Adorno in his *Minima Moralia: Reflections from Damaged Life* (1951), that Auschwitz marks a rift, an unbridgeable gap in the history of civilization. It was the only way we could get round the prohibition. Even so, Adorno's writing on the wall has retained its power to this day. All the writers of my generation did public battle with it. No one had the desire or ability to keep silent. It was our duty to take the goose step out of German, to lure it out of its idylls and fogged inwardness. We, the children who had had our fingers burned, we were the ones to repudiate the absolutes, the ideological black or white. Doubt and skepticism were our godparents and the multitude of gray values their present to us. In any case, such was the asceticism I imposed on myself before discovering the richness of a language I had all too sweepingly pronounced guilty: its seducible softness, its tendency to plumb the depths, its utterly supple hardness, not to mention the sheen of its dialects, its artlessness and artfulness, its eccentricities, and beauty blossoming from its subjunctives. Having won back this capital, we invested it to make more. Despite Adorno's verdict or spurred on by it. The only way writing after Auschwitz, poetry or prose, could proceed was by becoming memory and preventing the past from coming to an end. Only then could post-war literature in German justify applying the generally valid "To Be Continued…" to itself and its descendants; only then could the wound be kept open and the much desired and prescribed forgetting be reversed with a steadfast "Once upon a time."

The risk I referred to then has remained with me throughout the years. But what would the profession of writer be like without risk? Granted, the writer would have the security of, say, a cultural bureaucrat, but he would be the prisoner of his fears of dirtying his hands with the present. Out of fear of losing his distance he would lose himself in realms where myths reside and lofty thoughts are all. But the present, which the past is constantly turning into, would catch up to him in the end and put him through the third degree. Because every writer is of his time, no matter how he protests being born too early or late. He does not autonomously choose what he will write about, that choice is made for him. At least I was not free to choose. Left to my own devices, I would have followed the laws of aesthetics and been perfectly happy to seek my place in texts droll and harmless. But that was not to be. There were extenuating circumstances: mountains of rubble and cadavers, fruit of the womb of German history. The more I shoveled, the more it grew. It simply could not be ignored. Besides, I come from a family of refugees, which means that in addition to everything that drives a writer from book to book — common ambition, the fear of boredom, the mechanisms of egocentricity — I had the irreparable loss of my birthplace. If by telling tales I could not recapture a city both lost and destroyed, I could at least re-conjure it. And this obsession kept me going. I wanted to make it clear to myself and my readers, not without a bit of a chip on my shoulder, that what was lost did not need to sink into oblivion, that it could be resuscitated by the art of literature in all its grandeur and pettiness: the churches and cemeteries, the sounds of the shipyards and smells of the faintly lapping Baltic, a language on its way out yet still stable-warm and grumble-rich, sins in need of confession, and crimes tolerated if never exonerated.

A similar loss has provided other writers with a hotbed of obsessive topics. In a conversation dating back many years Salman Rushdie and I concurred that my lost Danzig was for me — like his lost Bombay for him — both resource and refuse pit, point of departure and navel of the world. This arrogance, this overkill lies at the very heart of literature. It is the condition for a story that can pull out all the stops. Painstaking detail, sensitive psychologizing, slice-of-life realism — no such techniques can handle our monstrous raw materials. As indebted as we are to the Enlightenment tradition of reason, the absurd course of history spurns all exclusively reasonable explanations.

Just as the Nobel Prize — once we divest it of its ceremonial garb — has its roots in the invention of dynamite, which like such other human headbirths as the splitting of the atom and the likewise Nobelified classification of the gene has wrought both weal and woe in the world, so literature has an explosive quality at its root, though the explosions literature releases have a delayed-action effect and change the world only in the magnifying glass of time, so to speak, it too wreaking cause for both joy and lamentation here below.

How can subversive writing be both dynamite and of literary quality? Is there time enough to wait for the delayed action? Is any book capable of supplying a commodity in so short supply as the future? Is it not rather the case that literature is currently retreating from public life and that young writers are using the internet as a playground? A standstill, to which the suspicious word "communication" lends a certain aura, is making headway. Every scrap of time is planned down to the last nervous breakdown. A cultural industry vale of tears is taking over the world. What is to be done?

My godlessness notwithstanding, all I can do is bend my knee to a saint who has never failed me and cracked some of the hardest nuts. "O Holy and (through the grace of Camus) Nobelified Sisyphus! May thy stone not remain at the top of the hill, may we roll it down again and like thee continue to rejoice in it, and may the story told of the drudgery of our existence have no end. Amen."

Appendix: List of Nobel Laureates in Literature

1901	Sully Prudhomme	France
1902	Theodor Mommsen	Germany
1903	Bjørnstjerne Bjørnson	Norway
1904	Frédéric Mistral	France
	José de Echegaray	Spain
1905	Henryk Sienkiewicz	Poland
1906	Giosué Carducci	Italy
1907	Rudyard Kipling	Great Britain
1908	Rudolf Eucken	Germany
1909	Selma Lagerlöf	Sweden
1910	Paul Heyse	Germany
1911	Maurice Maeterlinck	Belgium
1912	Gerhart Hauptmann	Germany
1913	Rabindranath Tagore	India
1914	NOT AWARDED	
1915	Romain Rolland	France
1916	Verner von Heidenstam	Sweden
1917	Karl Gjellerup	Denmark
	Henrik Pontoppidan	Denmark
1918	NOT AWARDED	
1919	Carl Spitteler	Switzerland
1920	Knut Hamsun	Norway
1921	Anatole France	France
1922	Jacinto Benavente	Spain
1923	William Butler Yeats	Ireland
1924	Władysław Reymont	Poland

1925	G.B. Shaw	Great Britain
1926	Grazia Deledda	Italy
1927	Henri Bergson	France
1928	Sigrid Undset	Norway
1929	Thomas Mann	Germany
1930	Sinclair Lewis	United States
1931	Erik Axel Karlfeldt	Sweden
1932	John Galsworthy	Great Britain
1933	Ivan Bunin	Stateless
1934	Luigi Pirandello	Italy
1935	NOT AWARDED	
1936	Eugene O'Neill	United States
1937	Roger Martin du Gard	France
1938	Pearl S. Buck	United States
1939	F.E. Sillanpää	Finland
1940	NOT AWARDED	
1941	NOT AWARDED	
1942	NOT AWARDED	
1943	NOT AWARDED	
1944	Johannes V. Jensen	Denmark
1945	Gabriela Mistral	Chile
1946	Hermann Hesse	Switzerland
1947	André Gide	France
1948	T.S. Eliot	Great Britain
1949	William Faulkner	United States
1950	Bertrand Russell	Great Britain
1951	Pär Lagerkvist	Sweden
1952	François Mauriac	France
1953	Winston Churchill	Great Britain
1954	Ernest Hemingway	United States
1955	Halldór Laxness	Iceland
1956	J.R. Jiménez	Spain
1957	Albert Camus	France
1958	Boris Pasternak [declined]	USSR
1959	Salvatore Quasimodo	Italy
1960	Saint-John Perse	France
1961	Ivo Andric	Yugoslavia
1962	John Steinbeck	United States
1963	Giorgos Seferis	Greece
1964	Jean-Paul Sartre [declined]	France

1965	Mikhail Sholokhov	USSR
1966	Shmuel Y. Agnon	Israel
	Nelly Sachs	Germany
1967	Miguel Ángel Asturias	Guatemala
1968	Yasunari Kawabata	Japan
1969	Samuel Beckett	Ireland
1970	Aleksandr Solzhenitsyn	USSR
1971	Pablo Neruda	Chile
1972	Heinrich Böll	Germany
1973	Patrick White	Australia
1974	Eyvind Johnson	Sweden
	Harry Martinson	Sweden
1975	Eugenio Montale	Italy
1976	Saul Bellow	United States
1977	Vicente Aleixandre	Spain
1978	Isaac Bashevis Singer	United States
1979	Odysseus Elytis	Greece
1980	Czesław Miłosz	Poland/United States
1981	Elias Canetti	Great Britain
1982	Gabriel García Márquez	Colombia
1983	William Golding	Great Britain
1984	Jaroslav Seifert	Czechoslovakia
1985	Claude Simon	France
1986	Wole Soyinka	Nigeria
1987	Joseph Brodsky	United States
1988	Naguib Mahfouz	Egypt
1989	Camilo José Cela	Spain
1990	Octavio Paz	Mexico
1991	Nadine Gordimer	South Africa
1992	Derek Walcott	Trinidad/United States
1993	Toni Morrison	United States
1994	Kenzaburō Ōe	Japan
1995	Seamus Heaney	Ireland
1996	Wisława Szymborska	Poland
1997	Dario Fo	Italy
1998	José Saramago	Portugal
1999	Günter Grass	Germany

Notes

Preface

1. Warren, Robert Penn. *New and Selected Essays.* New York: Random House, 1989.
2. Kerr, Walter. *The Decline of Pleasure.* New York: Simon & Schuster, 1962.
3. Ayers, Alex. *The Wit and Wisdom of Mark Twain.* New York: Nal-Dutton, 1989.
4. Dillard, Annie. *The Writing Life.* New York: Harper & Row, 1989.
5. Campbell, Joseph. *Transformations of Myth Through Time.* New York: Harper & Row, 1990.
6. Brueggemann, Walter. *Finally Comes the Poet.* Minneapolis: Augsburg Fortress, 1989.
7. *Ibid.*
8. Miller, Arthur. *Timebends.* New York: Grove Press, 1987.
9. Stipulation in Alfred Nobel's will.
10. O'Connor, Flannery. *Mystery and Manners.* New York: Farrar, Straus & Giroux, 1969.
11. Rodin, Auguste. *Rodin on Art and Artists.* Trans. Romilly Fedden. New York: Dover, 1983.
12. Kundera, Milan. *The Art of the Novel.* New York: Grove Press, 1988.

1. Bjørnstjerne Bjørnson (1903)

1. "The Aim of Poetry." In *The World's Best Essays: From Confucius to Mencken.* Ed. F.H. Pritchard, Albert and Charles Boni, 1929.
2. Koht, Havidan, and Sigmund Skard. *Twentieth Century Literary Criticism.* Vol. 37. Detroit: Gale, 1991.
3. Brandes, Georg. *Henrik Ibsen: A Critical Study.* London: W. Heinemann, 1899.
4. Koht, Havidan, and Sigmund Skard. *The Voice of Norway.* New York: Columbia University Press, 1944.
5. Payne, William Moreton. *Twentieth Century Literary Criticism.* Vol. 7. Detroit: Gale, 1982.

6. *The Voice of Norway.*
7. *Ibid.*
8. Koht and Skard. *Twentieth Century Literary Criticism.*
9. *The Aim of Poetry.*
10. *The Voice of Norway.*

2. William Butler Yeats (1923)

1. Ellmann, Richard. *Yeats: The Man and the Masks.* New York: Norton, 1978.
2. *Ibid.*
3. *United Ireland,* October 10, 1891, Dublin.
4. *Yeats: The Man and the Masks.*
5. Beckett, Samuel. *Waiting for Godot.* New York: Grove Press, 1954.
6. *Yeats: The Man and the Masks.*

3. Henri Bergson (1927)

1. Dodson, George Rowland. *Bergson and the Modern Spirit.* Boston: American Unitarian Association, 1913.
2. *Ibid.*
3. *Twentieth Century Literary Criticism.* Vol. 32. Detroit: Gale, 1989.
4. *Bergson and the Modern Spirit.*
5. Chevaline, Jacques. *Henri Bergson.* New York: Macmillan, 1928.
6. Untermeyer, Louis. *Makers of the Modern World.* New York: Simon & Schuster, 1955.
7. *Bergson and the Modern Spirit.*
8. *Twentieth Century Literary Criticism.*
9. *Makers of the Modern World.*
10. *Twentieth Century Literary Criticism.*
11. *Bergson and the Modern Spirit.*
12. *European Writers.* Vol. 8. New York: Scribner & Sons, 1989.

4. Sinclair Lewis (1930)

1. Lippmann, Walter. *Men of Destiny.* New York: Macmillan, 1927
2. Schorer, Mark. *Sinclair Lewis: An American Life.* New York: McGraw Hill, 1961.

6. T.S. Eliot (1948)

1. Aiken, Conrad. "An Anatomy of Melancholy." In *T.S. Eliot: The Man and His Work.* Ed. Allen Tate. New York: Delacorte Press, 1966.
2. Kermode, Frank, ed. *Selected Prose of T.S. Eliot.* New York: Harcourt, Brace, 1932.
3. Kermode, Frank. "A Babylonish Dialect." In *T.S. Eliot: The Man and His Work.*

4. T.S. Eliot centenary. *Contemporary Literary Criticism.* Vol. 55. Detroit: Gale Research, 1989.

7. William Faulkner (1949)

1. Meriwether, James, ed. *Essays, Speeches and Public Letters of William Faulkner.* New York: Random House, 1965.

8. Bertrand Russell (1950)

1. Wood, Alan. *Bertrand Russell: The Passionate Skeptic.* New York: Simon & Schuster, 1958.
2. *Ibid.*
3. *Ibid.*
4. *Ibid.*
5. *Ibid.*
6. Untermeyer, Louis. *Makers of the Modern World.* New York: Simon & Schuster, 1955.

9. Pär Lagerkvist (1951)

1. *European Authors.* New York: Scribner's & Sons, 1990.
2. Spector, Ronald Donald. *Pär Lagerkvist* (Twayne's World Author Series). London: 1973.
3. Sjöberg, Leif. *Pär Lagerkvist.* New York: Columbia Univ. Press, 1976.
4. Spector. *Pär Lagerkvist.*

11. Ernest Hemingway (1954)

1. *Conversations with Ernest Hemingway.* Jackson: University Press of Mississippi, 1986.
2. Hotchner, A.E. *Papa Hemingway.* New York: Random House, 1955.
3. *Ibid.*
4. *Ibid.*
5. Edmund Wilson on "In Our Time." *Contemporary Literary Criticism.* Vol. 34. Detroit: Gale, 1985.

13. John Steinbeck (1962)

1. Lisca, Peter. *Contemporary Literary Criticism.* Vol. 35. Detroit: Gale, 1986.

14. Mikhail Sholokhov (1965)

1. *Contemporary Authors.* Francis C. Locher, ed. Vol. 101. Detroit: Gale Research, 1981.

15. Miguel Ángel Asturias

1. Harss, Luis, and Barbara Dohmann. *Into the Mainstream: Conversations with Latin American Writers.* New York: Harper & Row, 1967.
2. *Seven Voices: Seven Latin American Writers Talk to Rita Gilbert.* New York: Knopf, 1973.
3. *Ibid.*
4. *Ibid.*
5. *Into the Mainstream.*
6. *Seven Voices.*
7. Callahan, Richard. *Miguel Ángel Asturias.* New York: Twayne, 1970.
8. *Into the Mainstream.*
9. *Ibid.*

18. Saul Bellow (1976)

1. "Distractions of a Fiction Writer." In *The Living Novel: A Symposium.* Granville Hicks, ed. New York: Macmillan, 1957.

19. Isaac Bashevis Singer (1978)

1. Kresh, Paul. *Isaac Bashevis Singer: The Magician of West 86th Street.* New York: Dial Press, 1979.

21. Gabriel García Márquez (1982)

1. Harss, Luis, and Barbara Dohmann. *Into the Mainstream.* New York: Harper & Row, 1966.
2. *García-Márquez: The Man and His Work.* Gene Bell-Villaoa. Chapel Hill: University of North Carolina Press, 1990.
3. *Ibid.*
4. *Ibid.*
5. *Ibid.*

23. Joseph Brodsky (1987)

1. Fromm, Erich. *Escape from Freedom.* New York: Avon, 1965.
2. "A Conversation." *National Review.* April 19, 1985.

24. Naguib Mahfouz (1988)

1. *Contemporary Literary Criticism.* Vol. 55. Detroit: Gale Research, 1988.

25. Nadine Gordimer (1991)

1. *Leopard II: Turning the Page: Essays, Memoirs, Fiction, Poetry, and One Sermon.* Christopher MacLehose, ed. Hammersmith, London: Harvill, 1993.

26. Derek Walcott (1922)

1. *Our Other Voices: Nine Poets Speaking.* John Wheatcroft, ed. Lewisburg, Pa.: Bucknell University Press, 1991.
2. Joseph Brodsky in *Contemporary Literary Criticism.* Vol. 76. Detroit, Mich.: Gale, 1993.
3. James Wieland in *Contemporary Literary Criticism.* Vol. 76. Detroit, Mich.: Gale, 1993.
4. Walcott, Derek. "The Caribbean: Culture or Mimicry?" *Journal of Interamerican Studies and World Affairs.* Vol. 16, no. 1, February 1974.

27. Toni Morrison (1993)

1. Reynolds, David. *Walt Whitman's America: A Cultural Biography.* New York: Knopf, 1995.

28. Kenzaburō Ōe (1994)

1. "Horizontal Lines to Other Worlds: An Interview with Kenzaburō Ōe." In *Poets and Writers,* vol. 24, issue 1, January-February, 1996.
2. "Japan Asks Why a Prophet Bothers." In *The New York Times,* November 6, 1994.

29. Dario Fo (1997)

1. Mitchell, Tony. *Dario Fo: People's Court Jester*. London: Methuen Theaterfile, 1984.
2. *Ibid.*
3. Nobel Lecture, 1997
4. Mitchell, Tony. *File on Fo*. London: Methuen Drama, 1989.
5. *Ibid.*
6. Twain, Mark. *A Connecticut Yankee in King Arthur's Court*. New York: C.L. Webster, 1889.
7. Twain, Mark. *Notebooks and Journals 1883–1891*. Berkeley and Los Angeles: University of California Press, 1979.

30. José Saramago (1998)

1. Borges, Jorge Luis. "An Examination of the Work of Herbert Quain." In *Ficciones*. New York: Grove Press, 1962.

Bibliography

Works listed by date of publication in English.

1. Bjørnstjerne Bjørnson (1903)

Ovind: A Story of Country Life in Norway. London: Simpkin, 1869.
The Fisher Girl. London: Trubner, 1871.
Arne: A Sketch of Norwegian Country Life. Boston: John Allyn, 1872; Boston: Houghton, Mifflin, 1881.
Life by the Fells and Fiords: A Norwegian Sketch-Book. London: Strahan, 1879.
A Happy Boy. Boston: Houghton, Mifflin, 1881; Boston: Macmillian, 1931.
Synnøve Solbakken. Boston: Houghton, Mifflin, 1881.
A Happy Boy and Later Sketches. New York: Doubleday-Page, 1882.
The Bridal March, and Other Stories. Boston: Houghton, Mifflin, 1882.
Captain Mansana and Other Stories by Bjørnstjerne Bjørnson. Boston: Houghton, Mifflin, 1882.
Magnhild. Boston: Houghton, Mifflin, 1883.
Synnøve Solbakken, Arne, and Early Tales and Sketches. Boston: Houghton, Mifflin, 1885.
Sigurd Slembe. New York: Houghton Mifflin, 1888
Pastor Sang. London: Longmans, Green, 1893.
Arne and the Fisher Lassie. London: G. Bell and Sons, 1894.
A Gauntlet. London: Longmans, Green, 1894.
Synnøve Solbakken. New York: Macmillan, 1895, 1912. As *Sunnyhill, a Norwegian Idyll.* New York: Macmillan, 1939.
The Bridal March and One Day. London: W. Heinemann, 1896.
Magnhild & Dust. London: W. Heinemann, 1897.
Bjørnson's Synnøve Solbakken. Chicago: J. Anderson, 1905; Minneapolis: The Lutheran Free Church, 1927.
Wise-Knut. New York: Brandu's, 1909.
When the New Wine Blooms. Boston: R.G. Badger, 1911.
Mary Queen of Scots. Chicago: Specialty Syndicate Press, 1912.
Plays by Bjørnstjerne Bjørnson (*The Gauntlet, Beyond Our Power, The New System*). New York: Scribner's, 1913. As *Three Plays.* New York: H. Fertig, 1989.
Plays, by Bjørnstjerne Bjørnson. Second series. (*Love and Geography, Beyond*

Human Might, Laboremus). New York: Scribner's, 1914; London: Duckworth, 1914.

Absalom's Hair & A Painful Memory. London: Heinemann, 1915.

Poems and Songs. New York: American-Scandinavian Foundation, 1915.

Arnljot Gelline. New York: American-Scandinavian Foundation, 1917.

Beyond Our Power. Volume 1 in *Modern Continental Plays*. New York: S.M. Tucker, 1929.

The Nobel Prize Treasury (*Synnøve's Song, Between the Battles, Over the Lofty Mountains, The Father*). Garden City, N.Y.: Doubleday, 1948.

Beyond Human Might. Volume 2 in *Nobel Prize Library*. New York: Gregory, 1971.

Three Comedies (*The Newly-Married Couple, Leonarda, A Gauntlet*). Westport: Greenwood Press, 1974.

Land of the Free: Bjørnstjerne Bjørnson's America Letters, 1880–1881. Northfield, Minn.: Norwegian-American Historical Association, 1978.

2. William B. Yeats (1923)

Poetry

Mosada: A Dramatic Poem. Sealy, Bryers & Walker, 1886; Shannon: Irish Univ. 1970; Ithaca, N.Y.: Cornell Univ. Press, 1987.

The Wanderings of Oisin and Other Poems. Kegan Paul, Trench, 1889; Ithaca, N.Y.: Cornell Univ. Press, 1994.

Poems. London: T. Fisher Unwin, 1895, 1899, 1901, 1912, 1927; London: A.H. Bullen, 1906; London: Macmillan, 1951, 1954.

The Wind Among the Reeds. London: E. Mathers, 1899.

In the Seven Woods: Being Poems Chiefly of the Irish Heroic Age. London: Macmillan, 1903; Shannon: Irish Univ. Press, 1970.

Sixteen Poems. Dundrum, Ire: The Dun Emer Press, 1905; Shannon: Irish Univ. Press, 1971.

The Poetical Works of William B. Yeats. London: Macmillan, 1906, 1912.

Poems: Second Series. London: A.H. Bullen, 1910.

The Green Helmet and Other Poems. Churchtown, Ire: Cuala Press, 1910; New York: Macmillan, 1912.

Poems Written in Discouragement, 1912–1913. Churchtown, Ire: Cuala Press, 1913; Shannon: Irish Univ. Press, 1971.

A Selection from the Poetry of W.B. Yeats. Bernard Tauschnitz, 1913.

A Selection from the Love Poetry of W.B. Yeats. Churchtown, Ire: Cuala Press, 1913.

Responsibilities. Churchtown, Ire: Cuala Press, 1914; London: Macmillan, 1916. As *Responsibilities: Poems and a Play*. Shannon: Irish Univ. Press, 1971.

Michael Robartes and the Dancer. Churchtown, Ire: Cuala Press, 1920; Shannon: Irish Univ. Press, 1971.

Selected Poems. London: Macmillan, 1921.

Later Poems. London: Macmillan, 1922, 1924.

Seven Poems and a Fragment. Churchtown, Ire: Cuala Press, 1922; Shannon: Irish Univ. Press, 1970.

The Cat and the Moon and Certain Poems. Dublin: Cuala Press, 1924; Shannon: Irish Univ. Press, 1970.

October Blast. Dublin: Cuala Press, 1927; Shannon: Irish Univ. Press, 1970.
The Tower. London: Macmillan, 1928.
The Winding Stair. New York: Fountain Press, 1929; Macmillan, 1933.
Words for Music Perhaps and Other Poems. Dublin: Cuala Press, 1932.
The Collected Poems. New York: Macmillan, 1933; Collier Books, 1989; Scribner Paperback Poetry, 1996.
Poems. Dublin: Cuala Press, 1935.
A Full Moon in March. New York: Macmillan, 1935.
New Poems. Dublin: Cuala Press, 1938; Shannon: Irish Univ. Press, 1970.
The Variorum Edition of the Poems of W.B. Yeats. New York: Macmillan, 1957, 1987.
Selected Poems and Three Plays. New York: Collier Books, 1966, 1973, 1986.
The Poems. New York: Macmillan, 1983, 1989; New York: Scribner, 1997.
Poems of W.B. Yeats: A New Selection. New York: Macmillan, 1984.
A Poet to His Beloved: The Early Love Poems of W.B. Yeats. New York: St. Martin's, 1985.
The Poems of W.B. Yeats. New York: Macmillan, 1989, 1990.
W.B. Yeats: Yeats' Poems. New York: Macmillan, 1990.
Selected Poems. Gramercy, 1992.
Early Poems. Dover, 1993.
Under the Moon: The Unpublished Early Poetry. New York: Scribner, 1995.

Plays

The Land of Heart's Desire. Chicago: Stone & Kimball, 1894; London: T.F. Unwin, 1922.
Cathleen ni Houlihan. London: A.H. Bullen, 1902.
Where There Is Nothing. A.H. Bullen, 1903; Washington, D.C.: Catholic Univ. Press of America, 1987.
On Baile's Strand. Dundrum, Ire: Dun Emer Press, 1903.
The King's Threshold. London: A.H. Bullen, 1904.
Deidre. London: A.H. Bullen, 1907.
The Shadowy Waters. London: A.H. Bullen, 1907.
The Unicorn from the Stars and Other Plays. London: Macmillan, 1908.
The Green Helmet: An Heroic Farce. Stratford-upon-Avon: Shakespeare Head Press, 1911.
The Countess Cathleen. London: T. Fischer Unwin, 1912.
The Hour Glass and Other Plays. Churchtown, Ire: Cuala Press, 1914; Shannon: Irish Univ. Press, 1970.
Two Plays for Dancers. Churchtown, Ire: Cuala Press, 1919; Shannon: Irish Univ. Press, 1970.
Four Plays for Dancers. London: Macmillan, 1921.
The Player Queen. London: Macmillan, 1922.
Sophocles' "King Oedipus." London: Macmillan, 1928.
Stories of Michael Robartes and His Friends. Dublin: Cuala Press, 1932.
The Collected Plays. London: Macmillan, 1934.
The Words Upon the Window Pane. Dublin: Cuala Press, 1934.
Wheels and Butterflies. London: Macmillan, 1934, 1935.
The King of the Great Clock Tower. Dublin: Cuala Press, 1934; London: Macmillan, 1935.

Nine One-Act Plays. London: Macmillan, 1937.
The Herne's Egg and Other Plays. London: Macmillan, 1938; Washington D.C.: Catholic Univ. Press of America, 1991.
Two Plays. Dublin: Cuala Press, 1939.
The Collected Plays of W.B. Yeats. London: Macmillan, 1952, 1953.
Eleven Plays of William Butler Yeats. New York: Macmillan, 1967.
The Death of Cuchulain. Ithaca, N.Y.: Cornell Univ. Press, 1981.
Purgatory. Ithaca, NY: Cornell Univ. Press, 1985.
The Herne's Egg. Washington D.C.: Catholic Univ. of America Press, 1991.

Poetry and Plays

The Countess Cathleen and Various Legends and Lyrics. Roberts Brothers, 1892.
The Wild Swans at Coole. Churchtown, Ire: Cuala Press, 1917; London: Macmillan, 1919.
"The Cat and the Moon" and Certain Poems. Dublin: Cuala Press, 1924.
Selected Poems and Two Plays. New York: Collier Books, 1931, 1935.
Last Poems and Two Plays. Dublin: Cuala Press, 1939.
Last Poems and Plays. London: Macmillan, 1940.
Selected Poems and Three Plays. Macmillan, 1987.

Fiction

John Sherman and Dhoya. New York: Cassell, 1891; Dublin: Lilliput Press, 1990.
The Secret Rose. Dodd, Mead, 1897. As *The Secret Rose: Stories by W.B. Yeats: A Variorum Edition.* Ithaca, N.Y.: Cornell Univ. Press, 1981; Macmillan, 1992.
The Tale of the Law and The Adoration of the Magi. London: Elkin Mathews, 1904.
Stories of Red Hanrahan. Dundrum, Ire: Dun Press, 1905; London: A.H. Bullen, 1913; Macmillan, 1914.
Mythologies. New York: Macmillan, 1959.

Autobiography

Reveries Over Childhood and Youth. Churchtown, Ire: Cuala Press, 1915; New York: Macmillan, 1916; Shannon: Irish Univ. Press, 1971. As *Autobiography Consisting of Reveries Over Childhood and Youth. The Trembling of the Veil and Dramatis Personae.* New York: Macmillan, 1944, 1953.
Four Years. Dundrum, Ire: Cuala Press, 1921; Shannon: Irish Univ. Press, 1971.
The Trembling of the Veil. London: T. Werner Laurie, 1922.
Autobiographies. London: Macmillan, 1926, 1927, 1955.
The Death of Synge and Other Passages from an Old Diary. Dublin: Cuala Press, 1928. As *Dramatis Personae.* Dublin: Cuala Press, 1935.
Pages from a Diary Written in Nineteen Hundred and Thirty. Dublin: Cuala Press, 1944.
The Autobiography of William Butler Yeats. New York: Collier Books, 1965, 1986.
Memoirs: Autobiography. New York: Macmillan, 1972, 1973.
The Collected Letters of W.B. Yeats. New York: Oxford Univ. Press, 1986.

Other

Ideas of Good and Evil. London: Macmillan, 1903; London: A.H. Bullen, 1907; New York: Russell and Russell, 1967.

Discoveries: A Volume of Essays. Dundrum, Ire: Dun Emer Press, 1907.
Synge and the Ireland of His Time. Dundrum, Ire: Cuala Press, 1911; Shannon Univ. Press, 1970.
The Cutting of an Agate. London: Macmillan, 1912, 1919.
Irish Fairy and Folk Tales. New York: Modern Library, 1918.
Per Amica Silentia Lunae (essays). London: Macmillan, 1918.
Essays. London: Macmillan, 1924.
The Bounty of Sweden. Dublin: Cuala Press, 1925.
A Packet for Ezra Pound. Dublin: Cuala Press, 1929.
Letters to the New Island. Cambridge, Mass.: Harvard Univ. Press, 1934; New York: Oxford University Press, 1970.
A Vision. London: Macmillan, 1937, 1938, 1978; New York: Collier Books, 1987.
Essays, 1931 to 1936. Dublin: Cuala Press, 1937; Shannon: Irish Univ. Press, 1971.
On the Boiler. Dublin: Cuala Press, 1939; Shannon: Irish Univ. Press, 1971.
If I Were Four-and-Twenty. Dublin: Cuala Press, 1940.
Essays and Introductions. New York: Macmillan, 1961.
Poetry and Ireland. Shannon: Irish Univ. Press, 1970.
Ah, Sweet Dancer. London: Macmillan, 1970.
Uncollected Prose by W.B. Yeats. New York: Columbia Univ. Press, vol. 1, 1970; vol. 2, 1976.
The Yeats Reader: A Portable Compendium of Poetry, Drama, and Prose. New York: Scribner Poetry, 1997.

3. Henri Bergson (1927)

Time and Free Will: An Essay on the Immediate Data of Consciousness. London: G. Allen, 1910, 1959; New York: Harper, 1960.
Creative Evolution. New York: Henry Holt, 1911; Modern Library, 1944; Lanham, Md.: University Press of America, 1983.
Laughter: An Essay on the Meaning of the Comic. New York: Macmillan, 1911. As *Comedy.* Garden City, N.Y.: Doubleday, 1956; Baltimore, Md.: Johns Hopkins Univ. Press, 1980.
An Introduction to Metaphysics. New York: G.P. Putnam, 1912; Indianapolis: Bobbs-Merrill, 1955.
Matter and Memory. New York: Macmillan, 1912; London: Allen & Unwin, Macmillan, 1950.
Dreams. London: T.F. Unwin, 1914. As *The World of Dreams.* New York: Philosophical Library, 1958.
Mind-Energy: Lectures and Essays. New York: H. Holt, 1920.
Two Sources of Morality & Religion. New York: H. Holt, 1935; Garden City, N.Y.: Doubleday, 1954; Notre Dame, Ind.: University of Notre Dame Press, 1977.
The Creative Mind. New York: Philosophical Library, 1946; Greenwood Press, 1968.
Selections from Bergson. New York: Appleton-Century-Crofts, 1949.
Duration and Simultaneity with Reference to Einstein's Theory. Indianapolis: Bobbs-Merrill, 1965.
"Aristotle's Concept of Place" in *Ancients and Moderns.* Washington, D.C.: Catholic University of America Press, 1970.
Philosophy of Poetry. New York: Philosophical Library, 1980.

4. Sinclair Lewis (1930)

Novels

Hike and the Airplane (juvenile, under pseudonym Tom Graham). New York: Stokes, 1912.

Our Mr. Wrenn: The Romantic Adventures of a Gentle Man. New York: Harper, 1914; Crowell, 1951.

The Trail of the Hawk: A Comedy of the Seriousness of Life. New York: Harper, 1915.

The Job: An American Novel. New York: Harper, 1917; Lincoln: Univ. of Nebraska Press, 1994.

The Innocents: A Story for Lovers. New York: Harper, 1917.

Free Air. New York: Harcourt, 1919; Scholarly Press, 1970.

Main Street: The Story of Carol Kennicott. New York: Harcourt, 1920, 1989; Library of America Press, 1992.

Babbitt. New York: Harcourt, 1922, 1989; Signet Classic, 1991.

Arrowsmith. New York: Harcourt, 1922, 1989; Cutchoque, N.Y.: Buccaneer, 1976, 1982; New York: New American Library, 1980. As *Martin Arrowsmith.* London: J. Cape, 1925, 1957.

Mantrap. New York: Grosset & Dunlap, 1926; London: J. Cape, 1926.

Elmer Gantry. New York: Harcourt, 1927; New York: New American Library, 1980.

The Man Who Knew Coolidge: Being the Soul of Lowell Schmaltz, Constructive and Nordic Citizen. New York: Harcourt, 1928.

Dodsworth. New York: Harcourt, 1929; London: J. Cape, 1929; New York: New American Library, 1972.

Ann Vickers. Garden City, N.Y.: Doubleday, Doran, 1933; Dell, 1962; Lincoln: Univ. of Nebraska Press, 1994.

Work of Art. Garden City, N.Y.: Doubleday, Doran, 1933; London: J. Cape, 1934; New York: Popular Library, 1962.

It Can't Happen Here. Garden City, N.Y.: Sun Dial Press, 1935; London: J. Cape, 1935; New York: New American Library, 1970.

The Prodigal Parents. New York: P.F. Collier, 1938.

Bethel Merriday. Garden City, N.Y.: Doubleday, Doran, 1940; New York: Popular Library, 1965.

Gideon Planish. New York: Random House, 1943; New York: Manor Books, 1974.

Cass Timberlane: A Novel of Husbands and Wives. New York: Random House, 1945; London: J. Cape, 1946; Cutchoque, N.Y.: Buccaneer, 1982.

Kingsblood Royal. New York: Random House, 1947; London: J. Cape, 1948.

The God-Seeker. New York: Random House, 1949; New York: Manor Books, 1975.

World So Wide. New York: Random House, 1951; New York: Manor Books, 1974.

Free Air. Lincoln: University of Nebraska Press, 1993.

If I Were Boss: The Early Business Stories of Sinclair Lewis. Carbondale: Southern Illinois Univ. Press, 1997.

Other

John Dos Passos' "Manhattan Transfer." New York: Harper, 1926; Folcroft, Pa.: Folcroft Library, 1977.

Cheap and Contented Labor: The Picture of a Southern Mill Town 1929. New York: United Textile Workers of America, 1929.

Selected Short Stories. New York: Doubleday, Doran, 1935, 1937. As *Selected Short Stories of Sinclair Lewis*. Chicago: I.R. Dee, 1990.

Jayhawker: A Play in Three Acts (with Lloyd Lewis). Garden City, N.Y.: Doubleday, Doran, 1935.

From Main Street to Stockholm: Letters of Sinclair Lewis, 1919–1930. New York: Harcourt, 1952.

The Man from Main Street: A Sinclair Lewis Reader: Selected Essays and Other Writings, 1904-1950. New York: Random House, 1953; London: Heinemann, 1954.

Moths in the Arc Light and The Cat of the Stars, Tokyo: Taishunkan, 1960.

Lewis at Zenith: A Three-Novel Omnibus: Main Street, Babbitt, Arrowsmith. New York: Harcourt, 1961.

I'm a Stranger Here Myself and Other Stories. New York: Dell, 1962.

Storm in the West (screenplay with Dore Schary). New York: Stein & Day, 1963

To Toby. St. Paul, Minn.: Macalester College, 1967.

5. Pearl S. Buck (1938)

East Wind: West Wind. New York: John Day, 1930, 1967.

The Good Earth. New York: John Day, 1931; Oxford Univ. Press, 1982.

Sons. New York: John Day, 1932; Pocket Books, 1975.

All Men Are Brothers (Shui-hu Chuan). New York: John Day, 1933; Crowell, 1968.

The First Wife, and Other Stories. New York: John Day, 1933; London: Methuen, 1963.

The Mother. New York: John Day, 1934, 1973.

A House Divided. New York: Reynal & Hitchcock, 1935, 1975.

House of Earth (contains *The Good Earth and Sons*). New York: Reynal & Hitchcock, 1935.

This Proud Heart. New York: Reynal & Hitchcock, 1938; New York: John Day, 1965.

The Patriot. New York: John Day, 1939.

Other Gods: An American Legend. New York: John Day, 1940; London: Severn House, 1976.

Today and Forever: Stories of China. New York: John Day, 1941.

Dragon Seed. New York: John Day, 1942; New York: Pocket Books, 1972.

China Sky. Philadelphia: Blakiston, 1942.

Twenty-seven Stories. Garden City, N.Y.: Sun Dial Press, 1943.

The Promise. New York: John Day, 1943.

The Story of Dragon Seed. New York: John Day, 1944.

The Townsman (under pseudonym John Sedges). New York: John Day, 1945; New York: Pocket Books, 1975. As *The Townsman: A "John Sedges" Novel*. New York: John Day, 1967.

Portrait of a Marriage. New York: John Day, 1945; New York: Pocket Books, 1975.

China Flight. Philadelphia: Triangle Books, 1945.

Pavilion of Women. New York: John Day, 1946; New York: Pocket Books, 1978.

Far and Near: Stories of Japan, China, and America. New York: John Day, 1947. As *Far and Near: Stories of East and West*. London: Methuen, 1949.

The Angry Wife (under pseudonym John Sedges). New York: John Day, 1947; New York: Pocket Books, 1975.

Peony. New York: John Day, 1948; New York: Pocket Books, 1978. As *The Bondmaid.* London: Methuen, 1949.

The Long Love (under pseudonym John Sedges). New York: John Day, 1949; New York: Pocket Books, 1975.

Kinfolk. New York: John Day, 1949; New York: Pocket Books, 1978.

God's Men. New York: John Day, 1952.

Bright Procession (under pseudonym John Sedges). New York: John Day, 1952.

Come, My Beloved. New York: John Day, 1953; New York: Pocket Books, 1975.

Voices in the House (under pseudonym John Sedges). New York: John Day, 1953; London: White Lion, 1977.

My Several Worlds. New York: John Day, 1954.

Imperial Woman. New York: John Day, 1956; London: White Lion, 1977.

Letter from Peking. New York: John Day, 1957; New York: Pocket Books, 1975.

American Triptych: Three "John Sedges" Novels. New York: John Day, 1958.

Command the Morning. New York: John Day, 1959; New York: Pocket Books, 1975.

Fourteen Stories. New York: John Day, 1961; New York: Pocket Books, 1976. As *with a Delicate Air, and Other Stories.* London: Methuen, 1962.

Satan Never Sleeps. New York: Pocket Books, 1962.

Hearts Come Home, and Other Stories. New York: Pocket Books, 1962.

The Living Reed. New York: John Day, 1963; New York: Pocket Books, 1979.

Stories of China. New York: John Day, 1964.

Escape at Midnight, and Other Stories. New York: Dragonfly Books, 1964.

Death in the Castle. New York: John Day, 1965.

The Water-Buffalo Children and The Dragon Fish. New York: Dell, 1966.

The Time Is Noon. New York: John Day, 1967.

The Beech Tree and Johnny Jack and His Beginnings. New York: Dell, 1967.

The New Year. New York: John Day, 1968.

The Three Daughters of Madame Liang. New York: John Day, 1969.

The Good Deed, and Other Stories of Asia, Past and Present. New York: John Day, 1969.

Mandala. New York: John Day, 1970.

The Chinese Story Teller. New York: John Day, 1971.

Once Upon a Christmas. New York: John Day, 1972.

The Goddess Abides. New York: John Day, 1972.

A Gift for the Children. New York: John Day, 1973.

Mrs. Starling's Problem. New York: John Day, 1973.

All Under Heaven. New York: John Day, 1973.

Words of Love (poetry). New York: John Day, 1974.

The Rainbow. New York: John Day, 1974.

East and West: Stories. New York: John Day, 1975.

Secrets of the Heart: Stories. New York: John Day, 1976.

The Lovers, and Other Stories. New York: John Day, 1976.

Mrs. Stoner and the Sea, and Other Works. New York: Ace Books, 1978.

The Woman Who Was Changed, and Other Stories. New York: Crowell, 1979.

The Old Demon. Mankato, Minn.: Creative Education, 1982.

Little Red. Mankato, Minn.: Creative Education, 1987.

Juvenile

The Young Revolutionist. New York: Friendship Press, 1932.
Stories for Little Children. New York: John Day, 1940.
The Chinese Children Next Door. New York: John Day, 1942.
The Water-Buffalo Children. New York: John Day, 1943.
The Dragon Fish. New York: John Day, 1944.
Ya Lan: Flying Boy of China. New York: John Day, 1945.
The Big Wave. Eau Claire, Wis.: 1948, 1961.
One Bright Day. New York: John Day, 1950. As *One Bright Day, and Other Stories for Children.* London: Methuen, 1952.
The Beech Tree. New York: John Day, 1954.
Johnny Jack and His Beginnings. New York: John Day, 1954.
Christmas Miniature. New York: John Day, 1957. As *The Christmas Mouse.* London: Methuen, 1958.
The Christmas Ghost. New York: John Day, 1960.
The Big Fight. New York: John Day, 1965.
The Little Fox in the Middle. New York: Collier Books, 1966.
Matthew, Mark, Luke, and John. New York: John Day, 1967.

6. T.S. Eliot (1948)

Poetry

Poems. London: Hogarth, 1919; New York: Knopf, 1920.
The Waste Land, and Other Poems. New York: Boni & Liveright, 1922; London: Faber & Faber, 1940; New York: Harcourt, 1955, 1988, 1997.
Poems, 1909–1925. London: Faber & Gwyer, 1925; Faber & Faber, 1932; New York: Harcourt, 1932.
Journey of the Magi. New York: Rudge, 1927.
A Song for Simeon. London: Faber & Faber, 1928.
Animula. London: Faber & Faber, 1929. Animula.
Ash-Wednesday. New York: Putnam, 1930; London: Faber & Faber, 1933.
Marina. London: Faber & Faber, 1930.
Triumphal March. London: Faber & Faber, 1931.
Words for Music. Bryn Mawr, Pa.: Bryn Mawr College Press, 1934.
Two Poems. Cambridge, U.K.: Cambridge Univ. Press, 1935.
Collected Poems, 1909–1935. New York: Harcourt, 1936, 1963, 1991.
Old Possum's Book of Practical Cats. New York: Harcourt, 1939, 1986; London: Faber & Faber, 1953, 1967.
East Coker. London: Faber & Faber, 1940.
Burnt Norton. London: Faber & Faber, 1941.
The Dry Salvages. London: Faber & Faber, 1941.
Later Poems, 1925–1935. London: Faber & Faber, 1941.
Little Giddings. London: Faber & Faber, 1943.
Four Quartets. New York: Harcourt, 1943, 1971.

A Practical Possum. Cambridge, Mass.: Harvard Printing Office, 1947.
Selected Poems. Hamondsworth, U.K.: Penguin, 1948; New York: Harcourt, 1967.
Poems Written in Early Youth. New York: Farrar, Straus & Giroux, 1967; London: Faber & Faber, 1967.
The Cultivation of Christmas Trees. London: Faber & Faber, 1954; New York: Farrar, Straus & Cudahay, 1956.
The Waste Land: A Facsimile and Transcript of the Original Drafts, Including the Annotations of Ezra Pound. New York: Harcourt, 1971.
Growltiger's Last Stand and Other Poems. New York: Farrar, Straus & Giroux, 1987; New York: Harcourt, 1987.

Plays

Sweeney Agonistes: Fragments of an Arisophanic Melodrama. London: Faber & Faber, 1932.
The Rock: A Pageant Play. Faber & Faber, 1934.
Murder in the Cathedral. New York: Harcourt, 1935, 1963; London: Faber & Faber, 1961.
The Family Reunion. New York: Harcourt, 1939, 1967.
The Cocktail Party. New York: Harcourt, 1950; London: Theater Book Club, 1951; London: Faber & Faber, 1974.
The Confidential Clerk. New York: Harcourt, 1954, 1982.
The Elder Statesman. New York: Farrar, Straus & Cudahay, 1959.

Anthologies

The Complete Poems and Plays, 1909–1950. New York: Harcourt, 1952, 1962, 1980.
Collected Plays. London: Faber & Faber, 1962.
The Complete Plays of T.S. Eliot. New York: Harcourt, 1967.

Prose

Ezra Pound, His Metric and Poetry. New York: Knopf, 1917.
Poetry in Prose: Three Essays by T.S. Eliot. London: The Poetry Bookshop, 1921.
The Sacred Wood: Essays on Poetry & Criticism. New York: Knopf, 1921; London: Faber & Faber, 1997.
Homage to John Dryden. London: L and Virginia Woolf, 1924; New York: Haskell House, 1966.
For Lancelot Andrewes: Essays on Style and Order. London: Faber & Gwyer, 1928; Garden City, N.Y.: Doubleday, 1929.
Selected Essays, 1917–1932. New York: Harcourt, 1932, 1950, 1951, 1964; London: Faber & Faber, 1951, 1972.
The Use of Poetry and the Use of Criticism. London: Faber & Faber, 1933, 1948, 1964.
Elizabethan Essays. London: Faber & Faber, 1934; New York: Haskell House, 1964.
After Strange Gods: A Primer of Modern Heresy. New York: Harcourt, 1934.
Essays, Ancient and Modern. New York: Harcourt, 1936.
The Idea of a Christian Society. London: Faber & Faber, 1939; New York: Harcourt, 1940.

Christianity and Culture. New York: Harcourt, 1940, 1949, 1960.
Points of View. London: Faber & Faber, 1941.
The Classics and the Man of Letters. Oxford, U.K.: Oxford Univ. Press, 1942.
The Music of Poetry. Glasgow: Jackson, 1942.
What Is a Classic? London: Faber & Faber, 1945.
From Poe to Vallery. New York: Harcourt, 1948.
Milton. Sewanee, Tenn.: Univ. of the South Press, 1948. As *Milton: Two Studies.* London: Faber & Faber, 1968.
Notes Towards the Definition of Culture. London: Faber & Faber, 1948, 1962; New York: Harcourt, 1949.
Poetry and Drama. Cambridge, Mass.: Harvard Univ. Press, 1951; London: Faber & Faber, 1951.
An Address to the Members of the London Library. London: Queen Anne Press, 1952.
The Modern Mind and Other Essays in Criticism. Tokyo: Nanun-Do, 1953.
Selected Prose. London: Penguin Books, 1953; Faber & Faber, 1975; New York: Farrar, Straus & Giroux, 1975.
Religious Drama: Mediaeval and Modern. New York: House of Books, 1954.
The Three Voices of Poetry. New York: Cambridge Univ. Press, 1954.
On Poetry and Poets. New York: Farrar, Straus & Cudahay, 1957.
Elizabethan Dramatists. London: Faber & Faber, 1963. As *Essays on Elizabethan Drama.* New York: Harcourt, 1956.
Knowledge and Experience in the Philosophy of F.H. Bradley. London: Faber & Faber, 1964.
The Aims of Poetic Drama. Folcroft, Pa.: Folcroft Library, 1971.
To Criticize the Critic & Other Writings. New York: Farrar, Straus & Giroux, 1965.
The Varieties of Metaphysical Poetry. London: Faber & Faber, 1993.

7. William Faulkner (1949)

Soldiers' Pay. New York: Boni & Liveright, 1926; New York: New American Library of World Literature, 1959.
Mosquitoes. New York: Boni and Liveright, 1927; New York: Garland Publishing, 1987; New York: Liveright, 1996.
Sartoris. New York: Harcourt, 1929; Nal-Dutton, 1983
The Sound and the Fury. London: J. Cape & H. Smith, 1929; New York: W.W. Norton, 1993.
As I Lay Dying. London: J. Cape & H. Smith, 1930; New York: Random House, 1964; New York: Vintage Books, 1987, 1991.
Sanctuary. London: J. Cape & H. Smith, 1931; New York: Random House, 1981; New York: Vintage Books, 1993.
Light in August. New York: H. Smith and R. Haas, 1932.
Pylon. New York: H. Smith and R. Haas, 1935; New York: Vintage Books, 1987.
Absalom, Absalom! New York: Random House, 1936; New York: Modern Library, 1993. As *William Faulkner's Absalom, Absalom!* New York: Garland, 1984.
The Unvanquished. New York: Random House, 1938, 1966; New York: Vintage Books, 1991.
The Wild Palms. New York: Random House, 1939.

The Hamlet. New York: Random House, 1940; New York: Vintage Books, 1991.
Go Down, Moses. New York: Random House, 1942; New York: Vintage Books, 1990; New York: Modern Library, 1990.
Intruder in the Dust. New York: Random House, 1948; New York: Vintage Books, 1991.
Requiem for a Nun. New York: Random House, 1951. As *Requiem for a Nun: A Play.* New York: Random House, 1959.
A Fable. New York: Random House, 1954; New York: Garland Publishing, 1987.
The Town. New York: Random House, 1957; New York: Vintage Books, 1961.
The Long Hot Summer. New York: New American Library, 1958.
Spotted Horses. New York: Random House, 1958.
The Mansion. New York: Random House, 1959
The Reivers: A Reminiscence. New York: Random House, 1962; New York: Macmillan Library Refernce, 1995.
Snopes: A Trilogy. Volume 1: *The Hamlet*; Volume 2: *The Town*; Volume 3: *The Mansion.* New York: Random House, 1965. As *Three Novels of the Snopes Family*, 1994.
Flags in the Dust. New York: Random House, 1973; New York: Garland Publishing, 1987.
Sanctuary & Requiem for a Nun. Mattituck, N.Y.: Amereon Ltd, 1976.
Mayday. Notre Dame, Ind: Univ. of Notre Dame Press, 1976, 1980.
Jealousy & Episode. Folcroft, Pa.: Folcroft Library Editions, 1977.
The Portable Faulkner. New York: Viking Penguin, 1977.
The Faulkner Reader. New York: Random House, 1989.
Novels, 1942–1954. New York: Library of America, 1994.
I Forget Thee, Jerusalem. New York: Random House, 1995.
The Marionettes. Ann Arbor, Mich.: Books on Demand, 1999.

Short Fiction

These Thirteen. London: J. Cape & H. Smith, 1931; New York: Garland, 1987.
Doctor Martino, and Other Stories. New York: H. Smith and R. Haas, 1934; New York: Garland, 1987.
Three Famous Short Novels (*Spotted Horses, Old Man, The Bear*). New York: Random House, 1942; New York: Vintage, 1978
Knight's Gambit. New York: Random House, 1949. As *Knight's Gambit: Six Stories.* London: Chatto & Windus, 1960; New York: Garland, 1987.
Collected Stories. New York: Random House, 1950. As *Collected Stories of William Faulkner.* New York: Vintage, 1977; New York: Demco Media, 1995.
Mirrors of Chartres Streets. Minneapolis: Faulkner Studies, 1953.
Big Woods. New York: Random House, 1955; Fowlerville, Mich.: Wilderness Adventure Press, 1996.
Jealousy, and Episode. Minneapolis: Faulkner Studies, 1955.
Uncle Willy, and Other Stories. London: Chatto & Windus, 1958.
Bear, Man and God: Seven Approaches to William Faulkner's "The Bear." New York: Random House, 1964.
The Wishing Tree (children's fiction). New York: Random House, 1964, 1967; New York: Garland, 1990.
The Marble Faun and A Green Bough. New York: Random House, 1965.
The Tall Men, and Other Stories. Kyoto: Apollonsha, 1965.

New Orleans Sketches. New York: Random House, 1968.
A Rose for Emily. New York: Merrill, 1970.
Fairchild's Story. London: Warren Editions, 1976.
Selected Short Stories of William Faulkner. New York: Modern Library, 1978, 1993.
Uncollected Stories of William Faulkner. New York: Random House, 1980; Vintage Books, 1997.
Helen. Oxford, Miss: Yoknapatawpha Press, 1981.
Vision in Spring. Arlington: Univ. of Texas Press, 1984.
Father Abraham. New York: Random House, 1984. As *Father Abraham, Nineteen Twenty-Six.* New York: Garland Publishing, 1987.
Country Lawyer and Other Stories for the Screen. Oxford: Univ. of Mississippi Press, 1987.
Unpublished Stories. New York: Garland Publishing, 1987.
Stallion Road. Jackson: Univ. Press of Mississippi, 1990.

Other

Art Today. New York: Harcourt Brace, 1963.
Each in Its Ordered Place: A Faulkner Collector's Notebook. Ann Arbor, Mich.: Ardis, 1975.
A Rose for Emily. Woodstock, Ill: Dramatic Publishing, 1983.
Tomorrow. New York: Dramatists Play Service, 1996.
Essays, Speeches and Public Letters. New York: Random House, 1996.

8. Bertrand Russell (1950)

German Social Democracy. London: Longmans, Green, 1896; New York: Simon & Schuster, 1966.
An Essay on the Foundations of Geometry. Cambridge, U.K.: Cambridge Univ. Press, 1897; New York: Dover, 1956.
A Critical Exposition of the Philosophy of Leibnitz. Cambridge, U.K.: Cambridge Univ. Press, Cambridge, 1900; London: Allen & Unwin, 1937.
Principia Mathematica (with Alfred North Whitehead). Vol. 1. Cambridge, U.K.: 1910, second edition, 1935; Vol. 2, 1912, second edition, 1927; Vol. 3, 1913, second edition, 1927; second in three volumes, 1950, 1962, 1976.
Philosophical Essays. London: Longmans, Green, 1910. As *Mysticism and Logic and Other Essays,* 1918. London: Allen & Unwin, 1966; New York: Simon & Schuster, 1967.
The Problems of Philosophy. New York: Henry Holt, 1912; Hackett, 1990.
Our Knowledge of the External World as a Field for Scientific Method in Philosophy. London: Open Court, 1914; London: Norton, 1929; London: Routledge & Kegan Paul, 1993.
The Philosophy of Bergson. London: Macmillan, 1914.
Why Men Fight. New York: Century, 1916; New York: Books for Libraries, 1971. As *Principles of Social Reconstruction.* London: Allen & Unwin, 1916, 1960.
The Policy of the Entente, 1904–1914. London: National Labor Press, 1916.
Justice in War-time. London: Open Court, 1916; London: Haskell, 1974.
Political Ideals. New York: Century, 1917; Simon & Schuster, 1964.

Roads to Freedom: Socialism, Anarchism, and Syndicalism. London: Allen & Unwin, 1918, 1919. As *Proposed Roads to Freedom: Socialism, Anarchism, and Syndicalism.* New York: H. Holt, 1919; New York: Barnes & Noble, 1966.
Introduction to Mathematical Philosophy. New York: Macmillan, 1919; New York: Simon & Schuster, 1971; London: Routledge & Kegan Paul, 1993.
Bolshevism: Practice and Theory. New York: Harcourt, 1920; Simon & Schuster, 1964. As *The Practice and Theory of Bolshevism.* London: Allen & Unwin, 1920, 1949.
The Analysis of Mind. New York: Macmillan, 1921; New York: Humanities Press, 1958.
The Problem of China. New York: Century, 1922.
A Free Man's Worship. Portland, Maine: T.B. Mosher, 1923.
The ABC of Atoms. New York: Dutton, 1923; London: Routledge & Kegan Paul, 1932.
Icarus; Or, the Future of Science. New York: Dutton, 1924.
How to Be Free and Happy. New York: Rand School of Social Science, 1924.
The ABC of Relativity. New York: Harper & Brothers, 1925; London: Allen & Unwin, 1969.
What I Believe. New York: Dutton, 1925.
Education and the Good Life. New York: Boni & Liveright, 1926, 1970. As *On Education Especially in Early Childhood.* London: Allen & Unwin, 1926.
Why I Am Not a Christian. New York: Watts, 1927; Freethought Press Association, 1940.
The Analysis of Matter. New York: Harcourt, 1927; Dover, 1954.
Philosophy. New York: Norton, 1927. As *An Outline of Philosophy.* London: Allen & Unwin, 1927; Singapore: World Publishing, 1961.
Selected Papers of Bertrand Russell. New York: Modern Library, 1927.
Skeptical Essays. New York: Norton, 1928; New York Barnes & Noble, 1961.
Marriage and Morals. New York: Liveright, 1929, 1970; London: Unwin Books, 1961.
A Liberal View of Divorce. Girard, Kans.: Haldeman-Julius, 1929.
The Conquest of Happiness. New York: Book League of America, 1930; New York: Liveright, 1971.
Has Religion Made Useful Contributions to Civilization? Girard, Kans.: Haldeman-Julius, 1930.
The Scientific Outlook. New York: Norton, 1931.
Education and the Modern World. New York: Norton, 1932. As *Education and the Social Order.* London: Allen & Unwin, 1932.
Freedom Versus Organization, 1814–1914. New York: Norton, 1934, 1962. As *Freedom and Organization, 1814–1914.* London: Allen & Unwin, 1934.
In Praise of Idleness and Other Essays. New York: Norton, 1935; New York: Simon & Schuster, 1972.
Religion and Science. New York: H. Holt, 1935; New York: Oxford University Press, 1961.
Determinism and Physics (lecture). Newcastle upon Tyne: The Librarian, Armstrong College, 1936.
Which Way to Peace? London: M. Joseph, 1936.
Power: A Social Analysis. New York: Norton, 1938, 1969.
An Inquiry Into Meaning and Truth. New York: Norton, 1940; New York: Allen & Unwin, 1966.
Let the People Think: A Selection of Essays. London: Watts, 1941; London: Rationalist Press Association, 1961.

How to Become a Philosopher: The Art of Rational Conjecture. Girard, Kans.: Haldeman-Julius, 1942.
How to Become a Logician: The Art of Drawing Inferences. Girard, Kans.: Haldeman-Julius, 1942.
How To Become a Mathematician: The Art of Reckoning. Girard, Kans.: Haldeman-Julius, 1942.
An Outline of Intellectual Rubbish: A Hilarious Catalogue of Organized and Individual Stupidity. Girard, Kans.: Haldeman-Julius, 1943.
How to Read and Understand History. Girard, Kans.: Haldeman-Julius, 1943.
A History of Western Philosophy: Its Connection with Political and Social Circumstances from the Earliest Times to the Present Day. New York: Simon & Schuster, 1945; London: Allen & Unwin, 1961.
Physics and Experience (lecture). Cambridge, U.K.: Cambridge Univ. Press, 1946.
Ideas That Have Harmed Mankind. Girard, Kans.: Haldeman-Julius, 1946.
Ideas That Have Helped Mankind. Girard, Kans.: Haldeman-Julius, 1946.
Is Materialism Bankrupt? Girard, Kans.: Haldeman-Julius, 1946.
Is Science Superstitious? Girard, Kans.: Haldeman-Julis, 1946.
Philosophy and Politics. Cambridge, U.K.: Cambridge Univ. Press, 1947.
Human Knowledge: Its Scope and Limits. New York: Simon & Schuster, 1948.
Authority and the Individual. New York: Simon & Schuster, 1949; Boston: Beacon Press, 1963; London: Unwin Paperbacks, 1977.
Unpopular Essays. London: Allen & Unwin, 1950; Simon & Schuster, 1951, 1966.
New Hopes for a Changing World. New York: Simon & Schuster, 1951.
The Wit and Wisdom of Bertrand Russell. Boston: Beacon, 1951.
The Impact of Science on Society. New York: Columbia University Press, 1952; AMS Press, 1968.
The Bertrand Russell Dictionary of Mind, Matter, and Morals. New York: Philosophical Library, 1952.
How Near Is War? London: D. Ridgway, 1952.
What Is Freedom? London: Batchworth Press, 1952.
What Is Democracy? London: Batchworth Press, 1953.
History as Art. Hand and Flower Press, 1954
Human Society in Ethics and Politics. London: Allen & Unwin, 1954; New York: Simon & Schuster, 1955; New York: New American Library, 1962.
John Stuart Mill. Oxford, U.K.: Oxford Univ. Press, 1956.
Logic and Knowledge: Essays, 1901–1950. New York: Macmillan, 1956.
Why I Am Not a Christian and Other Essays on Religion and Related Subjects. New York: Simon & Schuster, 1957, 1963.
Understanding History and Other Essays. New York: Philosophical Library, 1957.
The Good Citizen's Alphabet. New York: Philosophical Library, 1958.
The Will to Doubt. New York: Philosophical Library, 1958.
Wisdom of the West: A Historical Survey of Western Philosophy in Its Social and Political Setting. New York: Doubleday, 1959; New York: Fawcett, 1966.
The Philosophy of Logical Atomism (lectures). Minneapolis: Univ. of Minnesota Press, 1959.
My Philosophical Development. New York: Simon & Schuster, 1959.
The Future of Science. New York: Philosophical Library, 1959.
Common Sense and Nuclear Warfare. New York: Simon & Schuster, 1959; London: AMS Press, 1968.
Bertrand Russell Speaks His Mind. Singapore: World Publishing, 1960.

On Education. London: Allen & Unwin, 1960.
The Basic Writings of Bertrand Russell, 1903–1959. New York: Simon & Schuster, 1961.
Education and Character. New York: Philosophical Library, 1961.
Fact and Fiction. London: Allen & Unwin, 1961; New York: Simon & Schuster, 1962.
Has Man a Future? New York: Simon & Schuster, 1962.
Unarmed Victory. New York: Simon & Schuster, 1963.
War and Atrocity in Vietnam. London: Bertrand Russell Peace Foundation, 1965.
On the Philosophy of Science. New York: Bobbs-Merrill, 1965.
Appeal to the American Conscience. London: Bertrand Russell Peace Foundation, 1966.
War Crimes in Vietnam. Monthly Review Press, 1967.
The Art of Philosophizing and Other Essays. New York: Philosophical Library, 1968.
The Good Citizens Alphabet: And, History of the World in Epitome. London: Gaberbocchus Press, 1970.
Atheism: Collected Essays, 1943–1949. New York: Arno, 1972.
My Own Philosophy. Hamilton, Ont.: McMaster Univ. Press, 1972.
Russell's Logical Atomism. London: Collins, 1972.
Essays in Analysis. New York: Simon & Schuster, 1973.
Theory of Knowledge: The 1913 Manuscript. London: Allen & Unwin, 1984.
Philosophical Papers, 1896–1899. London: Unwin Hyman, 1990.
Logical and Philosophical Papers, 1909–1913. London: Routledge & Kegan Paul, 1992.
The Selected Papers of Bertrand Russell. New York: Houghton Mifflin, 1992.
The Quotable Bertrand Russell. Buffalo, N.Y.: Prometheus Books, 1993.
Foundations of Logic: 1903–1905. London: Routledge & Kegan Paul, 1993.
Principles of Mathematics 1900–1902. London: Routledge & Kegan Paul, 1993.

Other

Satan in the Suburbs and Other Stories. New York: Simon & Schuster, 1953.
Portraits from Memory and Other Essays. New York: Simon & Schuster, 1956.
Bertrand Russell's Best: Silhouettes in Satire. London: Allen & Unwin, 1958; London: New American Library, 1961.
Essays in Skepticism. New York: Philosophical Library, 1963.
The Autobiography of Bertrand Russell, Vol. 1 1872–1914. Boston: Little, Brown, 1967. *Vol. 2 1914–1944.* Boston: Little, Brown, 1968. *Vol. 3 1944–1969.* New York: Simon & Schuster, 1969.
The Collected Stories of Bertrand Russell. New York: Simon & Schuster, 1972.
Mortals and Others: Bertrand Russell's American Essays, 1931–1935. London: Allen & Unwin, 1975.

9. Pär Lagerkvist (1951)

Novels

The Eternal Smile. London: Gordon Fraser, 1934. As *The Eternal Smile and Other Stories.* London: Chato & Windus; New York: Random House, 1954.
Guest of Reality. London: J. Cape, 1936; London: Quartet, 1989.

The Dwarf. New York: Hill & Wang, 1945; New York: Random House, 1989.
Barabbas. Stockholm: Bonnier, 1951; New York: Random, 1951, 1968; New York: Bantam, 1972.
The Sibyl. London: Chato & Windus, 1958; New York: Random, 1958, 1963.
The Death of Ahasuerus. New York: Random, 1962.
Pilgrim at Sea. New York: Random, 1964.
The Holy Land. New York: Random, 1966; London: Chato & Windus, 1966.
Mariamne. Stockholm: Bonnier, 1967. As *Herod and Mariamne*, New York: Knopf, 1968; London: Chato & Windus, 1968.
Five Early Works. Roy Arthur Swanson, trans. Lewiston, N.Y.: St. David's Univ. Press, 1988.

Poetry

20th Century Scandinavian Poetry. Martin Allwood, ed. Mullsjo, Sweden: 1950.
Seven Swedish Poets. Fredric Fleischer, trans. Stockholm: B. Cavefors, 1963.
Eveningland (Aftonland). W.H. Auden and Leif Sjoberg, trans. Detroit: Wayne State Univ. Press, 1975.

Plays

Let Man Live. In *Scandinavian Plays of the Twentieth Century*. Princeton, N.J.: Princeton Univ. Press, 1951.
Midsummer Dream in the Workhouse. Alan Blair, trans. London: W. Hodge, 1953.
Pär Lagerkvist: Modern Theater: Seven Plays and an Essay (*The Difficult Hour I, II, III, The Secret of Heaven, The King, The Hangman, The Philosopher's Stone*). Lincoln: Univ. of Nebraska Press, 1966.
The Man Who Lived His Life Over. In *Five Modern Scandinavian Plays*. New York: Twayne, 1971.

Collections

The Eternal Smile: Three Stories ("The Eternal Smile," "Guest of Reality," "The Executioner"). London: Gordon Fraser, 1934. As *The Eternal Smile and Other Stories.* New York: Random House, 1954; London: Chatto & Windus, 1971.
The Marriage Feast ("The Marriage Feast," "Father and I," "The Adventure," "A Hero's Death," "The Venerated Bones," "Savior John," "The Experimental World," "The Lift That Went Down," "Love and Death," "The Basement," "The Evil Angel," "The Princess and All the Kingdom," "Paradise," "The Children's Campaign," "God's Little Traveling Salesman," "The Masquerade of Souls," "The Myth of Mankind," "On the Scales of Osiris," "The Strange Country"). London: Chato & Windus, 1955; New York: Hill & Wang, 1973.
Modern Theater: Seven Plays and an Essay. Lincoln: Univ. of Nebraska Press, 1966.

10. François Mauriac (1952)

The Kiss to the Leper. London: Heinemann, 1923. As *Kiss for the Leper.* London: Eyre & Spottiswoode, 1950. As *A Kiss for the Leper.* New York: Farrar, Straus & Giroux, 1968.

Thérèse. Boni & Liveright, 1928. As *Thérèse: A Portait in Four Parts.* New York: Farrar, Straus & Giroux, 1947, 1974; New York: Viking Penguin, 1995, 1999.

The Desert of Love. New York: Covici, Friede, 1929; London: Eyre & Spottiswoode, 1949; New York: Pellegrini & Cudahy, 1951; New York: Carrol & Graf, 1989.

Destinies. New York: Covici, Friede, 1929. As *Lines of Life.* New York: Farrar, Straus, 1957.

The Family. New York: Covici, Friede, 1930.

Vipers' Tangle. New York: Sheed & Ward, 1933. As *The Knot of Vipers.* London: Eyre & Spottiswoode, 1951; New York: Carrol & Graf, 1987.

A Woman of the Pharisees. New York; Farrar, Straus & Young, 1946; New York: Noonday Press, 1964; New York: Carrol & Graf, 1988.

The Unknown Sea. New York: Henry Holt, 1948; New York: Heath, 1953.

That Which I Lost and The Dark Angels. London: Eyre & Spottiswoode, 1951.

The Weakling and The Enemy. New York: Pellegrini & Cudahy, 1952.

The Little Misery. London: Eyre & Spottiswoode, 1952.

The Loved and the Unloved. New York: Pellegrini & Cudahy, 1952; New York: Noonday Press, 1967; London: Eyre & Spottiswoode, 1971.

The Frontenac Mystery. New York: Eyre & Spottiswoode, 1952, 1971. As *The Frontenacs.* New York: Farrar, Straus & Cudahy, 1961.

The Mask of Innocence. New York: Farrar, Straus & Young, 1953.

The River of Fire. London: Eyre & Spottiswoode, 1954.

Flesh and Blood. New York: Farrar, Straus, 1955; New York: Carroll & Graf, 1989.

The Lamb. New York: Farrar, Straus & Cudahy, 1955.

Questions of Precedence. London: Eyre & Spottiswoode, 1958; New York: Farrar, Straus, 1959.

The Stuff of Youth. London: Eyre & Spottiswoode, 1960.

Young Man in Chains. New York: Farrar, Straus, 1963.

The Holy Terror (juvenile). London: J. Cape, 1964; Funk, 1967.

Genetrix. Englewood Cliffs, N.J.: Prentice-Hall, 1966.

Five Novels. London: Eyre & Spottiswoode, 1969.

A Mauriac Reader. Farrar, Straus, 1968.

Maltaverne. New York: Farrar, Straus, 1970; London: University of London Press, 1972.

Plays

Asmodée: Or The Intruder (play). London: Secker & Warburg, 1939.

Nonfiction

Maundy Thursday. London: Burns & Oats, 1932.

God and Mammon. New York: Sheed & Ward, 1936.

Life of Jesus. New York: Longmans, Green, 1937.

Living Thoughts of Pascal. London: Cassell, 1940.

The Eucharist: The Mystery of Holy Thursday. New York: D. McKay, 1944; Manchester, N.H.: Sophia Institute Press, 1991.

Saint Margaret of Cortona. New York: Philosophical Library, 1948. As *Margaret of Cortona.* London: Burns & Oates, 1948.

Proust's Way. New York: Philosophical Library, 1950.
Men I Hold Great. New York: Philosophical Library, 1951. As *Great Men.* London: Rockliff, 1952; Kennikat, 1971.
The Stumbling Block. New York: Philosophical Library, 1952.
Letters on Art and Literature. New York: Philosophical Library, 1953; New York: Kennikat, 1970.
Words of Faith. New York: Philosophical Library, 1955.
The Son of Man. Cleveland: World, 1960.
Mémoires intérieures. London: Eyre & Spottiswoode, 1960, 1961.
Second Thoughts: Reflections on Literature and on Life. Cleveland: World, 1961; Philadelphia: Ayer, 1977.
Cain, Where Is Your Brother? New York: Coward-McCann, 1962.
What I Believe. New York: Farrar, Straus, 1963.
Anguish and Joy of the Christian Life. Wilkes-Barre, Pa.: Dimension, 1964; Notre Dame, Ind.: Notre Dame Univ. Press, 1967.
De Gaulle. Garden City, N.Y.: Doubleday, 1966.
The Inner Presence: Recollections of My Spiritual Life. New York: Bobbs-Merrill, 1968.
More Reflections from the Soul. Lewiston, N.Y.: Edwin Mellen Press, 1992.

11. Ernest Hemingway (1954)

Novels

The Torrents of Spring: A Romantic Novel in Honor of the Passing of a Great Race (paradox). New York: Scribner, 1926, 1972; New York: Macmillan, 1987; London: J. Cape, 1933, 1964.
The Sun Also Rises. New York: Scribner, 1926, 1970; New York: Collier Books, 1986. As *Fiesta.* London: J. Cape, 1959.
A Farewell to Arms. New York: Scribner, 1929, 1949, 1967; New York: Collier Books, 1986; New York: Scribner Paperback, 1995.
Winner Take Nothing. New York: Scribner, 1933, 1961, 1970; London: J. Cape, 1934.
To Have and Have Not. New York: Scribner, 1937; New York: Simon & Schuster, 1996; London: J. Cape, 1970.
For Whom the Bell Tolls. New York: Scribner, 1940, 1960; Collier Books, 1987.
Across the River and Into the Trees. New York: Scribner, 1950, 1987; New York: London: J. Cape, 1950, 1966.
The Old Man and the Sea. New York: Scribner, 1952, 1980; New York: Limited Editions, 1990; London: J. Cape, 1952, 1955 .
Islands in the Stream. New York: Scribner, 1970; New York: Bantam Books, 1972, London: Collins, 1970.
The Garden of Eden. New York: Scribner, 1986.
True at First Light. New York: Simon & Schuster, 1999.

Short Fiction

Three Stories and Ten Poems. Paris: Contact, 1923.
In Our Time. Paris: Three Mountain Press, 1924; London: J. Cape, 1926; New York: Scribner, 1925, 1930, 1970; New York: Collier Books, 1980.

Men Without Women. New York: Scribner, 1927, 1955; London: J. Cape, 1928.
Fifth Column and the First Forty-nine Stories. New York: Scribner, 1938. As *First Forty-nine Stories.* London: J. Cape, 1962. Play published separately as *The Fifth Column: A Play in Three Acts.* New York: Scribner, 1940; London: J. Cape, 1968.
The Short Stories of Ernest Hemingway. New York: Scribner, 1938.
Men at War. New York: Crown, 1942; New York: Berkeley, 1958.
The First Forty-nine Stories. London: J. Cape, 1944.
The Snows of Kilimanjaro and Other Stories. New York: Scribner, 1961, 1964.
The Short Happy Life of Francis Macomber and Other Stories. New York: Penguin, 1963.
Hemingway's African Stories: The Stories, Their Sources, Their Critics. John Howell, ed. New York: Scribner, 1969.
The Nick Adams Stories. New York, Scribner, 1972.
Along With Youth (biography). New York: Oxford Univ. Press, 1985.
The Complete Short Stories of Ernest Hemingway: The Finca Vigia Edition. New York: Scribner, 1987.
The Short Stories. New York: Simon & Schuster, 1995.
The Collected Stories. London: Everyman's Library, 1995.

Other

Death in the Afternoon. New York: Scribner, 1932, 1960.
Green Hills of Africa. New York: Scribner, 1935; London: J. Cape, 1936.
The Spanish War (monograph). London: Fact, 1938.
The Spanish Earth. Cleveland: J.B. Savage, 1938.
Voyage to Victory. New York: Crowell-Collier, 1944.
The Portable Hemingway. New York: Viking, 1944.
The Essential Hemingway. London: J. Cape, 1947, 1964.
The Hemingway Reader. New York: Scribner, 1953.
The Wild Years. New York: Dell, 1962.
A Moveable Feast. New York: Scribner, 1964, 1996; London: J. Cape, 1964.
The Suppressed Poems of Ernest Hemingway. New York: Book Awards, 1964.
The Collected Poems of Ernest Hemingway. New York: Gordon Press, 1972.
The Enduring Hemingway. New York: Scribner, 1974.
Eighty-Eight Poems. New York: Harcourt, 1979.
Ernest Hemingway, Selected Letters, 1917–1961. New York: Scribner, 1981.
Ernest Hemingway on Writing. New York: Scribner, 1984.
The Dangerous Summer. New York: Scribner, 1985; New York: Simon & Schuster, 1997.
Conversations with Ernest Hemingway. Jackson: Univ. Press of Mississippi, 1986.
Complete Poems. Lincoln: University of Nebraska Press, 1992.
By-Line: Ernest Hemingway. New York: Scribner, 1967; New York: Simon & Schuster, 1998.
Dateline Toronto: The Complete Toronto Star Dispatches, 1920–1924. New York: Scribner, 1985.

12. Albert Camus (1957)

The Outsider. Hamondsworth, U.K.: Penguin, 1942. As *The Fall.* New York: Knopf, 1946, 1957; New York: Vintage Books, 1991.

The Stranger. New York: Knopf, 1946, 1988; New York: Barron's, 1985.

Caligula and Cross Purpose. London: H. Hamilton, 1947.

The Plague. New York: Knopf, 1948; New York: Vintage Books, 1972; London: H. Hamilton, 1948.

The Rebel: An Essay on Man in Revolt. London: H. Hamilton, 1953; New York: Knopf, 1956; New York: Random House, 1991.

The Myth of Sisyphus and Other Essays. New York: Knopf, 1955; Random House, 1991; London: H. Hamilton, 1955.

Caligula and Three Other Plays (Misunderstanding, State of Siege, Just Assassins). New York: Knopf, 1958, 1966.

Exile and the Kingdom. New York: Knopf, 1958, 1977; New York. Random House, 1965, 1991; London: H. Hamilton, 1958.

The Possessed, a Play in Three Parts. New York: Knopf: 1960.

Resistance, Rebellion and Death. New York: Knopf, 1960; New York: Random House, 1974; London: H. Hamilton, 1961.

Neither Victims nor Executioners. New York: Liberation, 1960; Berkeley, Calif.: World Without War Council, 1968.

Collected Fiction (The Outsider, The Plague, The Fall, Exile and the Kingdom). London: H. Hamilton, 1960.

Caligula: A Drama in Two Acts. New York: French, 1961; London: Methuen, 1973.

State of Seige. New York: Random House, 1962.

The Just Assassins. New York: Random House, 1962.

Notebooks 1935–1941. London: H. Hamilton, 1963; New York: Modern Library, 1965; New York: Marlowe, 1994. As *Notebooks.* New York: Knopf, 1963; New York: Marlowe, 1998; Eastford, Conn.: Shooting Star, 1991.

Notebooks 1942–1951. New York: Knopf, 1965; Eastford, Conn.: Shooting Star, 1991.

Lyrical and Critical Essays. London: H. Hamilton, 1967; New York: Random House, 1970.

That Day in Budapest, October 23, 1956. New York: Funk & Wagnalls, 1969.

A Happy Death. New York: Knopf, 1972; New York: Vintage Books, 1973, 1995; London: H. Hamilton, 1972.

Youthful Writings. New York: Knopf, 1976; New York: Marlowe, 1994.

Albert Camus, the Essential Writings. New York: Harper Colophon Books, 1979.

The Guest. New York: Random House, 1982.

American Journals. New York: Paragon House, 1987; Eastford, Conn.: Shooting Star, 1994.

Between Hell and Reason: Essays from the Resistance Newspaper, "Combat." Middletown, Conn.: Wesleyan Univ. Press, 1991.

The First Man. New York: Knopf, 1995.

Tricks. London: Serpent's Tail, 1996.

13. John Steinbeck (1962)

Cup of Gold: A Life of Henry Morgan, Buccaneer. New York: Robert McBride, 1929; New York: Bantam Books, 1967.
The Pastures of Heaven. New York: Viking, 1932.
To a God Unknown. New York: Viking, 1933; New York: Penguin Books, 1976, 1995.
Tortilla Flat. New York: Viking, 1935, 1947; New York: Penguin, 1986, 1997.
In Dubious Battle. New York: Viking, 1936.
Of Mice and Men. New York: Viking, 1937, 1963; New York: Penguin Books, 1993.
The Red Pony. New York: Covici, Friede, 1937; New York: Viking, 1989.
The Grapes of Wrath. New York: Viking, 1939; New York: Penguin Books, 1992; London: David Campbell, 1993.
Sea of Cortez. New York: Viking, 1941. As *The Log from the Sea of Cortez.* New York: Penguin, 1986.
The Forgotten Village. New York: Viking, 1941.
The Moon Is Down. New York: Viking, 1942.
Cannery Row. New York: Viking, 1945, 1966.
The Portable Steinbeck. New York: Viking, 1946, 1971.
The Wayward Bus. New York: Viking, 1947.
The Pearl. New York: Viking, 1947, 1986.
Burning Bright: A Play in Story Form. New York: Viking, 1950.
East of Eden. New York: Viking, 1952; New York: Penguin Books, 1992.
Sweet Thursday. New York: Viking, 1954.
The Short Reign of Pippin IV: A Fabrication. New York: Viking, 1957.
The Winter of Our Discontent. New York: Viking, 1961.
Zapata: The Little Tiger. London: Heinemann, 1991.
Novels and Stories, 1932–1937. New York: Library of America, 1994.
Grand Babylon Hotel. New York: Viking Penguin, 1998.

Short Stories

Saint Katy the Virgin. New York: Covici, Friede, 1936.
Nothing So Monstrous. New York: Pynson Printers, 1936; Folcroft, Pa.: Folcroft Library, 1977.
The Long Valley. New York: Viking, 1938, 1964. As *Thirteen Great Short Stories from the Long Valley.* New York: Avon, 1943. As *Fourteen Great Short Stories from the Long Valley.* New York: Avon, 1947.
How Edith McGillicuddy Met R. L. S. Cleveland: Rowfant Club, 1943.
Short Novels: Tortilla Flat, The Red Pony, Of Mice and Men, The Moon Is Down, Cannery Row, The Pearl. New York: Viking, 1953, 1963.
The Acts of King Arthur and His Noble Knights. New York; Farrar, Straus & Giroux, 1976; New York: Ballantine, 1992; London: Heinemann, 1976.
The Grapes of Wrath and Other Writings. New York: Library of America, 1996.

Dramatizations

The Leader of the People. Luelle McMahon, dramatist. Chicago: Dramatic, 1952.

John Steinbeck's Molly Morgan. Reginald Lawrence, dramatist. Chicago: Dramatic, 1961.
Of Mice and Men: Play in Three Acts. New York: Dramatists Play Service, 1964.
John Steinbeck's The Pearl. William Frost, dramatist. Chicago: Dramatic, 1975.
Viva Zapata! The Original Screenplay. New York: Viking, 1975.
John Steinbeck's Grapes of Wrath. Frank Galati, dramatist. New York: Dramatists Play Service, 1991.

Other

A Letter to the Friends of Democracy. Stamford, Conn.: Overbrook Press, 1940.
Steinbeck. New York: Viking, 1943. As *The Portable Steinbeck.* New York: Viking 1946, 1971. As *Steinbeck Omnibus.* New York: Oxford University Press, 1946.
A Russian Journal. New York: Viking, 1948.
Once There Was a War. New York: Viking, 1958, 1977.
Travels with Charley: In Search of America. New York: Viking, 1962; New York: Penguin, 1986.
In Touch. New York: Knopf, 1969.
Journal of a Novel: The East of Eden Letters. New York: Viking, 1969.
Steinbeck: A Life in Letters. New York: Viking, 1975.
The Collected Poems of Amnesia Glasscock (pseudonym). South San Francisco: Manroot Books, 1976.
Conversations with John Steinbeck: Jackson: Univ. Press of Mississippi, 1988.
The Harvest Gypsies: On the Road to the Grapes of Wrath. Berkeley, Calif.: Heyday Books, 1988.
Working Days: The Journals of the Grapes of Wrath. New York: Viking, 1989.

14. Mikhail Sholokhov (1965)

And Quiet Flows the Don. London: Putnam, 1934; New York: Knopf, 1959; New York: Random House, 1965.
Virgin Soil Upturned. London: Putnam, 1935.
Seeds of Tomorrow. New York: Knopf, 1935.
The Don Flows Home to the Sea. London: Putnam, 1940; New York: Random House, 1989.
The Silent Don. New York: Knopf, 1941, 1946.
The Science of Hatred. New York: New Age, 1943.
Harvest on the Don. London: Putnam, 1960.
Tales from The Don. London: Putnam, 1961. As *Tales of the Don.* New York: Knopf, 1962.
The Fate of Man. Moscow: Progress, 1962.
Fierce and Gentle Warriors: Three Stories. Garden City, N.Y.: Doubleday, 1967.

15. Miguel Ángel Asturias (1967)

El Señor Presidente. New York: Atheneum, 1963, 1972; Prospect Heights, Ill: Waveland, 1997.
The Cyclone. London: Owen, 1967. As *Strong Wind.* New York: Delacorte, 1968.

Mulata. New York: Delacorte, 1967. As *The Mulatta and Mr. Fly.* London: Owen, 1967.
*The Green Pope. New York: Delacorte, 1971.
*The Eyes of the Interred. New York: Delacorte, 1973.
Men of Maize. New York: Delacorte, 1975; London: Verso, 1988.
The Mirror of Lida Sal. Pittsburgh: Latin American Literary Review Press, 1997.

*Banana Trilogy

Other

The Bejeweled Boy. Garden City, N.Y.: Doubleday, 1971.
The Talking Machine (juvenile). Garden City, N.Y.: Doubleday, 1971.
Guatemalan Sociology: The Social Problem of the Indian. Tempe: Arizona State Univ. Center for Latin American Studies, 1977.

16. Aleksandr Solzhenitsyn (1970)

One Day in the Life of Ivan Denisovich. New York: Dutton, 1963; Farrar, Straus & Giroux, 1991; New York: Nal-Dutton, 1998.
Aleksandr Solzhenitsyn's One Day in the Life of Ivan Denisovich: A Play in One Act. Robert Brome, dramatist. Chicago: Dramatic, 1963.
We Never Make Mistakes: Two Short Novels. (*An Incident at Krechetovka Station, Matryona's House*). Columbia: Univ. of South Carolina Press, 1963.
For the Good of the Cause. New York: Praeger, 1964, 1971.
The First Circle. New York: Harper & Row, 1968.
Cancer Ward. New York: New Dial, 1968; New York: Modern Library, 1983; New York: Random, 1995.
The Love Girl and the Innocent: A Play. New York: Farrar, Straus & Giroux, 1969; New York: Bantam, 1981.
Stories and Prose Poems by Aleksandr Solzhenitsyn. New York: Farrar, Straus & Giroux, 1971.
August 1914. New York: Farrar, Straus & Giroux, 1972, 1989; New York: Viking Penguin, 1992.
Nobel Lecture. New York: Farrar, Straus & Giroux, 1972. As *One Word of Truth ... the Nobel Speech on Literature.* London: Bodley Head, 1972.
A Lenten Letter to Pimen, Patriarch of All Russia. Minneapolis: Burgess, 1972.
Candle in the Wind. Minneapolis: Univ. of Minnesota Press, 1973.
The Gulag Archipelago, 1918–1956: An Experiment in Literary Investigation. Harper & Row, Vol. 1, 1974; Vol. 2, 1976; Vol. 3, 1979, 1985; Boulder, Colo.: Westview Press, 1997.
Aleksandr Solzhenitsyn's One Day in the Life of Ivan Denisovich: A Full Length Play. Richard France, dramatist. Elgin, Ill.: Performance, 1974.
Letter to the Soviet Leaders. New York: Harper & Row, 1974.
From Under the Rubble. Boston: Little, Brown, 1975; New York: Bantam, 1976.
Lenin in Zurich. New York: Farrar, Straus & Giroux, 1976.
Détente. New Brunswick, N.J.: Transaction Books, 1976; New York: Books on Demand, 1999.

Warning to the West. New York: Farrar, Straus & Giroux, 1976.
Prussian Nights: A Poem. New York: Farrar, Straus & Giroux, 1977.
A World Split Apart (commencement address). New York: Harper & Row, 1978.
Aleksandr Solzhenitsyn Speaks to the West. London: Bodley Head, 1978.
Solzhenitsyn: A Documentary Play. Alexsander Hausvater, dramatist. Toronto: Play-writes Canada, 1979.
The Oak and the Calf: Sketches of Literary Life in the Soviet Union. New York: Harper & Row, 1980.
The Mortal Danger. New York: Harper & Row, 1980, 1981.
East and West. New York: Harper & Row, 1980.
Prisoners: A Tragedy. London: Bodley Head, 1983.
Victory Celebrations: A Comedy in Four Acts. London: Bodley Head, 1983; New York: Farrar, Straus & Giroux, 1986.
Victory Celebrations: A Comedy in Four Acts and Prisoners: A Tragedy. London: Bodley Head, 1983.
Rebuilding Russia. New York: Farrar, Straus & Giroux, 1991.
The Russian Question at the End of the Twentieth Century. New York: Farrar, Straus & Giroux, 1995.
Invisible Allies. Washington, D.C.: Counterpoint, 1995.
November 1916. New York: Farrar, Straus & Giroux, 1998.

17. Heinrich Böll (1972)

Acquainted with the Night. New York: Holt, 1954. As *And Never Said a Word*. New York: McGraw, 1978; Evanston, Ill.: Northwestern Univ. Press, 1994.
Adam, Where Art Thou? New York: Criterion Books, 1955. As *And Where Were You, Adam?* McGraw, 1970; Evanston, Ill.: Northwestern Univ. Press, 1994.
The Train Was on Time. New York: Criterion Books, 1956; London: Secker & Warburg, 1973; Evanston, Ill.: Northwestern Univ. Press, 1994.
Traveller, If You Come to the Spa. London: Arco, 1956; Munich: Max Hueber, 1956.
Tomorrow and Yesterday. New York: Criterion Books, 1957; Evanston, Ill.: Northwestern Univ. Press, 1996. As *The Unguarded House*. London: Arco, 1957.
The Bread of Our Early Years. London: Arco, 1957. As *The Bread of Those Early Years*. McGraw, 1976; Evanston, Ill.: Northwestern Univ. Press, 1994.
Billiards at Half-Past Nine. London: Weidenfeld & Nicolson, 1961; New York: McGraw-Hill, 1962; Avon, 1975; New York: Viking Penguin, 1994.
The Clown. New York: McGraw, 1965, 1971; New York: Viking Penguin, 1994.
Absent Without Leave: Two Novellas. New York: McGraw, 1965; London: Weidenfeld & Nocolson, 1967; Evanston, Ill.: Northwestern Univ. Press, 1995.
Eighteen Stories. New York: McGraw-Hill, 1966, 1971.
Irish Journal. New York: McGraw-Hill, 1967; Evanston, Ill.: Northwestern Univ. Press, 1994.
The End of the Mission. New York: McGraw-Hill, 1968; Evanston, Ill.: Northwestern Univ. Press, 1994.
Children Are Civilians Too. New York: McGraw-Hill, 1970, London: Secker & Warburg, 1973; New York: Viking Penguin, 1995.
Adam and The Train: Two Novellas. New York: McGraw-Hill, 1970.
Group Portrait with Lady. New York: McGraw-Hill, 1973; New York: Viking Penguin, 1994.

The Lost Honor of Katharina Blum: How Violence Develops and Where It Can Lead. New York: McGraw-Hill, 1975; New York: Viking Penguin, 1994.
Missing Persons and Other Essays. New York: McGraw-Hill, 1977; Evanston, Ill.: Northwestern Univ. Press, 1994.
The Safety Net. New York: Knopf, 1982; Evanston, Ill.: Northwestern Univ. Press, 1995.
What's to Become of the Boy?, or Something to Do with Books. New York: Knopf, 1984; Evanston, Ill.: Northwestern Univ. Press, 1996.
A Soldier's Legacy. New York: Knopf, 1985; Evanston, Ill.: Northwestern Univ. Press, 1994.
The Casualty. New York: Farrar, Straus & Giroux, 1986; New York: W.W. Norton, 1989.
The Stories of Heinrich Böll. New York: Random House, 1986; Evanston, Ill.: Northwestern Univ. Press, 1995.
Women In a River Landscape. New York: Knopf, 1988; Evanston, Ill.: Northwestern Univ. Press, 1995.
The Silent Angel. New York: St. Martin's Press, 1994.
The Mad Dog. New York: St. Martin's Press, 1997.

18. Saul Bellow (1976)

Dangling Man. New York: Vanguard Press, 1944; New York: Penguin, 1988; New York: Viking Penguin, 1996.
The Victim. New York: Vanguard Press, 1947; New York: Viking Penguin, 1996; London: John Lehmann, 1948.
The Adventures of Augie March. New York: Viking Press, 1953; New York: Penguin, 1999; London: Weidenfeld & Nicolson, 1954.
Seize the Day and Other Stories. New York: Viking Press, 1956; New York: Penguin, 1996; London: Weidenfeld & Nicolson, 1957.
Seize the Day, with Three Short Stories and a One-Act Play. New York: Viking, 1956.
Henderson the Rain King. New York: Viking Press, 1959; New York: Viking Penguin, 1996.
Herzog. New York: Viking Press, 1964; New York: Viking Penguin, 1996; London: Weidenfeld & Nicolson, 1964.
The Last Analysis (play). New York: Viking Press, 1965; London: Weidenfeld & Nicolson, 1966.
The Arts and the Public: Essays by Saul Bellow (and others). James E. Miller & Paul D. Herring, eds. Chicago: Univ. of Chicago Press, 1967.
Mosby's Memoirs and Other Stories. New York: Viking Press, 1968; New York: Penguin, 1984; New York: Viking Penguin, 1996; London: Weidenfeld & Nicolson, 1969.
Mr. Sammler's Planet. New York: Viking Press, 1970; New York: Penguin, 1977; New York: Viking Penguin, 1996; London: Weidenfeld & Nicolson, 1970.
Zetland: By a Character Witness. New York: Viking Press, 1974.
The Portable Bellow. New York: Viking, 1974.
Humboldt's Gift. New York: Viking Press, 1976; New York: Viking Penguin, 1996; London: Secker & Warburg, 1975.

To Jerusalem and Back. New York: Viking Press, 1976; Viking Penguin, 1998; London: Secker & Warburg, 1976.

The Dean's December. New York: Harper & Row, 1982; New York: Pocket Books, 1983; New York: Viking Penguin, 1998.

Him with His Foot in His Mouth and Other Stories. New York: Harper & Row, 1984; Viking Penguin, 1998.

More Die of Heartbreak. New York: William Morrow, 1987; Garden City, N.Y.: Doubleday, 1997.

A Theft. New York: Viking Penguin, 1989.

The Bellarosa Connection. New York: Viking Penguin, 1989.

Something to Remember Me By: Three Tales. ("A Theft," "The Bellarosa Connection," "Something to Remember Me By"). New York: Viking, 1991.

It All Adds Up: From the Dim Past to the Uncertain Future. New York: Viking Penguin, 1994, 1995.

Conversations with Saul Bellow. Jackson: Univ. Press of Mississippi, 1994.

The Actual. New York: Viking, 1997.

Ravelstein. New York: Viking Penguin, 2000.

19. Isaac Bashevis Singer (1978)

The Family Moskat. New York: Knopf, 1950; New York: Farrar, Straus & Giroux, 1950, 1988.

Satan in Goray. New York: Noonday, 1955, 1996.

The Magician of Lublin. New York: Noonday, 1960; London: Penguin, 1979; Cutchoque, N.Y.: Buccaneer, 1992.

The Slave. New York: Farrar, Straus & Cudahy, 1962; Farrar, Straus & Giroux, 1988.

The Milk of a Lioness. New York: Harper & Row, 1966.

The Manor. New York: Farrar, Straus & Giroux, 1967, 1987.

The Estate. New York: Farrar, Straus & Giroux, 1969.

Elijah the Slave, Farrar, Straus & Giroux, 1970, 1988.

Enemies: A Love Story. New York: Farrar, Straus & Giroux, 1972; New York: New American Library, 1989.

Shosha. New York: Farrar, Straus & Giroux, 1978, 1996.

The Gentleman from Cracow: The Mirror. New York: Limited Editions, 1979.

Nobel Lecture. London: J. Cape, 1979.

Reaches of Heaven: A Story of the Baal Shem Tov. New York: Farrar, Straus & Giroux, 1980.

Isaac Bashevis Singer: Three Complete Novels (The Slave, Enemies: A Love Story, and Shosha). New York: Avenel Books, 1982.

The Golem. New York: Farrar, Straus & Giroux, 1982, 1996.

One Day of Happiness. New York: Red Ozier, 1982.

The Penitent. New York: Farrar, Straus & Giroux, 1983, 1993.

The King of the Fields. New York: Farrar, Straus & Giroux, 1988; New York: Viking Penguin, 1997.

Scum. New York: Farrar, Straus & Giroux, 1991; New York: Viking Penguin, 1996.

The Certificate. New York: Farrar, Straus & Giroux, 1992; New York: Viking Penguin, 1997, 1999.

Meshugah. New York: Farrar, Straus & Giroux, 1994; New York: NAL-Dutton, 1995.
The Complete Novels. New York: Random House, 1995.
Shadows on the Hudson. New York: Farrar, Straus & Giroux, 1997, 1998.
Mazel and Shlimazel: Or the Milk of a Lioness. New York: Farrar, Straus & Giroux, 1999.
One Night in Brazil. Princess Anne, Md.: Yestermorrow, 1999.

Short Stories

Gimpel the Fool and Other Stories. New York: Noonday, 1957; New York: Farrar, Straus & Giroux, 1978, 1988.
The Spinoza of Market Street and Other Stories. New York: Farrar, Straus & Giroux, 1961.
Short Friday and Other Stories. New York: Farrar, Straus & Giroux, 1964; Greenwich, Conn.: Fawcett, 1985.
Selected Short Stories. New York: Modern Library, 1966.
The Seance and Other Stories. New York: Farrar, Straus & Giroux, 1968.
A Friend of Kafka and Other Stories. New York: Farrar, Straus & Giroux, 1970, 1979, Greenwich, Conn.: Fawcett, 1984.
An Isaac Bashevis Singer Reader. New York: Farrar, Straus & Giroux, 1971.
A Crown of Feathers and Other Stories. New York: Farrar, Straus & Giroux, 1973.
Passions and Other Stories. New York: Farrar, Straus & Giroux, 1975; London: J. Cape, 1976.
Naftali the Storyteller and His Horse. New York: Farrar, Straus & Giroux, 1976, 1999; Oxford, U.K.: Oxford Univ. Press, 1977.
Old Love and Other Stories. New York: Farrar, Straus & Giroux, 1979.
The Collected Stories of Isaac Bashevis Singer. New York: Farrar, Straus & Giroux, 1982, 1996.
The Image and Other Stories. New York: Farrar, Straus & Giroux, 1985, 1996.
Gifts. Philadelphia: Jewish Publication Society of America, 1985.
The Death of Methuselah and Other Stories. New York: Farrar, Straus & Giroux, 1988.
"The Safe Deposit" and Other Stories About Grandparents, Old Lovers, and Crazy Old Men. New York: M. Wiener, 1989.

Autobiography

In My Father's Court. New York: Farrar, Straus & Giroux, 1966.
A Day of Pleasure: Stories of a Boy Growing Up in Warsaw. New York: Farrar, Straus & Giroux, 1969; Gloucester, Mass.: Peter Smith, 1994.
A Little Boy in Search of God: Mysticism in a Personal Light. Garden City, N.Y.: Doubleday, 1976.
A Young Man in Search of Love. Garden City, N.Y.: Doubleday, 1978.
Lost in America. Garden City, N.Y.: Doubleday, 1981.
Love and Exile. Garden City, N.Y.: Doubleday, 1984. As *Love and Exile: The Early Years — A Memoir.* London: J. Cape, 1985; New York: Bantam, Doubleday, Dell, 1987.
Conversations with Isaac Bashevis Singer. Garden City, N.Y.: Doubleday, 1985.

Isaac Bashevis Singer: Conversations. Jackson: Univ. Press of Mississippi, 1992.
Isaac Bashevis Singer. New York: Random House, 1995.

Juvenile

Zlateh the Goat and Other Stories. New York: Harper & Row, 1966; New York: Harper Collins, 1984.
The Fearsome Inn. New York: Scribner, 1967; New York: Simon & Schuster, 1984.
When Schlemiel Went to Warsaw and Other Stories. New York: Farrar, Straus & Giroux, 1968, 1986.
Elijah the Slave: A Hebrew Legend Retold. New York: Farrar, Straus & Giroux, 1970.
Joseph and Koza: Or, the Sacrifice to the Vistula. New York: Farrar, Straus & Giroux, 1970.
Alone in the Wild Forest. New York: Farrar, Straus & Giroux, 1971.
The Topsy-Turvy Emperor of China. New York: Harper & Row, 1971; New York: Farrar, Straus & Giroux, 1996.
The Wicked City. New York: Farrar, Straus & Giroux, 1972.
The Fools of Chelm and Their History. New York: Farrar, Straus & Giroux, 1973, 1988.
Why Noah Chose the Dove. New York: Farrar, Straus & Giroux, 1974, 1988.
A Tale of Three Wishes. New York: Farrar, Straus & Giroux, 1975.
Naftali the Storyteller and His Horse, Sus, and Other Stories. New York: Farrar, Straus & Giroux, 1976.
The Power of Light: Eight Stories for Hanukkah. New York: Farrar, Straus & Giroux, 1980, 1990.
Yentl the Yeshiva Boy. New York: Farrar, Straus & Giroux, 1983.
Stories for Children. New York: Farrar, Straus & Giroux, 1984, 1985.
Teibele and Her Demon. New York: Samuel French, 1984.

20. Czesław Miłosz (1980)

The Captive Mind. New York: Knopf, 1953; New York: Random House, 1981; Gloucester, Mass.: Peter Smith, 1992.
The Seizure of Power. New York: Criterion, 1955. As *The Usurpers.* London: Faber & Faber, 1955.
Native Realm: A Search for Self-Definition. Garden City, N.Y.: Doubleday, 1968.
Selected Poems. Harmondsworth, U.K.: Penguin, 1968; New York: Seabury, 1973. As *Selected Poems: Revised.* New York: Ecco Press, 1981, 1996.
The History of Polish Literature. New York: Macmillan, 1969; Berkeley: Univ. of California Press, 1983.
Emperor of the Earth: Modes of Eccentric Vision. Berkeley: Univ. of California Press, 1977.
The Bells in Winter. New York: Ecco Press, 1978, 1996.
The Issa Valley. New York: Farrar, Straus & Giroux, 1981; London: Sidgwick & Jackson, 1981.
Nobel Lecture. New York: Farrar, Straus & Giroux, 1981.
Visions from San Francisco Bay. New York: Farrar, Straus & Giroux, 1982.
Postwar Polish Poetry. Berkeley: University of California Press, 1983.

The Witness of Poetry (lectures). Cambridge, Mass.: Harvard Univ. Press, 1983.
The Land of Ulro. New York: Farrar, Straus & Giroux, 1984.
The Separate Notebooks. New York: Ecco Press, 1984, 1986.
The Rising of the Sun. San Francisco: Arion Press, 1985.
Unattainable Earth. New York: Ecco Press, 1986.
Conversations with Czesław Miłosz. San Diego: Harcourt Brace Jovanovich, 1987.
The Collected Poems, 1931–1987. New York: Ecco Press, 1988, 1990.
The World. San Francisco: Arion Press, 1989.
Collected Poems. New York: Ecco Press, 1990.
Provinces. New York: Ecco Press, 1991, 1993.
Beginning with My Streets: Essay and Recollections. New York: Farrar, Straus & Giroux, 1991.
A Year of the Hunter. New York: Farrar, Straus & Giroux, 1994.
Testimony to the Invisible and Other Essays on Swedenborg. New York: West Chester, Pa.: Swedenborg Foundation, 1995.
Facing the River: New Poems. Hopewell, N.J.: Ecco Press, 1995.
Striving Towards Being: The Letters of Thomas Merton and Czesław Miłosz. New York: Farrar, Straus & Giroux, 1997.
Road-side Dog. New York: Farrar, Straus & Giroux, 1998.
A Book of Luminous Things. San Diego: Harcourt Brace, 1998.

21. Gabriel García Márquez (1982)

No One Writes to the Colonel and Other Stories. New York: Harper & Row, 1968; London: Penguin, 1996.
One Hundred Years of Solitude. New York: Harper & Row, 1970; New York: Limited Editions, 1982; New York: Perennial Classics, 1998.
Leaf Storm and Other Stories. New York: Harper & Row, 1972, 1979.
The Autumn of the Patriarch. New York: Harper & Row, 1976; New York: Harper Perennial, 1991.
Innocent Eréndira and Other Stories. New York: Harper & Row, 1978.
In Evil Hour. New York: Harper and Row, 1979; New York: Harper Perennial, 1991.
Chronicle of a Death Foretold. New York: Knopf, 1982; New York: Ballantine, 1984.
Collected Stories. New York: Harper and Row, 1984; New York: Harper Perennial, 1991.
The Story of a Shipwrecked Sailor. New York: Knopf, 1986.
Clandestine in Chile: The Adventures of Miguel Littin. New York: Henry Holt, 1987.
Love in the Time of Cholera. New York: Knopf, 1988, 1997; New York: Viking Penguin, 1999.
The General in His Labyrinth. New York: Knopf, 1990.
Collected Novellas (*Leaf Storm, No One Writes to the Colonel, Chronicle of a Death Foretold*). New York: Harper & Row, 1990; New York: Harper Collins, 1991.
Strange Pilgrims. New York: Knopf, 1993.
Of Love and Other Demons. New York: Knopf, 1995; New York: Penguin, 1996; London: J. Cape, 1995.
News of a Kidnapping. New York: Knopf, 1997; New York: Viking Penguin, 1998.

22. William Golding (1983)

Lord of the Flies. London: Faber & Faber, 1954; New York: Putnam, 1964; New York: Coward-McCann, 1984; New York: Viking Penguin, 1999.

The Inheritors. London: Faber & Faber, 1955, 1964, 1972; New York: Harcourt Brace 1962.

Pincher Martin. London: Faber & Faber, 1955, 1972. As *The Two Deaths of Christopher Martin.* New York: Harcourt Brace, 1957.

Free Fall. New York: Harcourt Brace, 1960, 1962; London: Faber & Faber, 1959.

The Spire. New York: Harcourt Brace, 1964; London: Faber & Faber, 1964; Cutchoque, N.Y.: Buccaneer, 1991.

The Pyramid. New York: Harcourt Brace, 1967; London: Faber & Faber, 1967.

The Scorpion God: Three Short Novels (Clonk Clonk, Envoy Extraordinary, The Scorpion God). Harcourt, Brace, Jovanovich, 1971; London: Faber & Faber, 1971.

Darkness Visible. New York: Farrar, Straus & Giroux, 1979; London: Faber & Faber, 1979, 1999.

*Rites of Passage. New York: Farrar, Straus & Giroux, 1980.

The Paper Men. New York: Farrar, Straus & Giroux, 1984; London, Boston: Faber & Faber, 1984.

Lord of the Flies, Pincher Martin, Rites of Passage. London, Boston: Faber & Faber, 1984.

*Close Quarters. New York: Farrar, Straus & Giroux, 1987; London: Faber & Faber, 1987.

*Fire Down Below. New York: Farrar, Straus & Giroux, 1989; London: Faber & Faber, 1989.

To the Ends of the Earth: A Sea Trilogy Comprising "Rites of Passage," "Close Quarters," and "Fire Down Below." London: Faber & Faber, 1991.

The Double Tongue. New York: Farrar, Straus & Giroux, 1995; London: Faber & Faber, 1995, 1996.

*trilogy

Other

Sometime, Never: Three Tales of Imagination. William Golding, John Wyndham, Mervyn Peake. London: Eyre & Spottiswoode, 1956.

The Brass Butterfly: A Play in Three Acts. Chicago: Dramatic, 1957; London: Faber & Faber, 1958, 1963.

The Hot Gates, and Other Occasional Pieces. New York: Harcourt Brace, 1965; London: Faber & Faber, 1965; New Brunswick, N.J.: Transaction, 1990.

Talk: Conversations with William Golding. Jack Biles. New York: Harcourt Brace Jovanovich, 1970.

A Moving Target. New York: Farrar, Straus & Giroux, 1982; London: Faber & Faber, 1982, 1984.

Nobel Lecture: 7 December 1983. Leamington Spa, U.K.: Sixth Chamber Press, 1984.

An Egyptian Journal. London, Boston: Faber & Faber, 1985.

Franz Kafka's The Metamorphosis. New York: Chelsea House, 1989.

William Golding's "Lord of the Flies." Nigel Williams, dramatist. London, Boston: Faber & Faber, 1996.

23. Joseph Brodsky (1987)

Elegy to John Donne and Other Poems. New York: Longmans, Green, 1967.
Poems by Joseph Brodsky. Ann Arbor, Mich.: Ardis, 1972.
A Stop in the Desert. Ann Arbor, Mich.: Ardis, 1972.
Selected Poems, Joseph Brodsky. New York: Harper, 1973.
Brodsky. New York: Viking Penguin, 1974.
A Part of Speech. New York: Farrar, Straus & Giroux, 1980, 1981.
Verses on the Winter Campaign 1980. London: Anvil Press, 1981.
Mramor. Ann Arbor, Mich.: Ardis, 1984. As *Marbles: A Play in Three Acts.* New York: Farrar, Straus & Giroux, 1989; New York: Noonday, 1989.
Less Than One: Selected Essays. New York: Farrar, Straus & Giroux, 1984, 1986.
To Urania: Selected Poems: 1965–1985. New York: Farrar, Straus & Giroux 1988.
Watermark. New York: Farrar, Straus & Giroux, 1992, 1993.
On Grief and Reason: Essays. New York: Farrar, Straus & Giroux, 1995, 1997.
So Forth. New York: Farrar, Straus & Giroux, 1996, 1998.
This Prison Where I Live. London: Cassell Academic, 1996.
Homage to Frost. Joseph Brodsky, Seamus Heaney, Derek Walcott. New York: Farrar, Straus & Giroux, 1996.
Conversations with Joseph Brodsky: A Poet's Journey Through the Twentieth Century. Solomon Volkov, ed. New York: Free Press, 1998.

24. Naguib Mahfouz (1988)

The Beginning of the End. Cairo, Egypt: American Univ. of Cairo Press, 1951, 1985; New York: Doubleday, 1990.
Middaq Alley. Beirut: Khayats, 1966; Washington, D.C.: Three Continents, 1977, 1981, 1990; New York: Anchor, 1992.
God's World: An Anthology of Short Stories. Minneapolis: Bibliotheca Islamica, 1973, 1988.
Mirrors. Minneapolis: Bibliotheca Islamica, 1977, 1990.
Miramar. Washington, D.C.: Three Continents, 1978, 1983; New York: Doubleday, 1993, Pueblo, Colo.: Passeggiata Press, 1997.
Children of Gebelawi. Washington, D.C.: Three Continents, 1981, 1990; Pueblo, Colo.: Passeggiata Press, 1997.
Wedding Song. Cairo, Egypt: American Univ. of Cairo Press, 1984; New York: Doubleday, 1989.
The Thief and the Dogs. Cairo, Egypt: American Univ. of Cairo Press, 1985; New York: Doubleday, 1989.
Autumn Quail. Cairo, Egypt: American Univ. of Cairo Press, 1985.
The Beggar. Cairo, Egypt: American Univ. of Cairo Press; 1986, New York: Doubleday, 1990.
Respected Sir. London: Quartet, 1986, 1988; New York: Doubleday, 1990.
The Search. Cairo, Egypt: American Univ. of Cairo Press, 1987. As *Search.* New York: Doubleday, 1989.
Fountain and Tomb. Washington, D.C.: Three Continents, 1988.
Palace Walk. New York: Doubleday, 1989, 1990.

Novels (Middaq Alley, The Thief and the Dogs, Miramar). New York: Quality Paperback, 1989.
The Time and the Place and Other Stories. New York: Doubleday, 1991.
*Palace of Desire. New York: Doubleday, 1991.
*Sugar Street. New York: Anchor, 1992; New York: Doubleday, 1993.
The Journey of Ibn Fattouma. New York: Doubleday, 1992; New York: Anchor, 1993.
Adrift on the Nile. New York: Doubleday, 1993.
The Harafish. New York: Doubleday, 1994, 1997.
Arabian Nights and Days. New York: Doubleday, 1995.
Children of the Alley. New York: Doubleday, 1996; Pueblo, Colo.: Passeggiata Press, 1997.
Echoes of an Autobiography. New York: Doubleday, 1997.

*collectively known as The Cairo Trilogy

25. Nadine Gordimer (1991)

The Lying Days. New York: Simon & Schuster, 1953; New York: Viking Penguin, 1994; London: Virago, 1983.
A World of Strangers. New York: Simon & Schuster 1958; London: Gollancz, 1958; London: J. Cape, 1976.
Occasion for Loving. New York: Viking, 1963, 1983, 1994; London: Gollancz, 1963.
The Late Bourgeois World. New York Viking, 1966; New York: Penguin, 1982.
A Guest of Honor. New York: Viking, 1970; New York: Penguin, 1988.
The Black Interpreters: Notes on African Writing. Johannesburg: Spro-Cas/Raven, 1973.
The Conservationist. London: J. Cape, 1974; New York: Viking, 1975.
Burger's Daughter. New York: Viking, 1979; New York: Penguin, 1980.
July's People. New York: Viking, 1981; New York: Penguin, 1982; New York: Viking Penguin, 1999.
A World of Strangers. New York: Viking, 1984.
Lifetimes: Under Apartheid. New York: Knopf, 1986.
A Sport of Nature. New York: Knopf, 1987; London: J. Cape, 1987.
The Essential Gesture: Writing, Politics and Places. London: J. Cape, 1988; New York: Viking, 1989.
My Son's Story. London: Bloomsbury, 1990; New York: Farrar, Straus & Giroux, 1990; New York: Penguin, 1991.
Conversations with Nadine Gordimer. Jackson: Univ. Press of Mississippi, 1990.
Three in Bed: Fiction, Morals and Politics. Bennington, Vt.: Bennington College Press, 1991.
None to Accompany Me. London: Bloomsbury, 1994; New York: Viking Penguin, 1995.
Writing and Being. Cambridge, Mass: Harvard Univ. Press, 1995.
Harald, Claudia, and Their Son Duncan. London: Bloomsbury, 1996.
House Gun. New York: Farrar, Straus & Giroux, 1998; New York: Viking Penguin, 1999; London: Bloomsbury, 1998.

A Writing Life. London: Viking, 1999.
Living in Hope and History. New York: Farrar, Straus & Giroux, 1999.

Short Stories

Face to Face. Salt Lake City, Utah: Silver Leaf Books, 1949.
The Soft Voice of the Serpent, and Other Stories. New York: Simon & Schuster, 1952.
Six Feet of the Country: Fifteen Short Stories. New York: Simon & Schuster, 1956; New York: Penguin, 1982; London: Gollancz, 1956.
Friday's Footprint, and Other Stories. New York: Viking, 1960.
Not for Publication and Other Stories. New York: Viking, 1965.
Livingstone's Companions. New York: Viking, 1971.
Selected Stories. London: J. Cape, 1975; New York: Viking, 1976. As *No Place Like: Selected Stories.* New York: Penguin, 1978.
Some Monday for Sure. London: Heinemann Educational, 1976.
A Soldier's Embrace. New York: Viking, 1980, 1982; London: J. Cape, 1980.
Something Out There. New York: Viking, 1984; London: J. Cape, 1984; London: Bloomsbury, 1994.
Armies of Conscience: Selected Short Stories. London: Heinemann, 1991.
Crimes of Conscience. Oxford: Heinemann, 1991.
Jump and Other Stories. London: Bloomsbury, 1991; New York: Farrar, Straus & Giroux, 1991; New York: Viking Penguin, 1992.
Why Haven't You Written?: Selected Stories, 1950–1972. New York: Viking, 1993.

26. Derek Walcott (1992)

Poetry

Twenty-Five Poems. Boston, U.K.: Guardian Commercial Printery, 1948.
Epitaph for the Young: A Poem in XII Cantos. Bridgetown, Barbados: Advocate, 1949.
Poems. Kingston, Jamaica: Kingston City Printery, 1953.
In a Green Night: Poems, 1948–1960. London: J. Cape, 1962.
Selected Poems. New York: Farrar, Straus & Giroux 1964.
The Castaway and Other Poems. London: J. Cape, 1965.
The Gulf and Other Poems. London: J. Cape, 1969.
Another Life. New York: Farrar, Straus & Giroux, 1973; Washington, D.C.: Three Continents Press, 1982.
Sea Grapes. London: J. Cape, 1976.
Selected Verse. London: Heinemann, 1976.
The Star-Apple Kingdom. New York: Farrar, Straus & Giroux, 1979.
The Fortunate Traveller. New York: Farrar, Straus & Giroux, 1981.
Selected Poetry. London, Kingston: Heinemann, 1981, 1993.
The Caribbean Poetry of Derek Walcott, and the Art of Romare Bearden. New York: Limited Editions Club, 1983.
Midsummer. New York: Farrar, Straus & Giroux, 1984; London; Boston: Faber & Faber, 1984.
Collected Poems, 1948–1984. New York: Farrar, Straus & Giroux, 1986, 1987.

The Arkansas Testament. New York: Farrar, Straus & Giroux, 1987, 1989.
Omeros. New York: Farrar, Straus & Giroux, 1990; New York: Noonday, 1992.
Odyssey. New York: Farrar, Straus & Giroux, 1993.
The Bounty. New York: Farrar, Straus & Giroux, 1996, 1998; London; Boston: Faber & Faber, 1997.

Plays

Henri Christophe: A Chronicle in Seven Scenes. Bridgetown, Barbados: Advocate, 1950.
Harry Dernier: A Play for Radio Production. Bridgetown, Barbados: Advocate, 1951.
Wine of the Country. Mona, Jamaica: Univ. College of the West Indies, 1953.
The Sea at Dauphin: A Play in One Act. Mona, Jamaica: Univ. College of the West Indies, 1954.
Ione: A Play with Music. Mona, Jamaica: Univ. College of the West Indies, 1957.
Drums and Colours: An Epic Drama. Caribbean Quarterly, March-June 1961.
Malcochon: or, Six in the Rain. Mona, Jamaica: University of West Indies, 1966.
Dream on Monkey Mountain and Other Plays. New York: Farrar, Straus & Giroux, 1970; New York: Noonday, 1991.
The Joker of Seville and O Babylon!: Two Plays. New York: Farrar, Straus & Giroux, 1978.
Remembrance and Pantomime: Two Plays. New York: Farrar, Straus & Giroux, 1980.
Three Plays (The Last Carnival, Beef, No Chicken, A Branch of the Blue Nile). New York: Farrar, Straus & Giroux, 1986.
The Odyssey: A Stage Version. New York: Noonday, 1993; London, Boston: Faber & Faber, 1993.
The Capeman (with Paul Simon). New York: Farrar, Straus & Giroux, 1997.

Other

The Antilles: Fragments of Epic Memory. New York: Farrar, Straus & Giroux, 1993.
Monsters, Tricksters and Sacred Cows. Charlottesville: Univ. Press of Virginia, 1996.
Conversations with Derek Walcott. Jackson: Univ. Press of Mississippi, 1996.
Homage to Robert Frost (with Joseph Brodsky and Seamus Heaney). New York: Farrar, Straus & Giroux, 1997.
What the Twilight Says: Essays. New York: Farrar, Straus & Giroux, 1998; London: Faber & Faber, 1998.

27. Toni Morrison (1993)

The Bluest Eye. New York: Holt, Rinehart & Winston, 1969; New York: Washington Square, 1972; New York: Knopf, 1993; New York: Plume, 1994; New York: Chelsea House, 1999.
Sula. New York: Knopf, 1973, 1974, 1989, 1991; New York: New American Library, 1982; New York: Penguin, 1987; New York: Chelsea House, 1999.

Song of Solomon. New York: Knopf, 1977, 1995; New York: Signet, 1978; New American Library, 1987, New York: Chelsea House, 1999.

Tar Baby. New York: Knopf, 1981; New York: Plume, 1982; New York: New American Library, 1983, 1987.

Beloved. New York: Knopf, 1987; New York: New American Library, 1987; New York: Plume, 1988; New York: Signet, 1991; New York: Penguin, 1998; New York: Viking Penguin, 2000.

Jazz. New York: Knopf, 1992; New York: Plume, 1993.

Playing in the Dark: Whiteness and the Literary Imagination. Cambridge, Mass.: Harvard University Press, 1992.

Nobel Prize Speech. New York: Knopf, 1994.

Conversations with Toni Morrison. Jackson: Univ. Press of Mississippi, 1994.

The Dancing Mind (Speech at National Book Foundation). New York: Knopf, 1996, 1997.

Paradise. New York: Random House, 1998; New York: Plume, 1999.

Big Box. New York: Disney Press, 1999.

28. Kenzaburō Ōe (1994)

A Personal Matter. New York: Grove, 1968, 1982.

The Silent Cry. Tokyo: Kodansha, 1974, 1994.

Teach Us to Outgrow Our Madness: Four Short Novels (The Day He Himself Shall Wipe My Tears Away, Prize Stock, Teach Us to Outgrow Our Madness, Aghwee the Sky Monster). New York: Grove, 1977.

Hiroshima Notes. Tokyo: YMCA Press, 1981; New York: Marion Boyers, 1995; New York: Grove, 1996.

Atomic Aftermath. New York: Grove Press, 1985.

An Echo of Heaven. New York: Farrar, Straus & Giroux, 1986; Tokyo: Kodansha, 1996.

The Pinch Runner Memorandum. Armonk, N.Y.: M.E. Sharpe, 1994.

The Catch and Other War Stories (contributor). New York: Kodansha America, 1995.

Nip the Buds Shoot the Kids. New York: Marion Boyars, 1995; New York: Grove, 1996.

Japan, the Ambiguous, and Myself and Other Lectures. New York: Kodansha, 1995.

17 and J. Tucson, Ariz., Blue Moon Books, 1996.

A Healing Family. New York: Kodansha, 1996.

A Quiet Life. New York: Kodansha, 1996; New York: Grove, 1996, 1998.

29. Dario Fo (1997)

We Can't Pay? We Won't Pay! London: Pluto, 1978; New York: S. French, 1984.

Accidental Death of an Anarchist. London: Pluto, 1980; Wolfeboro, N.H.: Longwood, 1986; New York: S. French, 1987.

Ulrike Meinhof and Tomorrow's News. In *Gambit,* vol. 9, no. 36, 1980 (Tony Mitchell, trans.).
Dario Fo and Franca Rame: Theatre Workshops at Riverside Studios, London. London: Pluto, 1981.
Female Parts: One Woman Plays (with Franca Rame). London: Pluto, 1981.
About Face. In *Theater,* vol. 14, no. 3, Summer-Fall, 1983. New York: S. French, 1989.
Elizabeth: Almost by Chance a Woman. London: Methuen, 1987; New York: S. French, 1989.
Archangels Don't Play Pinball. London: Methuen, 1987, New York: S. French, 1989.
Mistero Buffo: Comic Mysteries. London: Methuen, 1988.
The Open Couple and An Ordinary Day (with Franca Rame). London: Methuen, 1990.
The Tricks of the Trade. New York: Routledge, 1991.
A Woman Alone and Other Plays (with Franca Rame). London: Methuen, 1991.
Dario Fo: Plays 1 (*Mistero Buffo, Accidental Death of an Anarchist, Trumpets and Raspberries, The Virtuous Burglar, One Was Nude and One Wore Tales*). London: Methuen, 1992, 1997.
Dario Fo: Plays 2 (*We Cant Pay? We Won't Pay!, Elizabeth, The Open Couple, An Ordinary Day*). London: Methuen, 1994.
Abducting Diana. London: Oberon, 1994; New York: Theatre Communications, 1997.
The Pope and the Witch, The First Miracle of the Boy Jesus. London: Oberon, 1994, 1997; New York: Theatre Communications, 1997.

30. José Saramago (1998)

Baltasar and Blimunda. New York: Harcourt Brace, 1987, 1998; New York: Harvest, 1996.
The Year of the Death of Ricardo Reis. New York: Harcourt Brace, 1990, 1992; New York: Harvest, 1992.
Manual of Painting and Calligraphy. Manchester, U.K.: Carcanet, 1994.
The History of the Siege of Lisbon. New York: Harcourt Brace, 1994; New York: Harvest, 1998; London: Harvill, 1996.
The Gospel According to Jesus Christ. New York: Harcourt Brace, 1994; New York: Harvest, 1994.
The Stone Raft. New York: Harcourt Brace, 1995, 1996; New York: Harvest, 1996.
Blindness. New York: Harcourt Brace, 1998; New York: Macmillan, 1999.
All the Names. London: Harvill, 1999.
The Tale of the Unknown Island. New York: Harcourt, 1999.

31. Günter Grass (1999)

The Tin Drum. New York: Random House. 1961, 1980; New York: Vintage Books, 1964, 1990; New York: Knopf Everyman's Library, 1993; Gloucester, Mass.: Peter Smith, 1992.

*Cat and Mouse. New York: Harcourt, Brace, 1963, 1991; New York: Dutton, 1964.
Dog Years. New York: Harcourt, Brace, 1965, 1989; New York: Fawcett, 1986.
Local Anaesthetic. New York: Harcourt Brace, 1970, 1989; New York: Fawcett, 1981.
The Flounder. New York: Harcourt Brace, 1978, 1989; Gloucester, Mass.: Peter
    Smith, 1993. As Günter Grass's Der Butt. New York: Oxford Univ. Press, 1990.
The Meeting at Telgte. New York: Harcourt Brace Jovanovich, 1981, 1990; New
    York: Fawcett, 1982.
The Rat. New York: Harcourt, 1987, 1989.
The Danzig Trilogy (The Tin Drum, Cat and Mouse, Dog Years). New York: Pan-
    theon Books, 1987; New York: Fine Communications, 1996.
Show Your Tongue. New York: Harcourt, 1989.
The Call of the Toad. New York: Harcourt Brace, 1992, 1993.
Cat and Mouse and Other Writings. New York: Continuum, 1994.
My Century. New York: Harcourt, Brace, 1999.

*Danzig Trilogy

Plays

The Plebeians Rehearse the Uprising: A German Tragedy. New York: Harcourt Brace,
    1966.
Four Plays (Flood; Mister, Mister; Only Ten Minutes to Buffalo; The Wicked Cooks).
    New York: Harcourt, Brace, 1967.
The Wicked Cooks. New York: Harcourt, 1968.
Only Ten Minutes to Buffalo. New York: Harcourt, 1968.
Mister, Mister. New York: Harcourt, 1968.
Flood. New York: Harcourt, 1968.
Davor. New York: Harcourt College, 1969, 1973.
Max. New York: Harcourt Brace Jovanovich, 1970, 1972.

Poetry

Selected Poems. New York: Harcourt, 1966.
Inmarypraise. New York: Harcourt, 1974.
In the Egg and Other Poems. New York: Harcourt Brace Jovanovich, 1977.
Kinderlied. Northridge, Calif.: Lord John Press, 1983.
Novemberland. New York: Harcourt, Brace, 1996.

Other

On Writing and Politics 1967–1983. New York: Harcourt, Brace, Jovanovich, 1966,
    1985, 1986.
Speak Out! New York: Harcourt, Brace, 1968, 1969.
From the Diary of a Snail. New York: Harcourt, 1976.
Headbirths, or, The Germans Are Dying Out. New York: Harcourt, 1982, 1983, 1990.
Graphics and Writing. New York: Harcourt, 1983, 1985.
Drawings and Words 1954–1977. New York: Harcourt, 1983.
Etchings and Words 1972–1982. New York: Harcourt, 1985.
Two States — One Nation. New York: Harcourt, 1991.
The Future of German Democracy. New York: Continuum, 1993.

Index

Defoe, Daniel 43
dehumanization 132, 133
delight, capacity for 129
delusions 169
despair 68, 79, 90, 91, 92, 99, 102, 156,
  179, 191, 209, 213, 236
Destre, Gabrielle 204
The Devil with Tits 215
devotion 159
Dickens, Charles 30, 43, 77, 150, 169, 233
dignity 105
Dillard, Annie 1
discipline 97
disdain 123
dissociation of sensibility 48, 49
The Divine Comedy 142
Döblin, Alfred 234
Dodsworth 29
Dog Years 230, 231, 235
dogma 161, 217
The Don Flows Home to the Sea 101
Don Quixote 142
Donne, John 161
doom 198
Dos Passos, John 37
Dostoevsky, Fydor 53, 111, 116, 117, 125,
  166
*Dream on Monkey Mountain and Other
  Plays* 183
dreams 97, 110, 217, 218, 221, 224
Dreiser, Theodore 32, 33
The Dry Salvages 48
duration 24
The Dwarf 67, 69, 70

East Coker 47
East of Eden 95
eccentricity 65, 135, 121, 163, 230, 237
Echegaray, Jose de 4
echo 186, 227
Écriture 146
ecstasy 15, 129, 218; canned 162; religious
  10, 114
education 16, 27
egoist 13
élan vital 24
Eliot, George 77
Elmer Gantry 29
emotions 16, 24, 49
enchantment 155
endurance 129, 133, 191
enemies 15
An Enemy of the People 5

Enlightenment 16, 141, 180, 238
envy 219
Erasmus 204
Escape from Freedom 161
Essays and Introductions 15, 16
estrangement 183
eternal damnation 68
The Eternal Smile 69, 70
eternal values 122
ethical relativism 59
evil 11, 36, 39, 60, 75–77, 80, 133, 162,
  171, 174, 192; mystery of 79; source of
  114
excitement 63, 64
exile 162, 163, 179, 180
Exile and the Kingdom 91
existentialism 89
exultation 187

fable 110, 170
Facing the River 141
Fah Shu Ching 42
faith 25, 68
The Fall 90, 91
fallacy 177
The Family Moskat 135, 136, 137
fantasy 151, 214
farce 214
A Farewell to Arms 84
Faulkner, William 5, 23, 37, 53–56, 150,
  153, 261–263
fear 13, 59, 64, 83, 99; driven by 156
fearless 104
Ferber, Edna 35
Fielding, Henry 43
Finnegans Wake 137
Fire Down Below 156
The First Circle 85, 111, 112, 114
The First Man 90
The First Miracle of the Boy Jesus 209
A Flaming Green Tree 201
Flaubert, Gustave 43, 180
The Flounder 229, 230, 231, 232
flux 24, 25
Fo, Dario 3, 207–215, 286
folly 169
Fontane, Theodor 233
foolishness, parody of 30
Ford, Ford Maddox 85
forgetfulness 114, 120, 170, 191
forgiveness 127, 172, 173, 219
Forster, E. M. 179
The Fortunate Traveller 184, 185